Glimpses of a Great Soul

1. Swami Saradananda

Glimpses of a Great Soul
A Portrait of Swami Saradananda

by

Swami Aseshananda

The Vedanta Society of Portland, Oregon

Copyright © 1982 by The Vedanta Society of Portland. All rights reserved including the right to reproduce in whole or part in any form without prior written permission from the publisher.

Library of Congress Catalog Card Number 81-53018
ISBN 0-87481-039-6
   2 3 4 5 6 7 8 9 10

      Address all inquiries to:
      The Vedanta Society of Portland, Oregon
      1157 S.E. 55th Avenue
      Portland, Oregon 97215

Dedicated
to
Sri Sarada Devi
(My teacher)
Whom the devotees of Sri Ramakrishna
lovingly called Holy Mother. I have
seen her face, I have heard her words;
now I seek her grace with all the longing
of my heart.

Contents

Preface	xi
1. Swami Saradananda's Bodyguard	1
2. Sarat	9
3. The Trip to America	19
4. General Secretary of the Ramakrishna Math and Mission	29
5. Holy Mother and the *Udbodhan*	41
6. Western Visitors	57
7. Caring for Others	63
8. Swami Saradananda's Sense of Humor	71
9. Samadhi and Mahasamadhi	79
Epilogue	99
Swami Saradananda's Writings	101
Letters to Holy Mother	101
The Harmony of All Religions	104
Individuality and Philosophy in Vedanta	108
The Spiritual Teachings of Swami Saradananda	115
Comments on Karma Yoga	118
Spiritual Precepts of Swami Saradananda	120
Need for Spiritual Practice	120
Supreme Knowledge	121
Resignation to God	121
Need for Meditation	122
Power of Faith	123
Marriage or Renunciation	125
The Power of the Divine Name	126
On Japa	126
Directions for Meditation	128
Freedom through Desirelessness	131
Preparing the Ground	134
The Concept of Maya (the Dynamic Power of God)	136

The Balance of the Yogas 137
The Ideal and Application of Modern Vedanta 137
Paths of Affirmation and Negation 138
Control of Lust 139
Pranayama 141
Rules about Food 142
Self-effort and Self-surrender 143
Action and Contemplation 145
Patience in Suffering 147
Work as a Means to Perfection 148
Spiritual Consolation 151
The Letters of Swami Saradananda 153
Comments on Spiritual Experience (Adapted from *Sri Ramakrishna, The Great Master*) 180
A Conversation 183
Notes from the Lectures 188
"On Sri Ramakrishna and the Yoga of Devotion" (adapted from *Sri Ramakrishna, the Great Master*) 188
"Bigotry, Religion, and Philosophy in the Light of the Teachings of Sri Ramakrishna and Swami Vivekananda" 190
Address of Welcome 192
Spiritual Talks with Swami Saradananda 196
The Literary Beauties of the Vedas 211
Swami Saradananda and Girish Chandra Ghosh 220
Other Reminiscences of Swami Saradananda 237
Swami Nikhilananda 237
Swami Saradeshananda 250
The editor of the *Prabuddha Bharata* 255
A Grandson of Jogin Ma 255
Glossary 259
Notes on Illustrations 273

Illustrations

For notes on illustrations see page 273

1. Swami Saradananda — *frontispiece*
2. Studio portrait of Sri Ramakrishna — *following page 28*
3. Sri Sarada Devi
4. Sri Sarada Devi
5. Swamis Brahmananda and Saradananda
6. Swamiji: Swami Vivekananda
7. Group picture of monks
8. Swami Saradananda in his Udbodhan office
9. Saradananda as a young sannyasin — 78
10. On tour in America
11. Dressed for Western audiences
12. Swami Saradananda
13. Swamis Shivananda, Brahmananda, Saradananda
14. Girish Ghosh
15. Swamis Saradananda and Shivananda
16. Sarat Chandra Chakravarty: Swami Saradananda
17. Swami Aseshananda

Preface

IT IS DIFFICULT for us to understand those who have realized God. They see what we cannot see because they have experienced what we only hope to experience. But if we surrender ourselves to such individuals, keep their company and follow their teachings, they will heighten our awareness and shape our lives.

Now, some fifty years later, I can see that Swami Saradananda blessed me during my first meeting with him, giving me a firm shove toward my chosen path. But at the time, I saw nothing and felt only fear.

It was 1917. I was a student at St. Paul's Christian College in Calcutta, with no thought of becoming a monk. But I had heard of Sri Sarada Devi, the widow of Sri Ramakrishna and a great holy woman in her own right, so I was interested when my friends brought me news that she had come to Calcutta from her rural village of Jayrambati. On impulse, I went to the Udbodhan House where she was staying, with some of my friends on a day when male devotees could pay their respects and receive her blessings.

After a wait, a monk told us that we could go upstairs to have the *darshan* of Holy Mother. We went to the shrine, where she received male visitors, prostrated before her, and touched her feet. Afterwards, we came downstairs and began talking with Swami Dhirananda, a senior monk. While we were talking, I heard a voice call out from the next room, "Let the boy who has left his shoes on the threshold come here." Since I had left my shoes on the threshold, I rose and followed the voice through the doorway. There, dominating the room, was the large, imposing figure of Swami Saradananda.

"Do these shoes belong to you?" he asked me severely.

"Yes, Maharaj."

"Why have you left them on the threshold? You should have put them where they belong—below the staircase. Keeping them at the doorstep causes inconvenience to others. You should be more careful."

Those stern words, given force by the swami's somber appearance, cut me deeply. Out of fear, I avoided him for the next four years, staying away from the Udbodhan House unless Holy Mother was there. Instead, I often went to the home of Balaram Bose, the great devotee, to see Swami Brahmananda, the spiritual son of Sri Ramakrishna and the President of the Ramakrishna Order.

Swami Saradananda was methodical about everything. He could not bear a casual, haphazard way of doing things. In turn he had learned this quality from *his* master, Sri Ramakrishna. On one such occasion Swami Saradananda had returned to the Master's room after taking leave of him.

"Why have you returned so quickly?" Sri Ramakrishna asked.

"Sir, I have come to get my shoes, which I forgot to take."

"My boy, always remember things and never leave anything behind. All the fun and joy of attending the Panihati festival would have been marred if you had gone home and found that your shoes were missing, and you did not know where you had left them."

Swami Turiyananda had a similar experience when he borrowed a penknife from Sri Ramakrishna in order to peel fruits and cut vegetables for a picnic at the Panchavati. When he returned the penknife, he put it in a different place from where he got it. Sri Ramakrishna asked him to put it where it belonged. "If you put it in a different place, I will have to hunt for it everywhere," Sri Ramakrishna said. "Always remember to return a thing where you found it."

I believe that Swami Saradananda used harsh treatment to impress me with the need for responsibility. He was the embodiment of responsibility and the precision that brings orderliness to the inner life as well as the outer life. I believe he saw my future and knew that I would have to be responsible for a large spiritual family and alert to the welfare of others.

Holy Mother's departure from Calcutta for her home village of Jayrambati put me in a quandry. Without her presence, my fear of Swami Saradananda prevented me from visiting the Udbodhan House and receiving the benefit of their advice and example. In my perplexity I turned to Holy Mother for help, praying silently, "O Mother, your name is Abhaya, the bestower of fearlessness. Please remove this fear, which is troubling me so much." Like most prayers, its fulfillment took time and came in increments. First, by the Mother's grace, in 1921 I was able to join the Ramakrishna Order. Then, destiny in the form of malaria sent me back to the Udbodhan House to act as assistant to the office manager. Once there, I began hearing stories of Swami Saradananda's compassionate heart from those who worked under his direction, but still I felt uneasy and went out of my way to avoid him.

One day, the swami called me to his upstairs room. His stern look was gone; in a sweet voice he asked, "Would you be able to write letters for me? I will dictate and you will write. I will sign after reading what you have written. But you must not divulge the contents of the letters to anyone, not even your best friend." My fear vanished; that was the beginning of my association with Swami Saradananda as his private secretary and personal attendant.

As I write, my mind goes back to the years 1921–1927 when I lived with the swami in Calcutta. In memory I see him enter the shrine at the Udbodhan House and prostrate in front of the portrait of Holy Mother before returning to his room to become absorbed in meditation. Once again I hear his voice as he dictates to me and watch him sign the completed letter in his careful hand. I relive the time, when in replying to a request for spiritual instructions, the swami had me write, "I am dictating this letter to a person who would never divulge its contents, even at the cost of his life." Even now that memory sends a thrill through my body. As does the memory of his resonant and melodious chanting when, as the *tantradharak,* he assisted the *pujari* on a Shiva Ratri night.

I came to love and respect him. In him I found all that was great and true. He was a living exemplar of the teachings of Vedanta.

I believe he had a special role in the mission that Sri Ramakrishna was born to accomplish. Swami Saradananda's role had five distinct facets:

1. He defended the Ramakrishna Order from governmental criticism and repression by convincing the British governor

that the Order was not involved in politics in any way. It was solely a religious brotherhood whose only secular function was to render service to all mankind irrespective of creed, color, or nationality.

2. He defended the Ramakrishna Order against inner laxness and apathy in his training of the young monks. The 1980 convention at Belur Math was a replica on a grand scale of the convention that Swami Shivananda and Swami Saradananda sponsored for the purpose of rededicating the monks of the Ramakrishna Math and Mission to work for the good of mankind and for the awakening of *Brahma-Kundalini,* universal divine consciousness.

3. He preserved the memory of Sri Ramakrishna's spiritual life in his monumental biography, *Sri Ramakrishna, the Great Master,* which not only details accurately the events of Sri Ramakrishna's life but describes the Master's spiritual explorations that ranged from the purest dualistic *bhakti* to the ultimate expression of nondualism. Only one who has himself known the highest samadhi could interpret these experiences, and only one as methodical as the swami could present them in such a rational and convincing style. His biography is a priceless treasure for mystics all over the world.

4. He joyfully assumed the responsibilities and burdens of Holy Mother. He arranged for her financial support and built a house for her to stay in when visiting Calcutta and another in her home village, Jayrambati. He made it possible for her to meet with the throngs of devotees who came daily to receive her blessing and to initiate those who were ready to begin their spiritual life. And as his final token of love and esteem, after her passing, he built two temples, one at Belur Math and the other at Jayrambati to perpetuate her memory.

5. He interpreted the true significance of the Ramakrishna Order for Western visitors who came to Belur Math. His experience in America and Europe made him an ideal representative of the Order's role in working for unity among the world's various religious movements and especially in bridging the sense of separateness between the spiritual traditions of the East and the religious consciousness of the West. Because Swami Saradananda exemplified the practical Vedantist who lives in the

world, serving others and seeing God in all people, Swami Brahmananda chose him to meet with Western visitors, while he, Maharaj, prayed for the beneficial outcome of the meeting.

Swami Saradananda's work brought him into contact with people of many different temperaments. He was a perceptive and compassionate observer of human nature. I never saw him condemn or lose his inner calm, no matter how great the provocation. He teaches best who teaches through shining example: That was Swami Saradananda. He molded the lives of those who came into his sphere. He captured us all with his sweetness and his forgivingness. His presence always brought me hope and cheer. On one occasion when I could not pray or meditate due to lack of enthusiasm for such activities, the swami advised me:

> Hold on to God even in gloom. Never miss meditation or forget to repeat the name of the Lord. Meditation is the anchorage of the soul. Meditation will purify your mind. Continue *japa* and meditation without losing heart. You belong to the Master. By his grace you will be able to achieve everything when the time is ripe.

In Benares, I used to chant this hymn to Shiva:

> By telling Thy glories, O Shiva,
> I have become richer than the richest
> By thinking of Thy virtues
> I have purified my heart and uplifted my soul.
> I do not know Thy true nature,
> Nor do I know Thy powers.
> Whatever Thou art, O Mahadeva,
> Please accept my salutations and give refuge to me.

Similarly I feel inadequate to describe the greatness of Swami Saradananda. Therefore, I must say,

> Accept my salutations, O Great One,
> And bless me and my endeavor out of
> The generosity of thy heart.

I am indebted to Swami Saradeshananda for his kindness in writing down his reminiscences of Swami Saradananda. I am thankful to Mr. and Mrs. Shelly Lowenkopf of Santa Barbara for taking the responsibility of editing my manuscript. But for their help, my reminiscences would not have taken this shape and order.

If this book starts you reflecting on the infinite riches and beauty of the spirit and helps you find your inner Self, I shall consider myself fortunate and I will be eternally grateful to the Lord.

1

Swami Saradananda's Bodyguard

DESPITE THE FACT that he weighed 195 pounds and I weighed only 115, Swami Saradananda took to calling me his bodyguard. I would be working in the Udbodhan office, and he would summon me, saying, "I am going to Belur Math to see Mahapurush Maharaj (Swami Shivananda, who was then President of our Order). You must come with me. I cannot go without my bodyguard."

Immediately I would put all work aside and go, making the manager of the office angry with me for leaving without his permission. He warned me repeatedly that if my absences continued, he would replace me. The situation was becoming serious.

Finally, after I went out with Swami Saradananda on another one of his visits, the office manager fired me and gave my job to someone else. Marshalling apologies and pleas for another chance, I approached him, but he refused to speak to me. My only hope was Swami Saradananda. The swami listened gravely to my story, then smiled and said, "Go to the manager and tell him, 'I am a prince. I am not a beggar. I have every right to claim my heritage.'"

Somehow I knew that I had won. My feeling was borne out when I repeated the words to the office manager exactly as the swami had tutored me. He understood immediately that the "Supreme Court" had ruled in my favor. I was back in my old job.

Later I learned that the lines Swami Saradananda had me memorize were part of a speech by Rahula, the son of Buddha, from a play written by Bengal's great dramatist and a disciple of

Sri Ramakrishna, Girish Chandra Ghosh. My lines had been taken from the scene where Rahula had been sent to meet his father after Buddha had attained his enlightenment. The swami had playfully compared himself to Buddha and me to his son—just to make the office manager relent and give me back my job.

In 1923 my father became so ill that Swami Saradananda asked me to go to Dehri-on-Sone, the health resort where he was being treated, to nurse him. My efforts could not stop the disease; his condition grew worse, and his doctors gave up hope. I persuaded my father to go to Benares, where the Ramakrishna Mission had a large, modern hospital. Even there, his condition continued to deteriorate. Finally all we could do was to make him comfortable until his death and to lift up his mood by reading from The Gospel of Sri Ramakrishna. He passed away on a day considered auspicious in India, and his body was cremated at the famous Manikarnika Ghat.

Shortly after the cremation rites and *shraddha* ceremonies were over, Swami Shivananda arrived in Benares. "It's a good thing your father died here," he said, alluding to the belief that a person who dies in Benares is certain to gain union with God. "But," he added, "you had better do the traditional mourning rituals for your father for a year before you take your final vows as a monk." I returned to our Benares Sevashram to teach at the orphanage there.

Teaching and taking dictation are not the only duties of young monks of the Ramakrishna Order. I joined the Order at Belur Math on Swami Vivekananda's birthday and had worked and undergone my training there until Swami Saradananda (in his role as Secretary of the Order) received a report of a famine in the Khulna District of East Bengal (which is now a part of Bangladesh). At once he requested Swami Shivananda to send three young monks or *brahmacharis* from the Math to him. Three of us, Swami Jyotirmayananda, Brahmachari Moksha Chaitanya, and I—who at the time was known as Brahmachari Kiran*—received Swami Shivananda's blessings and left for the Udbodhan.

---

* Swami Aseshananda's nonmonastic or "civilian" first name is Kiran. As a young monk, he was known as Bramachari Kiran; young monastics were called bramachari even though they had not taken appropriate vows. After formal bramachari vows and ceremony, he was known as Kalyana Chaitanya.

At the Udbodhan House we attended vesper service and had supper. Afterwards, Swami Saradananda talked to us as a father to his sons, detailing how to organize relief work for the distressed area and reminding us to look upon those we helped as a symbol and expression of God. We boarded the train from Scalda Station; our first stop was Khulna, where we stayed overnight as guests of Bharat Sevasram Sangha. The following day we hired a country boat and arrived at a small village called Nakipur in the Satkhira Division of the Khulna District.

At first we were guests of a gentleman of the village, but when we discovered his hospitality was not absolutely unselfish, Swami Jyotirmayananda, the head of our party, decided to rent a room in the bazaar. That plan worked out very well. Swami Jyotirmayananda stayed at the room, which became our center, to meet the villagers, and we two *brahmacharis* went to all the villages within a radius of 10 to 15 miles, giving needy people tickets for doles of rice on our center's days of distribution.

Our journeys were often difficult and sometimes dangerous. Once a cobra hurtled over my feet. I did not see the snake as I was looking ahead towards the village we were trying to reach. Fortunately (the scriptures say the Lord protects his devotees at the time of their need), the village watchman did. He cried out, "Sir, be careful! There is a cobra." But by that time the snake had moved away; after a few minutes it slid into a stream and disappeared. Another time, while I was wading through a creek, a villager called to me, "Sir, you should not wade there. The other day a shark bit off part of a villager's leg." I had heard that hungry sharks from the Bay of Bengal frequently swam up the brackish waters of the creek, foraging for food, but I thought, if the Lord keeps, who can kill? So, taking the Lord's name, I waded across the creek and came unhurt to the other side.

The experience in Khulna was not all hard work and danger. About three miles from our camp site at Nakipur, there was a beautiful old temple dedicated to the Yasoreswari Kali, which had been erected by Pratapaditya, a famous king of Bengal. When I had some free time, I would walk to the temple, perform a ritual worship, offering flowers to the deity, and pray for her blessings. The priest became very friendly after a couple of visits. He began inviting me to lunch, giving me delicious *prasad,* food that has become sanctified by being offered to God.

For six months we worked silently and steadily, despite swarms of mosquitos which fed on us, infecting my brother *brahmachari* and me with malaria. What bothered us even more than the aches and fever of the disease was that we had so little to give. When the Ramakrishna Mission has the funds, in times of need we distribute rice, donate clothing, and, if necessary, build houses. This time we had been able to collect only enough money to distribute rice. A conservative Hindu organization wrote that they would be glad to give clothing for the poor under the condition that we would give the clothing only to the Hindus and not to the Moslems. But we refused, writing back, "All gifts must be unconditional; we will show no discrimination between Hindus and Moslems; and the majority of the villagers *are* Moslems." Under those terms, they refused to send anything. Fortunately a little later on, a liberal Hindu organization enabled us to distribute clothing as well as rice.

Seeing the conditions of the village people with my own eyes broadened my outlook and evoked sympathy for underprivileged people. It made me understand more deeply the tradition of the Ramakrishna Order to renounce the world, not to escape from hard work and responsibility, but to worship God by serving human beings, who are a tangible manifestation of Brahman. The Bhagavad Gita says, "He who looks upon the pleasure and pain of all beings by the same standards as he applies to himself, O Arjuna, that yogi is regarded by me as the highest."

At the end of six months, all the educated people of the locality gathered together to thank us and the Ramakrishna Mission for our help. Swami Jyotirmayananda asked me to reply; probably that was the first time I spoke in public.

Even after we returned to Belur Math, I could not shake off the malaria and was weak and feverish. The obstinate malady proved to be a blessing in disguise; it was responsible for my superiors sending me to the Udbodhan in order to receive better medical treatment. More than any medicine, Swami Saradananda's loving care helped me to fight the malaria.

Before my year of mourning rituals was up, the time for the celebration of Sri Ramakrishna's birthday approached. I was in

Benares at the time. Preparations were in full swing, and many of my brother *brahmacharis* asked Swami Saradananda to give them their vows of *sannyasa* in Benares on that auspicious day. The swami called me to him. "Many have asked for *sannyasa,* but you have not," he said. "Tell me what is on your mind."

"Mahapurush Maharaj (Swami Shivananda) has ordered me to purify myself for a year on account of my father's death," I replied. "That is why I have not approached you."

"Such things are for householders. Those rules don't apply to *brahmacharis* and monks of our Order. You should write to Mahapurush Maharaj and tell him that if he permits it, I will have no objection to giving you *sannyasa* on Sri Ramakrishna's birthday."

I wrote immediately; then anxiously awaited a reply. It didn't arrive.

When the ceremony took place, Swami Saradananda gave me the final vows along with the others. I worried about the consequences, but he knew better. There was such a trusting sweetness between him and Swami Shivananda that whatever Saradananda did, Shivananda approved unquestioningly.

"Don't worry," Swami Saradananda told me after the ceremony. "Sri Ramakrishna used to say, 'Now the marriage is performed. Whatever they may say, they cannot alter it.'"

The next day Swami Shivananda's reply arrived: "Sarat Maharaj wants to give you *sannyasa.* You have my wholehearted approval. Accept my blessings. May Sri Ramakrishna grant you the inmost desire of your heart so that you can live the life of renunciation and realize the goal through his grace."

In a separate letter to Swami Saradananda, Swami Shivananda had listed the new monastic names he had bestowed upon the monks who had taken their *sannyasa* vows at Belur Math the same day. The very name that Swami Saradananda had given me—Aseshananda—had been given by Swami Shivananda to Jogesh Maharaj. Saradananda asked Shivananda to allow me to keep my name, and Shivananda, the President of the Order, changed Jogesh Maharaj's name to Ashokananda.

Before our *sannyasa* ceremony, Swami Saradananda addressed us: "You should study the mantras beforehand and learn their meanings from your teacher. Vows become effective when they are done with right understanding and knowledge of their meaning."

Swami Atmanananda, a senior swami, was listening with great attention. Suddenly he spoke up. "Maharaj, you are going to give these *brahmacharis sannyasa*," he said. "Are they qualified? Have they acquired such guru *bhakti* that whatever you say they would do immediately and without hesitation? Suppose you asked them right now to go to the bank of the Ganges and plunge headlong into the river on this cold night. Would anyone here be prepared to do so?"

I don't know why, but I spoke up immediately. "If Swami Saradananda asks me to go the bank of the Ganges and plunge into the river, I will surely do it," I said. I still had not completely recovered from malaria and feared that making good on my pledge would likely be the death of me. I told myself that to die in Benares was auspicious and to follow the wish of a man whom I had come to love and respect from the bottom of my heart was a great privilege. However, Swami Saradananda said in a joking tone, "Kiran knows very well that I would never give an unreasonable order that would endanger the life of any man, not to speak of our *brahmacharis*." Later I discovered that it is not nearly so difficult to be willing to die for one whom we love as it is to live according to the ideals embodied by a truly dedicated, selfless person who has given himself to God.

After our *sannyasa,* several of us returned to Calcutta with Swami Saradananda by train. The sun was going down on the western horizon. Night was approaching fast. The swami asked me to sing a song with him. He began singing and I tuned my voice to his:

> I have made thee, O Lord, the pole star of my life.
> No more shall I lose my way on the world's trackless sea.
> Wherever I wander here, thy brilliance shines undimmed;
> With thy serene and gracious light
> Thou drivest all the tears out of my troubled soul.

"You have a good voice," Swami Saradananda told me. "We will sing the whole song together. Swamiji (Swami Vivekananda) used to sing this song before Sri Ramakrishna, and the Master would go into samadhi. What a great singer Swamiji was." He began singing and I tuned my voice to create harmony.

> In my heart's inmost shrine thy face forever beams;
> If, for a moment even, I cannot find it there,
> My soul is overwhelmed with woe;
> And when my witless mind strays from the thought of thee,
> the vision of thy face strikes me with deepest shame.

Swami Saradananda was a gifted musician who learned his art from Swamiji. In Puri I saw Swami Saradananda teaching that style of singing and chanting to the senior swamis, passing along a legacy of beauty that still remains and is treasured by our Order.

The swamis who attended Holy Mother told me that she was very fond of listening to Swami Saradananda's songs. The Mother would send word through Golap Ma: "Ask Sarat to sing a few songs." And strumming the *tanpura*, the swami would sing:

> Why should I go to Ganga or Gaya, to Kasi, Kanchi, or Prabhas
> So long as I can breathe my last with Kali's name upon my lips?
> What need of rituals has a man, what need of devotions any more
> If he repeats the Mother's name at the three holy hours?
> Rituals may pursue him close, but never can they overtake him.
> Charity, vows, and giving of gifts do not appeal to Madan's mind;
> The Blissful Mother's lotus feet are his whole prayer and sacrifice.
> Who could ever have conceived the power Her name possesses?
> Shiva himself, the God of Gods, sings Her praise with His five mouths!

Another song lingers in my memory. It is the nativity song of Sri Ramakrishna, composed by Girish Chandra Ghosh. Swami Saradananda sang it on Sri Ramakrishna's birthday in Benares on the day I was ordained as a monk of our Order.

> Who is that child that illumines my heart
> Seated on the lap of a Brahmin mother,
> Lowly and forlorn and beaming with a face of love?

2

Sarat

"How do you want to realize God?" Sri Ramakrishna once asked Sarat, the young man who would become Swami Saradananda. "What divine visions do you want to see in meditation?"

"Sir," Sarat replied, "I don't want to see any particular form of God in meditation. I want to see Him manifested in all the creatures of the world. I don't like visions and raptures."

"But seeing God in all creatures is the last word of spiritual realization," Sri Ramakrishna said, smiling. "You can't have it all at once."

"I won't be satisfied with anything short of that," Sarat said.

The man who refused to be satisfied with anything short of the highest was born Sarat Chandra Chakravarty on 23 December 1865, the son of Nilmani Devi and Girish Chandra Chakravarty, a successful proprietor of the Druggist's Hall, a pharmacy in Calcutta. Sarat was a quiet youngster of wide-ranging interests. He scored at the top of most of his school examinations, played a leading role in his school debating society, and developed a strong physique, the result of enthusiastic exercise. "His deep religious nature expressed itself in early boyhood," wrote Swami Gambhirananda, general secretary of the Ramakrishna Math and Mission. "He would sit quietly by the side of his mother when she was engaged in worshipping Narayana, the family deity, and afterwards repeat the ritual before his friends."* Most children long for toys; Sarat wanted the images of the deities so that he could set up a shrine of his

---

* Gambhirananda, Swami, ed., *Apostles of Sri Ramakrishna*. (Calcutta: Advaita Ashrama), pp. 169–194.

own and pretend to be a *pujari*. He had to wait until he was nine and had been invested in the sacred thread ceremony of the Brahmins to begin formal ritual worship.

His instinct to take care of others also showed up early in life. He often spent his lunch money on presents for his poorer classmates, sometimes even giving away his own clothing to those who needed it. When relatives, friends, and neighbors fell ill, Sarat was a frequent visitor and nurse. Once he discovered one of their neighbor's maidservants had been stricken with cholera and that her master, fearing contagion, had moved her up on the roof and left her to her fate. Sarat hurried to the woman's side and did what he could for her. When she died, he made the arrangements for her last rites.

Although he came from an orthodox Brahmin family, towards the end of his studies at the Hare School, he was drawn to the rationalism of the New Dispensation Movement of the Bramho Samaj of Keshab Chandra Sen, and he began practicing meditation according to the Brahmo system. After he entered St. Xavier's College in Calcutta, his interest in religion so impressed its principal, Father Laffront, that he tutored Sarat in Christianity and the Bible.

At this time Sarat's cousin, Sashi Bhoshan Chakravarty, was living with the family.* One of Sashi's friends read an article in the Brahmo Samaj newspaper by Keshab Chandra Sen about a great holy man who was living at nearby Dakshineswar. The three students decided to investigate the story for themselves. They arrived at the Kali temple on October 1883; Sri Ramakrishna appeared to be waiting for them, and he captured their interest immediately by his personal warmth and illumined spiritual discourses. The Master told them: "Bricks and tiles, if burnt after the trademark has been stamped on them, retain these marks forever. But nowadays parents marry their boys too young. By the time they finish their education, they are already fathers of children and have to run hither and thither in search of a job to maintain the family."

When someone asked if it were wrong to marry, Sri Ramakrishna requested two readings from the New Testament

---

* He later became Swami Ramakrishnananda.

(Matthew 19:12): "... and there be some eunuchs, which were so born from their mother's womb; there be some eunuchs, which were made eunuchs of men; and there be eunuchs, which have made themselves eunuchs for the kingdom of heaven's sake. He that is able to receive it, let him receive it." And St. Paul's famous injunction: "I say therefore to the unmarried and widows, it is good for them if they abide even as I. But if they cannot contain, let them marry: for it is better to marry than to burn." A man interrupted saying, "Do you mean to say, Sir, that marriage is against the will of God? And how can His creation go on if people cease to marry?" Sri Ramakrishna smiled and said, "Don't worry about that. Those who like to marry are at perfect liberty to do so. What I said just now was between ourselves. I speak on what I have got to say; you take as much of it as you like and no more."*

After that, Sarat visited Dakshineswar almost every Thursday, a school holiday. Sri Ramakrishna not only welcomed him, he began giving the young man spiritual instructions, suggesting one day that Sarat model himself after Shiva because Shiva represents patience, equanimity, and compassion. "Did not Shiva, according to our Puranas, accept poison from the world while the ocean was being churned and give nectar in return?" the Master asked. "You too should do the same thing in your life. Always give love where there is hatred, sympathy where there is bitterness, compassion where there is resentment."

However, when he heard the Master praise the integrity of Ganesha, the "Ideal Devotee" and the God of Success, for his devotion to his mother, Durga, Sarat told Sri Ramakrishna that he would like to make Ganesha his model. "No, my child, Ganesha is not your model. Your model is Shiva. You possess the beneficent attributes of Shiva, the God of renunciation and universal compassion. Think of yourself always as Shiva and me as *Shakti*. I am the ultimate source—the very reservoir of all your powers. Remember this!"

Before coming to Dakshineswar, Sarat had met Narendra Nath Datta, who was to become Swami Vivekananda. Sarat's first impression was that Narendra was bad mannered and conceited. Then a few months later, Sarat heard Sri Ramakrishna praise a

---

* *The Life of Sri Ramakrishna.* (Calcutta: Advaita Ashrama. 1973).

young man named Naren so highly that, not realizing this was the same Narendra he had already met and disliked, Sarat got his address and called on him. Despite the shock of recognition, the two became fast friends. They would often walk the streets of Calcutta until the early morning hours, too excited about their exchange of ideas to break away from each other and go to bed. One day in the winter of 1884 Sarat and Sashi came to Narendra's house about noon. Swami Gambhirananda described the meeting:

> In the course of the conversation the day passed into evening. Narendra took them to Cornwallis Square for an evening stroll. There also the conversation continued, broken by a song sung by him. Suddenly, Sarat woke up to the consciousness of time as he heard a clock strike nine at night. Narendra proceeded with them to give them his company for a little distance. But engaged in talk, he came actually to the house of Sarat Chandra, and Sarat requested him to take his meal there. Narendra agreed. But as he entered the house, he stopped in astonishment. It seemed as if he had been in this house before, and knew every corridor, every room there! He wondered if it could be the remembrance of any past life."

The Master, delighted that such a deep love had sprung up between his two disciples, remarked, "The mistress of the house knows which cover will go with which cooking utensil."

Sarat passed his first arts examination at St. Xavier's College in 1885. His father wanted him to study medicine so he could work with him at his pharmacy. Although Sarat had no interest in becoming a doctor, he took Narendra's advice and enrolled at Calcutta Medical College. In the middle of that year, Sri Ramakrishna became debilitated with the throat cancer that would later claim his life. His devotees rented a garden house for the Master at Cossipore on the banks of the Ganges in the hopes that the refreshing air and the quiet would speed his recovery. Sarat abandoned his medical studies to help nurse Sri Ramakrishna.

Sarat's father was alarmed. He felt his son was behaving foolishly as a result of Sri Ramakrishna's bad influence. He begged his son to be guided by the family guru, Jagannath

Tarkalankar, a famous pundit and Tantrika scholar. Sarat's father took the pundit to meet Sri Ramakrishna at Cossipore. Swami Gambhirananda commented about the meeting:

> His idea was that in the course of conversation between the family preceptor and Ramakrishna it would transpire what a pigmy the latter was in comparison with the former, and Sarat would clearly see his folly in giving up the family guru. But in a moment's talk, an adept like the pundit found that he was in the presence of a blazing fire. Secretly he told Girish (Sarat's father) that his son should be considered blessed to have such a guru.

At the Cossipore house Sarat witnessed many of the Master's high spiritual states. One day in January, 1886, Sri Ramakrishna went into ecstasy while walking in the garden of the house and devotees rushed to him to receive his blessings. Sarat and Latu,* another young disciple, saw the joy and ecstasy the devotees were experiencing from the Master's touch but, characteristically, stayed upstairs to clean Ramakrishna's room while he was out. Asked years later why he didn't go downstairs to participate in the joyful scene, Swami Saradananda said, "I did not feel any necessity for that. Why should I? Was not the Master dearer than the dearest to me? Then, what doubt was there that he would give me, of his own accord, anything that I needed?"

While Sarat and his brother disciples were nursing Sri Ramakrishna, the Master was giving them their final instructions in spiritual life. During this time, one of Sri Ramakrishna's devotees, Gopal Senior, stopped by the Cossipore house for a visit, bringing with him some rosaries and a pile of ochre cloths—the traditional garb of monks in India—explaining that he was planning to distribute the clothing and rudraksha rosaries among *sannyasins*.

"You won't find better monks than these anywhere," Sri Ramakrishna told Gopal, pointing to his young disciples. "Give your cloths and rosaries to them."

Instead, Gopal offered the cloths and beads to Sri Ramakrishna, who then personally gave each of his young disciples the

---

* He later became Swami Adbhutananda.

ochre cloth of renunciation. After they were distributed, one cloth remained; Sri Ramakrishna ordered it set aside for Girish Ghosh because the dramatist had acquired the true spirit of renunciation.

Sri Ramakrishna followed this symbolic act some evenings later with a brief ceremony and then sent the young men out to beg for food—also traditional among the monks of India—to teach them to rely on God and purge pride from their minds. So it was that Sri Ramakrishna set in motion the events culminating in the future Ramakrishna Order.*

Sri Ramakrishna left the body on August 16, 1886, plunging his devotees into grief. Nevertheless, the spiritual training the Master had given his young disciples was already shaping their lives. Sri Ramakrishna embodied the method as well as the principle of the philosophy of the Upanishads. Now that his living presence had been taken from them, they were determined to make that method their own by achieving the goal of the Upanishads, which their Master had exemplified in his daily life.

Narendra and a few brother disciples rented a house at Baranagore, not far from Cossipore, and started a monastery. Sarat had returned home after Sri Ramakrishna's death—reluctantly—but his resolve to obey his parents couldn't stand firm against the pull of Ramakrishna's influence. He began spending more and more time at the monastery, absorbed in spiritual practices and discussions of the Master's teachings. Swami Gambhirananda wrote:

> Apprehending that his eldest son Sarat was tending to be a recluse, and failing to turn his mind toward worldly life by arguments, Sarat's father, Girish Chandra, took the extreme step of cutting off all contact of his son with his fellow disciples by locking him up in a room. Unruffled, Sarat Chandra accepted the unenviable solitary confinement in his own house, and fully utilized his loneliness in focusing his mind on his spiritual objective. However, one day when one of his sympathetic younger brothers furtively unlocked the room, Sarat Chandra silently walked out of the house and went straight to the Baranagore monastery.

---

* Source of information—*The Life of Sri Ramakrishna* (Calcutta: Advaita Ashrama).

Not long after that, Sarat and most of Sri Ramakrishna's other young disciples gathered at Antpur, the home village of Baburam,* which was in the district of Hooghly, Bengal. Inspired by Narendra, they took mental vows of *sannyasa* during a night-long vigil around a sacred fire. Later they discovered that their vigil had taken place on Christmas Eve. Back in Baranagore, the young monks plunged deeply into spiritual practice, filling their days and nights with meditation, prayer, hymns, religious discussions, and scriptural study. It was during this period that Sarat's parents, sensing that he had gone beyond their recall, visited Baranagore to give him their blessing.

Ochre cloth, a brief ceremony, and mental vows did not satisfy the legal procedure of British India. The band of brothers discovered that to be recognized in a court of law, *sannyasa* had to be undertaken through the *viraja homa* ceremony. For this reason Swami Vivekananda was eager to have the ceremony performed.

There was a problem about the ceremony, however. Each of the ten orders of the monastic system founded by Shankara has mantras and rituals that are specific to it; they are secret and are passed along only from the initiating monk to the initiate. Sri Ramakrishna was initiated into the non-dualistic Puri Order (one of Shankara's ten orders) by the *sannyasin* Totapuri, but when Sri Ramakrishna gave his young disciples their ochre cloth of monasticism shortly before he died, he did not give them the secret mantras. Nevertheless, his disciples did receive the mantras they needed—in a strange way. Kaliprasad, one of their number, who later became Swami Abhedananda, went on pilgrimage to a shrine in the Barabar Hills near Gaya. While he was there, he met a monk of the Puri Order. This monk gave Kaliprasad the formal rituals of the *viraja homa* ceremony and some other esoteric designations of that Order. In his book *History of the Ramakrishna Math and Mission,* Swami Gambhirananda quotes from Swami Abhedananda's unpublished autobiography:

> One day Narendra said, "We shall take orders in accordance with the scriptural injunctions." When I was consulted, I said, "The Vedic Sannyasa requires Viraja Homa." I had

---

* Later he took the name Swami Premananda.

secured the mantras for this Homa. With the help of these, the Viraja Homa was performed one day (beginning of Magh, 1293 Bengali Era—third week in January, 1887 A.D.) in the shrine in front of the Master's slippers. Naren as our leader poured the oblation, and by the grace of the Lord, I, after sanctifying the fire, went on reading out the Mantras for him; and the Lord made me utter the sacred formula of Sannyasa for all to repeat. Niranjan, Naren, Sashi, Sarat, Rakhal, Sarada, Baburam, and I poured oblations simultaneously in the Viraja Homa, and we became brother-disciples.

I believe they assumed monastic names at the end of the ceremony, except Naren who waited until 1893 to adopt the name Vivekananada. They became Swami Niranjananda, Swami Ramakrishnananda, Swami Saradananda, Swami Brahmananda, Swami Trigunatitananda, Swami Premananda, and Swami Abhedananda.

Soon Saradananda and most of his brother monks were seized by the need to wander in the Hindu monastic tradition, depending completely on God for food and shelter and practicing intense spiritual disciplines. Swami Saradananda went to Puri, the holy seaside city where the temple of Jagannath is located. For the next three years he wandered throughout northern India, visiting the great religious sites, staying or moving on as an inner voice led him. In the summer of 1890 he met Swami Turiyananda and Vaikuntha Nath Sannyal; later they joined Swami Vivekananda at Almora and with other brother monks pilgramaged to Garhwal, Tehri, Rajpur, Rishikesh, Meerut, and Delhi. Alone again, he wandered from shrine to shrine, returning at last to Benares, where he became so absorbed in meditation that he stayed for several months. His example attracted an earnest young devotee who took *sannyasa* vows from him, becoming Swami Satchitananda. Swami Abhedananda joined him in the summer of 1891, and the three young monks made a ritual procession on foot around the circumference of the holy city, which covered an area of about forty miles. All three men came down with fever. The years of austerity had taken their toll; not long after he had recovered from the fever, a severe attack of dysentary forced Saradananda to end his pilgrimage and return in September 1891 to Baranagore. The next year, the monastery was moved to Alambazar to be closer to the Dakshineswar temple.

In 1893 Swami Vivekananda left on his first trip to the West carrying the message of Vedanta to the United States and England. His electrifying speeches at the Parliament of Religions in Chicago that September forged a bridge of understanding between the East and the West. When the Parliament was over, Swamiji was besieged with invitations to speak throughout the east coast and middlewest of America. The tour was a sensation; people thronged to hear the dynamic mystic from India and his message of the divinity of the human spirit and the brotherhood of religion. A nucleus of devotees and admirers formed around Swamiji, and finally, they were able to persuade him to open a center for teaching Vedanta in New York City.

Meanwhile, he was writing to his brother monks at Alambazar, urging them to break away from the traditional monastic seclusion to begin a new kind of monastic order that would serve humanity as well as instruct the seekers of liberation. From its inception, the New York Center progressed steadily. Swamiji was invited to England by the scholar E.T. Sturdy. He arrived in London in July 1894 and soon was attracting audiences of scientists, philosophers, theologians, and educators. He was in such demand that he wrote to Swami Brahmananda, who had taken on the task of heading the Alambazar monastery, for an assistant. The monk he asked for was Swami Saradananda.

3

The Trip to America

AT FIRST SWAMI Saradananda felt reluctant to accept Swamiji's call to teach in the West. He pleaded that he wasn't competent to lecture.

Finally he went to Holy Mother, who was then living in Jayrambati, and asked for her advice. She was hesitant to give permission to her beloved spiritual son to travel to a far-off country. But she sought for the answer to the problem in meditation, and then she told him, "My child, be not afraid. You should go to the West. Sri Ramakrishna will protect you. Sri Ramakrishna will be with you wherever you go. He will always look after you and shield you from all dangers and difficulties." The Mother placed her hand on his head and repeated his name, as is the custom of all Hindu mothers bidding their children goodbye.

Swami Saradananda sailed for England from a port near Calcutta. In the Mediterranean Sea a hurricane buffeted the vessel. "All the passengers were in a great panic," the swami recalled. "Some were crying; some were running here and there in fear; some were shaking with nervous excitement. The whole scene was frightening, but I was not afraid in the least. My mind was steady and calm as the needle of a compass." Sri Ramakrishna was indeed protecting him, just as Holy Mother had promised.

He arrived in London on 1 April 1896 and lived with E.T. Sturdy while waiting for Swamiji (who after three months of lecturing in London had returned to New York to lecture there and give classes in karma yoga). When Swamiji's ship docked, the brother monks embraced, remaining still as statues for a minute before launching into a lively conversation about what was needed to bring Sri Ramakrishna's message to the West.

One of Swami Saradananda's first tasks in London was supplying Professor Max Mueller, the famous authority on Oriental philosophy, with material about the life of Ramakrishna. Years later, talking to devotees in his small room at the Udbodhan, the swami described his work:

> At the invitation of Max Mueller, Swamiji went to Oxford and stayed in his home as a guest. Max Mueller wrote an article in the *Nineteenth Century* on Sri Ramakrishna entitled "The Real Mahatma." He asked Swamiji to furnish him with enough material for a book so he could write about Sri Ramakrishna in greater detail. Swamiji agreed to help. When he returned, he asked me to undertake the job forthwith. I worked hard and gathered all the incidents in the life of the Master and the teachings of the Master and showed the manuscript to Swamiji. I thought Swamiji would edit it and make extensive corrections. He didn't do that. He simply changed a few words for fear of exaggeration and sent the whole manuscript to Professor Mueller. As I remember, Professor Mueller incorporated the completed manuscript in his book and published it without making any alterations.

After Swami Saradananda had delivered a few lectures and held classes on the Bhagavad Gita in London, his initial nervousness disappeared. Observing this, Swamiji sent him to New York City in late June as the head of the Vedanta Society there. He was accompanied by J.J. Goodwin, Swamiji's disciple and stenographer.

In New York, Swami Saradananda continued Swamiji's work, lecturing at Sunday services, holding classes on the Gita and the Upanishads, and giving interviews. Spiritual aspirants came in large numbers to discuss personal problems. One incident illustrates the swami's straightforward advice. A woman asked the swami's help in dealing with her psychic experiences. At night, she said, the furniture in her room would move around and her windows would fly open, and she would feel an unknown presence. Once, she concluded, she was standing in her room when some formless being lifted her bodily a few inches off the floor.

After reflecting a few moments, the swami said, "I am glad

that you have come. But if you ask my opinion, I will say that these experiences are the outcome of a weakened state of mind. Please train your mind firmly to think thoughts that are wholesome, good, and beneficial. By invigorating thoughts alone, these occult phenomena and psychic experiences can be averted." He suggested she practice self-control, read inspiring books, and meditate on the Divine Spirit every day. She followed his advice and became a changed person.

Swami Saradananda was invited to be one of the teachers at the Greenacre Conference of Comparative Religions in Maine. He lectured extensively throughout New England and New York State. "Everywhere," one observer noted, "his dignity of bearing, gentle courtesy, readiness to meet questions of all kinds and, above all, the spiritual height from which he could talk, won for him a large number of friends, admirers, and devotees." Among his staunchest friends during those years in America were Mrs. Sara Bull of Boston, Miss Josephine McLeod of New York City, and Mrs. Wheeler of Montclair, New Jersey.

In his Bengali book on Swami Saradananda, Brahmachari Ashaya Chaitanya quoted the swami as telling devotees: "The famous violinist Mr. Ole Bull, was one of the pioneers who worked hard for bringing independence to Norway. While playing the violin in his performances, so absorbed he would be in his music that quite often he would lose all outer consciousness. Mr. Bull's manager used to deceive him of his earnings. A lady, out of sympathy for the great artist and to set things aright, married him."

Swamiji, who had also been helped by Mrs. Bull during his stay in America, had lovingly called her Dhira Mata (Steady Mother). Mrs. Bull invited Swami Saradananda to her home in Boston and introduced him to her friends, including William James and other members of the Harvard faculty. Mrs. Bull often said that Swamiji was like the brilliant, scorching sun and Saradananda, the cool, refreshing moon. "She has tremendous faith in Sarat," Swamiji wrote Swami Brahmananda when Mrs. Bull donated "a magnificent sum" for the construction of Belur Math. Saradananda returned her esteem; in his Udbodhan room there were two photographs—one of Holy Mother, the other of Mrs. Bull.

When Mrs. Bull came to India, Holy Mother met her and became very fond of her. She invited Holy Mother to the little cottage at Belur Math where she was staying with Miss McLeod and Margaret Noble (Sister Nivedita). They couldn't speak Bengali and the Mother couldn't speak English, but they all understood the language of the heart. Later, the three Western women (all disciples of Swamiji) were visited by Holy Mother once again. She greeted each of them affectionately as "my daughter" and when Miss McLeod said, "Won't you eat with us?" Holy Mother readily agreed. Swamiji was tremendously pleased when he heard about it. "Sri Mother is here," he wrote Swami Ramakrishnananda, "and the European and American ladies went the other day to see her and what do you think, Mother even ate with them! Is not that great?"

Holy Mother had been born a Brahmin and made a widow with the death of Sri Ramakrishna, and should, according to scriptures, observe the rules of strict vegetarianism, cook her own meals, and eat only once a day, but never with non-Brahmins or foreigners. Swamiji's delight was in learning that the Mother had demonstrated Sri Ramakrishna's teaching, "Among the devotees of God there should not be any distinction of caste. Devotees are all one by the tie of love for God." Nevertheless, the Mother herself said later, "I did not take rice—I took only fruits and sweets. I did not violate the rules of Hindu scriptures in spirit when I gladly accepted the invitation of Miss McLeod for lunch and ate with the devotees of our Master on that day at Belur."

Miss McLeod's brother-in-law, Frank Leggett, was president of the New York Vedanta Society. When Saradananda came to New York, he was a guest of Mr. and Mrs. Leggett, enjoying the peaceful atmosphere of Ridgely Manor, their country estate. Once while the swami was conducting the Sunday service, he saw Miss McLeod in the front row, fast asleep. After the service, as he was shaking hands with members of the congregation, Miss McLeod appeared and extended her hand in greeting. The swami with a grave face asked, "Did you sleep well?" Both laughed heartily.

I never met Mrs. Bull, but I spent time with Miss McLeod, both in India and in this country. I used to visit her at the

Barbazon Plaza, the hotel that was her home, when I was associated with the Ramakrishna-Vivekananda Center in New York City. She was very gracious to me because I had been an attendant of Swami Saradananda. A world traveller and full of vitality to the very end, she brimmed with the desire and with ideas for helping India and our Order; her inspiration resulted in Vedanta Centers in France and Argentina. We younger monks called her Tantine because she was like a great-aunt to us all. I had the honor of performing the funeral ceremony for Tantine after she passed away in Hollywood, California, at the age of ninety in 1949.

Swami Saradananda used to go regularly to Montclair, New Jersey, to hold classes. He stayed at the home of Mr. and Mrs. Wheeler. Swami Atulananda, a Western monk of our Order, described their home in his book, *With the Swamis in America:* "It was a home of culture, piety and cheerfulness—one of those healthy, balanced American homes, rich with mutual love and consideration, with a great deal of freedom, but perfectly regulated, the children full of life and enterprise, adoring the parents and very free with them, a home of mutual understanding." Swami Saradananda was held in high esteem by every member of the Wheeler family; there he saw American life at its best.

It was Mrs. Wheeler who had dreamed of Sri Ramakrishna when she was a young girl—long before she had seen his picture in Swami Saradananda's album.* Swami Turiyananda used to speak of her as one of the most spiritual women he had ever met. One time he told Swami Atulananda, "She is so *sattvic*, firm, quiet; she always does the right thing at the right time without the least fuss." While staying with the Wheelers, Swami Turiyananda received a letter from India informing him that part of Bengal was being devastated by famine. Mrs. Wheeler quietly collected money among her friends and presented the swami with a large amount to send for relief work in Bengal.

Swami Saradananda told us, "The Master chooses his own men and women. We are mere instruments in his hands. It is a privilege to work under his banner. In America he already prepared the ground for me; I was not alone. He brought to me men

---
*See Page 152.

and women of exalted character who helped me in our work and bore great love for our Master."

After Swami Saradananda had been in the United States for two and a half years, Swamiji, who had returned to India in January 1897, wrote and asked him to return home. Although Swamiji gave him the option to stay if he wanted, the swami felt that the mere wish of Swamiji was as good as a command. He sailed for India on 12 January 1898, leaving Swami Abhedananda in charge of the New York Center.

Dr. Lewis G. Janes, director of the Cambridge Conference, wrote the editor of the *Bramavadin* in appreciation of the swami's work:

> The many friends of the Swami Saradananda in Cambridge and vicinity cannot permit him to return to India without expressing through your columns their hearty appreciation of the excellent educational work which he accomplished in this country, and the fine accompaniment of personal character and influence which greatly strengthened the effect of the work wherever it was conducted. On every hand, the friends of the Swami express a sense of personal loss in his departure, and hope that he may some time return to America where his work is so heartily appreciated.
>
> In Cambridge, the classes in the Vedanta philosophy, constituting a single feature in the broad field of comparative study outlined for the Cambridge Conferences, attracted large and intelligent audiences, in part made up of professors and students of the Harvard University. The swami's exposition of the principles of the Advaita doctrine, in just comparison with other views which are held in India, was admirably lucid and clear. His replies to questions were always ready and satisfactory. His great fairness of mind and soundness of judgment enabled him to present the doctrine in a manner which at once convinced all of his sincerity, while it disarmed the factious opposition which is sometimes stirred up by a more dogmatic and assertive manner. In Boston, Waltham and Worcester, Mass., the Swami Saradananda conducted courses of lectures which were largely attended and which everywhere manifested a sustained interest in his subject.

On his return trip to India, the swami revisited France and Italy, this time as the escort to Mrs. Ole Bull and Miss McLeod, who wanted to see Swamiji and to help him in his work in founding the Belur Math and constructing a temple for Sri Ramakrishna. Swami Saradananda followed his Master's teaching: "Always adjust yourself to time, place, and circumstances. Be keen about helping others in fulfilling their plans and wishes, instead of holding fast to your own wishes and plans and being an obstacle in their way."

Broadmindedness was one of the swami's characteristics; he enjoyed cultures and traditions different from his own. I have never heard him criticize a civilization that produced men and women of breadth and vision and nobility of character. He studied history with understanding and delighted in meeting people, talking with them, and discovering their heritage through their reminiscences of daily life, their achievements, and their dreams of a brighter future. Here are some entries in his diary of his return journey after working in the West from 1896 to 1898:

Wednesday, 12 Jan. 1898	Sailed (from New York).
Wednesday, 19 Jan.	Last day and night on board *Teutonic*.
Thursday, 20 Jan.	Liverpool and London. Hotel Midland Grand. Saw Mrs. Sturdy and the Galsworthys.

(The swami admired the art, music, and other creative talents of the French people.)

Saturday, Jan. 22, 1898	Paris — the theatre — Sara Bernhardt as the blind wife — La Belle — Paris — the artistic in French life — the Notre Dame — Theatre Renaissance — La Villa Morte.

(Swami Saradananda once mentioned that he heard the singing of Madame Emma Calvé while he was in Paris. His hotel was next to the hotel where Madame Calvé lived and was practicing for a big performance.)

    Sunday, 23 Jan.   Left Paris at 8 p.m. In the train from Paris to Naples. Madeleine Church. Acquaintance with Mr. Niblack, the American Embassy. A ride of two nights and one day to Rome from Paris.

(Swami Saradananda liked Rome for its historic past and its spiritual influence on the minds and hearts of the Roman Catholic followers of Christ, not only in Europe but all over the world: A devout Catholic dreams of seeing the holy city and receiving the blessing of the Pope one day. I believe the swami felt there was a close similarity between the Catholic concept "The logos then which is begotten of the Father, proceeds consubstantial with the Father, that is having precisely the same divine nature of the Father, and yet really distinct from the Father in personality as every son is distinct from the father who begets him"—and the verses from the Gita—"Whenever there is a decline of spirituality and an uprise of materialism, I incarnate myself for the protection of the good and for the establishment of righteousness. I am born in every age.")

    Tuesday, 25 Jan. 1898   Arrival at Rome early in the morning. The Hotel Continental. St. Peter. View from the top of Mount Janiculum. The Catacomb of Saint Sebastian. The theatre at night—Signora Elinora Duse, the greatest actress. Santa Scolla—the Sistine Chapel—the masterpieces of Michael Angelo. The Moses.

(From studying his diary I note how modern the swami was. I am rather old-fashioned. I came here in 1947. Thirty-four years have passed, but I have not been to any theatre up to this time. A great soul comes for the whole world. We come for a few selected souls. Their capacity is big, ours is small. We must be content with what little we can do. In the eyes of God, perhaps that is sufficient and quite acceptable.)

Wednesday, 26 Jan. 1898	Colosseum in the morning. Left Rome for Naples by 1:35 p.m. train, reaching there at 5:35 p.m. The Hotel Continental.
Thursday, 27 Jan. 1898	The morning in the Vatican library and the Sculpture Gallery at the Vatican. St. Peter for the last time.
Friday, 28 Jan.	Went to the Vesuvius.
Saturday, 29 Jan.	Left Naples by 7:35 a.m.—rain, arrival at Brindisi at 6 p.m. after a ride of 10 hours in the train through beautiful Italian landscapes.
Sunday, 30 Jan.	*The Peninsular* left Brindisi at 10:30 p.m.
Monday, 31 Jan.	In the steamer. Copied the prayers for S. The Ionian Islands are very beautiful.

("S" perhaps means Sanyal. Vaikuntha Nath Sanyal was a lay disciple of Sri Ramakrishna. While I was there he visited the swami at the Udbodhan almost every evening. I have heard many stories about Swami Saradananda and his innate generosity and unbounded love from Sri Sanyal, whom we affectionately used to call Sanyal Mahasay. Swami Saradananda would sometimes call me and say, "Prepare tea and also prepare tobacco for Sanyal. That will please me.")

As he traveled from city to city the swami had the habit of praying to the Divine Mother to give love, peace, and harmony to the hearts of those who lived there. Perhaps he chanted the Sanskrit prayer:

> May good betide all.
> May happiness come to all.
> May all see the face of truth.
> And may all be protected by the Lord,
> Who is the Father and Mother of all mankind.

2. *Sri Ramakrishna*

3. *Sri Sarada Devi*

4. *Sri Sarada Devi*

5. *Maharaj (l) and Sarat (r): Swamis Brahmananda and Saradananda*

6. *Swamiji: Swami Vivekananda*

7. Brother monks: (l to r) Swamis Brahmananda, Trigunatitananda, Premananda, Turiyananda, and Saradananda

8. *Swami Saradananda in his* Udbodhan *office*

9. *Saradananda as a young sannyasin*

4

General Secretary of the Ramakrishna Math and Mission

WHEN SWAMI SARADANANDA stepped onto the Howrah railroad station, six kilometers south of Belur Math, and saw Swamiji, Swami Saradananda felt he was truly home. Swamiji saw that living in the comfort of the West had not made his brother disciple materialistic; rather he had grown spiritually from the experience.

Swami Saradananda was just the man Swamiji needed at the moment—a man whose work in the West had added a knowledge of organizational efficiency to his spiritual depth. Swamiji had not slacked the pace of his work since returning to India. He had traveled the subcontinent from Colombo in the south to Almora in the north, lecturing to large crowds. These tours laid the foundation for the Ramakrishna Order of monks and the Ramakrishna Mission, an organization of lay and monastic members dedicated to carrying out spiritual and humanitarian work, which Swamiji had officially inaugurated on 1 May 1897.

Swamiji appointed Swami Saradananda General Secretary of both institutions in 1899; Swami Saradananda's power of organization was so effective that Mission centers were established throughout India to serve the poor. Both the general public and the British colonial government valued the Mission's work. At the monastery, Saradananda played two roles—General Secretary and spiritual teacher. First and foremost, feeling that this was the foundation for everything else, he looked after the spiritual well-being of the Ramakrishna monastics. Then, using his experience in organization, he brought the internal affairs of the monastery into order. Finally his experiences in America and England helped him train monks for service in the West.

Friday, 3 February 1899	Decided (by Swamiji) that we (Swami Turiyananda and I) go to Gujarat to preach and collect funds (for Belur Math).
Tuesday, 7 Feb.	Preparation for starting for Junagarh. Left Math by 5 p.m. Saluted Mother at Calcutta. Left by Punjab Mail.
Wednesday, 8 Feb.	Reached Cawnpur by 6:16 p.m. Put up in a very poor inn. A bad night.
Thursday, 9 Feb.	A flying visit round the city. Cooper Allen Tannery. Two pairs of slippers for Hari and myself. Interview with Pundit Prithvinath, his words of discouragement.
Friday, 10 Feb.	In the train all day — travelled to Jeypore. Reminded of my travel with the same line with Y and N few months before (Perhaps *Y* means Swami Yogananda and *N* means Swami Niranjananda, but I cannot be sure because I have not heard it from his own lips.)
Sunday, 12 Feb.	The meeting with the Raja of Khetri in the morning— his coldness — questions about Miss Muller's withdrawal.

I never asked Swami Saradananda the reason Miss Henrietta Muller of London cut off her connection with Vedanta. I inferred from Mary Lewis Burke's book, *Swami Vivekananda and His Second Visit to the West*,* that Miss Muller equated "religion with self-mortification." Vedanta teaches that strength is the antidote to life's ills; self-mortification weakens the body. To attain Self-enlightenment, the supreme goal of life, we need a healthy body and a vigorous mind. After Buddha's severe self-mortification caused him to faint one day, he renounced extreme asceticism to preach the doctrine of the Middle Path, warning his disciples that extremes lead to failure. The Atman cannot be reached by the weak. The Bhagavad Gita is explicit:

> Yoga is not for the man who overeats, or for him who fasts excessively. It is not for him who sleeps too much, or for the keeper of excessive vigils. Let a man be moderate in his eating and recreation. Moderately active, moderate in sleep and in wakefulness. He will find that yoga (power of mind through concentration) takes away all his unhappiness.
>
> [chapter 6, verse 17]

The Ramakrishna Order is grateful to Miss Muller for her handsome gift to Swami Vivekananda with which he purchased the extensive grounds on the bank of the Ganges for the Belur Math. I believe Swamiji always prayed for Miss Muller's spiritual growth and discovery that the real meaning of religion is the realization of God. The bond between Swamiji and Miss Muller is unbreakable while these details of history are as ephemeral as drifting clouds. Swamiji's love was absolutely unselfish. Sri Ramakrishna once said to Swamiji, "Don't think of your personal salvation. You are meant for great things by the Divine Mother. Be like a Banyan tree. Many weary souls will come to take shelter under your wide branches. Never refuse any of them. Accept them all and give them peace and abiding rest."

Monday, 13 Feb.   The Raja cordial last evening and offered two second class tickets to Ahmedabad.

---

* Published by the Advaita Ashram, Calcutta.

Wednesday, Feb. 22	We do not know how people are receiving us and our work.
Sunday, 26 Feb.	The librarian Dully Rao came and informed us of the meeting at 4 p.m. My first attempt at speaking Hindustani.
Thursday, 6 April	Nivedita's letter about Yogin's (Swami Yogananda's) sad death on 28 March, Tuesday at 3 p.m. Spoke at night in the town hall in Hindustani.

Swami Saradananda stayed in Ahmedabad for three months. Then all of a sudden, a telegram came from Swamiji to return to Belur Math, for he was planning to go the West again and needed to have Swami Saradananda at the Math to supervise the monastary activities and to help in the training of the young *brahmacharis* and swamis.

Monday, 17 April	The S.V.'s telegram to return directly. Decided to start tomorrow.
Tuesday, 18 April	Started by the 8 a.m. train.
Wednesday, 3 May	Calcutta by 8 a.m. Saluted Mother. Started for Math by 4 p.m. Met Swamiji — he anxious to start (for America on his second trip to the West. He took Swami Turiyananda and Sister Nivedita along with him for a definite purpose, which can be known from reading Miss Burke's book).

In those early days his work forced Swami Saradananda to travel a great deal. Swami Gambhirananda recalled:

> In all places his presence created a great stir. In Barisal he stayed for eight days. Here he delivered three public lectures, but day and night he had to talk with crowds of eager souls who would come to him to solve their spiritual problems. Ashwini Kumar Datta, a great devotee and a political leader in Barisal, was beside himself with joy to have a brother disciple of Swamiji and a disciple of Sri Ramakrishna in his town. At Ashwini Kumar's house, Saradananda spent most of his time receiving visitors and discussing various problems with them. He returned to Belur Math in January 1900.

Swamiji fell ill while lecturing in Kashmir and wired Swami Saradananda to come and nurse him. Without delay, Swami Saradananda hurried to his side, hiring a tonga, a small one-horse carriage, to drive him from Rawalpindi to Srinagar in Kashmir. It wasn't long before the coachman began acting peculiarly, whipping and urging the horse to go faster and faster, muttering to himself, "I will see whether Allah protects me this time." The horse was running frantically when another carriage suddenly appeared in the road directly in front of them. The startled animal jumped in the air, one of the wheels of the carriage came loose and bounced away and the baggage was thrown off.

Swami Saradananda wasn't shaken. Of his self-control, Swamiji used to say humorously, "Sarat's is the blood of a fish; it will never warm up." Noting that the carriage was rapidly approaching a tree, he bided his time until the tree was overhead, then caught hold of a limb and swung to the ground. The carriage fell over and disintegrated; the unfortunate horse was killed by a dislodged boulder. What happened to the coachman? I believe he was only badly bruised: Allah had protected him.

On that occasion Swamiji responded well to the nursing, and the crisis passed. But his health was failing and his head-long plunge into work and spiritual practices and the increasing intensity of his spiritual experiences were fast using up what strength remained.

Swamiji died on 4 July 1902. Swami Vivekananda planted the ideal of worshipping God through service to mankind in Swami Saradananda's heart. After Swamiji's *mahasamadhi*, Swami Saradananda practiced that ideal in such large-scale projects as flood and famine relief, the Mission's educational programs, and protecting the monks who had given up their revolutionary politics from the government. And still, he never stopped caring for individuals and watching over those around him; supervising the upbringing of Yogin Ma's three orphan grandchildren was one of his last domestic concerns.

Swami Brahmananda became head of the Math and Mission. A senior swami said of him, "Sri Ramakrishna has brought Swami Vivekananda for the whole world and Swami Brahmananda for himself." But we younger monks felt that Maharaj, as he was known in the Order, had been brought for us, too. It was he who first inspired me to live a life of renunciation for the realization of God and service to humanity, and it was Maharaj who gave me, as he gave so many others, my vows of *bramacharya*.

Swami Saradananda delivered a series of lectures on the Bhagavad Gita at Albert Hall in Calcutta in 1906. The lectures were later published under the title *The Essence of the Bhagavad Gita*. He was an effective speaker in Bengali, English, and Hindustani, which he used in his tours of northwestern India. Sometimes he wrote down his speeches, but often he spoke extemporaneously. He drafted the two speeches he gave for the Ramakrishna Mission Convention of 1926 and asked for my opinion of them. I told him I thought they were very good. "You may say so, but will the public endorse your opinion?" he replied. They did. His audiences at Belur Math remained spellbound in introspective silence for several minutes after he had finished.

During a lecture of a series on Vedanta philosophy in East Bengal, Swami Saradananda was asked to speak about Sri Ramakrishna. He replied with a smile, "As long as there is the slightest trace of egotism it is futile to try to understand Ramakrishna. We were fortunate to sit at the feet of such a man, in whom there was no body consciousness, not the slightest touch of lust and desire. He looked upon all women as the manifested symbol of the Divine Mother. His senses were so pure and so well tuned that even the least thought wave emanating from the

Divine Mother was recorded and would move him automatically like a machine. Every pulsation of thought, every rhythm of his activity was at the bidding of the Supreme Mother. The command of the Mother he felt, not merely in meditation, but heard constantly as a human voice. That voice, incarnated in sound, entered into his ears so that he acted accordingly to teach mankind. Meditate on Sri Ramakrishna. Dwell on his qualities. Then he will reveal himself to you and make you understand everything. There is not the slightest doubt about it. Have faith. How much have we understood of Ramakrishna, of his infinite moods, of his infinite expressions? To tell the truth, very little."

After saying these words, his voice failed and he became motionless like a statue. He stayed in this exalted mood without uttering a single word for some time. The audience was struck with wonder and pondered how great Ramakrishna must be when the thought of him would throw his disciple into samadhi.

An ideal monk must be courageous. He must hold fast to justice and truth both in his inner and outer lives. Swami Saradananda demonstrated these qualities in his dealings with the British colonial office.

In 1909 the swami accepted into the Ramakrishna Order two men who were former revolutionaries. (Later a few other revolutionaries would follow.) By doing so, he invited retaliation from the British and the local police. The two former revolutionaries received spiritual initiation from Holy Mother and later became Swamis Prajnananda and Chinmoyananda. They never betrayed the trust Swami Saradananda placed in them and were valued workers for the Math as long as they lived.

Another former revolutionary, Swami Atmaprakasananda, wrote in his reminiscenses: "But for Swami Saradananda I would have no place in this Order, and the service that I have rendered to the suffering people through the years during flood, famine, epidemics, and earthquakes would not have been possible without his compassionate help. I don't know how to repay my debt of gratitude to the swami, who has been a strong support to me in my difficult days and a worthy benefactor to my soul in my spiritual life."

The presence of the former revolutionaries did bring police surveillance down on the Order. Swami Atmaprakasananda, who had joined in 1912, recalled that when the police learned that he was at the Udbodhan, they summoned Swami Saradananda for questioning. The police official did not offer the swami a chair nor speak courteously to him. Standing, Swami Saradananda gently assured the police official that the young men who joined the Ramakrishna Order give up all political activities. When they were returning to Belur Math, one of the former revolutionaries, who had accompanied the swami to the police department, said in an aggrieved tone, "Swami, I am extremely sorry. It is for my sake that you have had to put up with an insult unworthy of your position."

"Who can insult me?" Swami Saradananda replied. "If my mind does not accept the rudeness, how can I be insulted? Have I kept anything for myself? I have already offered body, mind, and soul at the blessed feet of our Lord, where there cannot be any room for good and bad, honor and dishonor. Be at ease. You need not worry on my behalf."

Later, police officials visited Belur Math. The swami received them cordially and talked to them about the ideals of the Ramakrishna Mission. They were impressed by his genial temperament and candid behavior. Gradually the cloud of suspicion was lifted from their minds.

But the problem did not end there. A few years later some government sedition committee's investigators, who had not met with authorities at Belur Math, filed a report insinuating that the writings of Swami Vivekananda inspired young revolutionaries. The report was followed in 1916 by a speech by Lord Ronaldshay, the governor of Bengal, charging that the Ramakrishna Mission gave shelter to revolutionaries. One part of the speech stated that revolutionaries "often seized the opportunity which membership in a charitable society like the Ramakrishna Mission, or participation in the relief of distress, gives them to meet and influence the boys who have noble ideas, but who have not enough experience to judge where a particular course might lead.... Mean and cruel men do join these societies in order to corrupt the minds of young men who would, if only they were not interfered with, be benefactors to their fellow countrymen."

The governor's statement could have been disastrous. It could have easily provoked the Executive Council of the Viceroy of India to ban the Ramakrishna Order for harboring cruel and mean men with revolutionary tendencies to overthrow the British government. They had done this to the "Anushilan Samitti," a revolutionary movement of Dacca, a few years before, effectively wiping out the movement. At the least our foreign activities would have been stifled by the withholding of passports to swamis. The centers in America, England, and Europe would have suffered a terrible setback. In India, our philanthropic activities would have been hurt. Although the government never gave us substantial money, they did help us in many ways to initiate, expand, consolidate, and execute our relief projects. Employees of the government could not have openly sympathized with our humanitarian activities for fear of prosecution or of losing their jobs. The British government had the full power to curb our Mission work; they could have put an end to our flood and famine relief projects. In the hope of mitigating the damage, Swami Saradananda wrote to the governor, giving him the true story of what had happened. After some time, the swami received a letter asking him to come to the governor's residence to answer questions. When Swami Saradananda arrived, he was received by the governor's secretary, W.R. Gourlay. The swami told Gourlay that the Mission had not deviated from its high spiritual principles and did not engage in political activities, emphasizing the Order's right to accept novices according to its own discretion.

As a result of this interview Lord Ronaldshay did change his official position, a unique reversal in the history of the British government during its regime in India. The governor wrote the swami, "... my object was not to condemn the Ramakrishna Mission and its members. I know the character of the Mission work is entirely nonpolitical, and I have heard nothing but good of its work of social science for the people ... I have full sympathy with the real aims of the Ramakrishna Mission, and it was this abuse of the name of the Mission that I wished to prevent. I hope the words I used will help the Mission to guard against the illegitimate use of its name by unscrupulous people."

Indeed, Swami Saradananda had taken great pains to see that the Order did not become entangled with politics. He knew from studying history that religious movements often lost their power to do good by entering the political arena. Jesus told his disciples, "Render unto Caesar what is Caesar's and unto God what is God's" and "My kingdom is not of this world."

In 1921 Mahatma Gandhi started his noncooperation movement as part of the campaign to free India from British rule. Gandhi's followers wanted the Ramakrishna Mission to boycott British goods, British courts—everything British. Swami Saradananda admired Gandhi for his sincerity, unselfishness, and service to India, but he knew Gandhi's sphere of action was very different from his own. The swami knew the Mission's message must be universal. It must be delivered for the good of all, not just for the good of the Hindus and India. It must be a spiritual, not a political, message. Thus, despite criticism from some of Gandhi's followers, he kept the Mission free of the noncooperation movement.

Because Swami Saradananda was able to remain unperturbed during crisis, he was able to penetrate to the heart of matters and make quick, constructive decisions. He was the embodiment of the Bhagavad Gita's definition of a seer:

>   Not shaken by adversity,
>   Not hankering after happiness;
>   Free from fear, free from anger,
>   Free from the things of desire.
>   I call him a seer, and illumined.
>   The bonds of his flesh are broken.
>   He is lucky, and does not rejoice.
>   He is unlucky, and does not weep.
>   I call him illumined.
>   I call him illumined.

The swami's physical courage was an easy match for his moral courage. Once a sudden storm struck a country boat that was taking Swami Saradananda and Dr. Kanjilal up the Ganges to Belur Math so that the doctor, a devotee, could perform some minor surgery on Swami Brahmananda. Swami Saradananda sat at his ease, smoking a pipe. Halfway across the river, the boat was in danger of swamping. Dr. Kanjilal became panicky, but the swami continued sitting imperturbably, smoking his pipe. Dr. Kanjilal's nerves and the storm worsened. Finally, the doctor flew into a rage at the swami's composure in the face of death and threw the swami's tobacco container into the river. Swami Saradananda kept on smoking.

"Sir," the doctor shouted at him. "Don't you know enough to be afraid? Death is knocking at our door and you sit smoking!"

"What next?" the swami replied with a twinkle. "Are you going to throw away my pipe, too?"

Nothing that ordinary men fear seemed to bother him. Swami Turiyananda used to tell the story of the time when he and Vaikuntha Nath Sannyal—a lay disciple of Sri Ramakrishna—and Swami Saradananda, pilgrimaging to the shrines of the Himalayas, took longer worshipping Shiva at the famous Virupaksha Temple than they had planned. Darkness fell as they made their way down a mountain path toward the rest home for pilgrims. Suddenly a tiger roared.

After a short conference, they decided to split up so that at the worse only one of them could be killed by the tiger. With the tiger roaring close at hand, Swami Saradananda went on his way. Finally, after traveling some distance, he climbed a rock and decided to stay there for the night. He repeated the name of Sri Ramakrishna and went into deep meditation.

In the morning, Swami Turiyananda and Vaikuntha Nath Sannyal, who had both spent the night in safer places, found their friend seated on the rock, still totally unconscious of the outer world.

5

Holy Mother and the Udbodhan

IN 1902 WHEN Swami Trigunatitananda, the chief editor of the *Udbodhan*, left for America, Swami Saradananda took over the responsibility for publishing the Bengali magazine that was one of the chief voices of the Ramakrishna movement. At that time the magazine was printed by Girindra Vasak from his own home in Maitra Lane, where he had a small press called Sarada Press. In November 1906 Girindra passed away, and the *Udbodhan* was moved to a rented house in Bosepara Lane, Baghbazar, Calcutta. The owner saw what he thought was a golden opportunity and increased the rent enormously. Contrary to his expectations, his move prompted Swami Saradananda to think of building a home for the magazine and consolidating its management with the editorial work on the books published by the Ramakrishna Mission.

There was an even more important reason to build in Calcutta—Holy Mother badly needed a place to stay during the periods she set aside to give her blessings to the increasing number of devotees who were seeking her out. Going against opposition from some quarters, the swami borrowed money on his own initiative to finance the construction of a building that would house the publishing house downstairs and Holy Mother upstairs. Towards the end of 1908 the work was finished and the publishing enterprise was installed in its new building at Mukherjee Lane (which has since been changed to the Udbodhan Lane). Depending on whether the speaker was thinking of the downstairs offices or the upstairs residence, the building was variously referred to as the Udbodhan Office, the Udbodhan House, or even Holy Mother's house.

Holy Mother first came there on 23 May 1909. From the house she could easily walk to the Ganges for her daily bath, and she could see the towers of the temple at Dakshineswar, where Sri Ramakrishna had completed his spiritual explorations and where he had taught and shared his experiences with her and his devotees.

Her arrival gave Swami Saradananda great joy. Since the death of Swami Yogananda and the departure of Swami Trigunatitananda to the West, Swami Saradananda had taken up Holy Mother's comfort as his most important work. She was more than the wife of his guru; she was Sri Ramakrishna's first and foremost disciple, who applied his teachings to her day-to-day life, despite all obstacles and discomforts. Now that Sri Ramakrishna was dead, she took up his role of guru—spiritual teacher and guide—uplifting the lives of those who came in contact with her in ways and to an extent that surprised the persons themselves and all who knew them. To Swami Saradananda, Sri Sarada Devi was the Divine Mother in human form. Swami Saradananda's devotion to Holy Mother is a legend to the monks of the Ramakrishna Order. His devotion inspired their understanding of her and deepened their trust in her. Swamiji, writing from America to a brother monk, spoke for both of them when he said, "None of you have understood Mother. Her grace upon me is one hundred thousand times more great than that of the Master's. About Mother I am a little fanatic. I can do anything if she gives the order. I shall give a sigh of relief when you purchase a piece of land and install the living Durga there...."

The necessity of a guru as an awakener of the soul and a dispeller of darkness has been recognized from the early Vedic days down to our modern times. Holy Mother's special quality was that she could not refuse anyone who came to her door for help. Swami Premananda, a disciple of Sri Ramakrishna, once said in astonishment, "What a power Holy Mother is! The poison we cannot digest we send to Holy Mother. But how wonderful it is, the very person whom all gave up as hopeless turned over a new leaf and became a regenerated soul by the magic of her words and the power of her touch."

The words of Holy Mother had an irresistible force because they came from her own experiences. The gift of highest realization, which arose from inner purity and divine contemplation, made her competent to solve the most intricate problems of spiritual life in an infallible manner. When asked how one could lead a spiritual life while performing humdrum duties, she replied, "You must do your normal work. Many are known to do great works under the stress of some strong emotion, but a man's true character is revealed from the manner in which he does his insignificant daily duties. But then prayer and meditation are also necessary. You must meditate twice a day despite your heavy activities. That will be like a helm to a boat. It is idle to expect that dangers and difficulties will not come. But for a man of prayer, they will pass away under the feet like water. One who makes a habit of prayer will easily overcome all difficulties and remain calm and unruffled in the midst of the trials of life."

The art of living lies in one word—simplicity. But we associate greatness with grandeur. To us a great person should have a halo and be able to perform miracles. That is not true, for all the great things of life are very simple. Great literature is simple. When ornate style comes, literature fails to achieve its noble purpose of creativity. It becomes stagnant like a river that has ceased to flow. Similarly good music is also simple. The Fifth Symphony of Beethoven is simple; its music came spontaneously from the inmost depths of his soul, and he gave expression to its flow freely without hindrance by the manipulation of restless thought. Only geniuses can create good literature and first-class music, for they have struggled hard, "scorning delight and living laborious days," to develop their talent, while preserving the freshness and simplicity of inspiration.

Sister Nivedita found this quality in Holy Mother. While she was in Boston taking care of Sara Bull (Mrs. Ole Bull), who had fallen ill, Sister Nivedita took the time to write Holy Mother:

> Dec. 11, 1910
> Dearest Mother—I wish we could send you a wonderful hymn, or a prayer. But somehow even that would seem too loud, too full of noise! Surely you are the most wonderful thing of God—Sri Ramakrishna's own chalice of His Love for the world—a token left with his children, in these lonely days, and we should be very still and quiet before you—ex-

cept indeed for a little fun! Surely the "wonderful things of God" are all quiet—stealing unnoticed into our lives—the air and the sunlight and the sweetness of gardens and of the Ganges. These are the silent things that are like you! Isn't your thought, now and then, of the high calm that neither loves nor hates? Isn't that a sweet benediction that trembles in God, like the dew-drop on the lotus-leaf, and touches not the world?

Swami Saradananda translated this letter into Bengali and read it to Holy Mother. While listening to the words of Nivedita, she entered into a high introspective mood and blessed both Nivedita and Sara from the depth of her heart. Swami Saradananda bowed down and touched the feet of the Mother and went downstairs to return to work. Perhaps he pondered over the words, "the 'wonderful things of God' are all quiet—stealing unnoticed into our lives" and prayed silently that God make us all simple and truly beautiful.

Seated in a small, downstairs room at the Udbodhan House, the swami regulated Holy Mother's visitors. Sometimes he jestingly introduced himself to strangers as her doorman. Assuming the responsibility for her care had not been easy. It involved not only looking after Mother's person but her family, four or five monastic members when she was at Jayrambati and at all times her three nieces, who were eccentric and infirm. Radhu's protracted illness had cost the Mother heavily, draining away her slender and unstable income. Most of her devotees came from middle class families and, regardless of their desire to help, they could not donate liberally. Finally Swami Saradananda wrote to Sara Bull in Boston for help. Immediately, Sara Bull arranged to send 250 rupees a month to meet the Mother's expenses.

Once Holy Mother told Swami Arupananda, "I shall be able to be at the Udbodhan so long as Sarat is there. I don't see anyone who can be responsible for me after that; Sarat can in every respect. He is the man to bear my burden." Swami Arupananda asked if Swami Brahmananda could look after her needs. "No, my child, that is not in his temperament," the Mother answered. "He is cast in a different mold. It is difficult for him to bring his mind down to meet situations which are of a complicated nature.

His mind soars always very high. He can look after me mentally or attend to my needs through someone else."

"What about Swami Premananda?" Arupananda asked.

"No, he can't either."

"But he is running the Belur Math."

"That may be; but looking after women is a bother. He can keep an eye on me only from a distance."

Her remarks remind me of the time when Sri Ramakrishna sat on Sarat's lap for a little while and remarked as he got up, "I was testing to see how much weight you can bear." I believe he was doing more than testing; by that touch he gave the swami the power to bear the heavy responsibility for Holy Mother's care and the administration of the Ramakrishna Math and Mission.

Holy Mother called the swami her Vasuki, the mythical snake, who protected her with a thousand hoods. If anyone tried to persuade the Mother to go to Calcutta when the swami was absent, she would say, "There can be no question of my going to Calcutta when Sarat is not there. To whom shall I go? Suppose I am in Calcutta and Sarat says that he wants to go elsewhere for a few days. Then I tell him, 'Wait a little, my child. First of all, let me leave this place and then you may go.'" In her last days she was heard to remark, "I am tired of this life. I shall now depart, taking Sarat in my arms and carrying him wherever I go." The swami wept like a child on hearing this.

Swami Saradananda always kept Holy Mother informed about efforts of the Ramakrishna Mission to provide relief in drought, famine, and other calamities. In 1919, the swami wrote a long letter to the Mother describing the suffering of people throughout India from a terrible famine and an influenza epidemic. He sought her blessings and prayed to her that the Mission would get the necessary funds from the public for relief activities. Holy Mother burst into tears when an attendant read her the letter. With a choked voice she said, "I cannot bear the suffering of the people anymore. Oh Lord, may you be pleased to do something for them. Be kind enough to put an end to all their sorrows and pain."

Then she looked at the devotees seated around her and said, "Have you seen the heart of Sarat? You will not find another person with so big a heart as Sarat's excepting surely Naren's.

There may be illumined souls, knowers of Brahman, but you will not find another man in India, or elsewhere, so kind, so compassionate, so generous as you see in the personality of Sarat. His heart cries for the suffering of man. He is like the great protector, protecting people with food, shelter, and clothing—whatever may be their needs. No one can be compared to him. As his heart is big, so his love is vast and all-embracing."

In her conversations with her lay disciples, Holy Mother instructed them to live active lives while maintaining inner calm. She used Swami Saradananda to show it could be done. One day she said, "Just see Sarat—how much work he is doing. How many burdens he is bearing on his shoulders. But he does not whisper a word [of complaint] to anybody. His mouth is shut—he is truly a holy man. Why should he bother about all these things? Men like him, if they wish, can easily sit quietly and concentrate on God, devoting their time to meditation for hours and hours together. Why do they not do that? It is only for your good that they bring their minds to a lower plane and engage themselves in all kinds of activities for the sake of suffering humanity."

Holy Mother had absolute trust in the swami. Sometimes she would be hesitant to initiate a devotee, but if the devotee were eager and persistent, she would invariable say, "Go to Sarat. If he says yes, I will give." For his part, Swami Saradananda implicitly obeyed every one of the Mother's instructions and carried out unquestioningly her wishes—with one exception. It happened this way: In 1920 Holy Mother was stricken with kalaazar, a dangerous and painful fever-ridden disease. Her doctors had prescribed a bitter Western medicine to be taken several times a day and a bland diet, consisting mainly of barley water and milk. She followed this regime without complaint for a long time, but finally, it caused her to lose both her appetite and her temper. She scolded her attendant, Sarala Devi, "You know only two things—bring the thermometer to see the temperature and bring barley water and milk, coaxing me to drink more and more. I am tired of all this!" She asked a niece to buy her some puffed rice and food fried in mustard oil—which Jayrambati people are very fond of but which is harmful to kalaazar patients—from a neighborhood shop, one that had a reputation of selling food of not the best quality. When the food was brought to her, she gave some to her niece and put the rest in a cup for herself. She was about to savor the food fried in mustard oil when Swami Saradananda entered the room. (One of her attendants had run to him for help, and as he had climbed the stairs he wondered how he was going to say no to Holy Mother, and yet his sense of responsibility for her well-being compelled him to do just that.)

Seeing him coming, Holy Mother hid the cup behind her back and said, "My child, why have you come? What can I do for you?"

The swami, who had entered her presence with folded hands, knelt down before her, saying, "Mother, I have come for a purpose and I beg you to fulfill it. I request you to give me the cup that is behind your back. All of your children downstairs, including me, will eat its contents joyfully and we will fill it for you again when you are well."

At first Mother, like a little village girl holding onto her favorite thing, was reluctant to yield it up, but she did finally, with the knowledge that Swami Saradananda was asking for it only to serve her.

The incident reminds me of a few lines from a poem: "Who can fathom the depth of the heart of an illumined soul? Sometimes softer than a flower, sometimes harder than a thunderbolt, he walks and moves in the world, spreading the aroma of sweetness and compassion, standing solidly on the firm rock of responsibility that he considers a gift from God as a token of His love."

It was because of the efforts of Swami Saradananda that the Mother consented to have her birthday observed at Vedanta centers throughout the world. One day in December 1919 he approached her with folded hands, saying, "Mother, the devotees have for a long time expressed their desire to me to celebrate your birthday here. If you would permit, we will have the festival here and perform a special worship of Sri Ramakrishna, and the devotees will be invited to participate with their families." Holy Mother replied, "If all want it, let it be done."

The construction of the Udbodhan House put a heavy burden of debt on Swami Saradananda, but the debt caused him to write a biography of Sri Ramakrishna that acquainted many with the Master for the first time and clarified his moods and message for even long-time devotees.

The swami carefully collected all that was known about Sri Ramakrishna and sifted through it painstakingly to give an accurate account of his life up to the year before his death. The book was written under conditions that would have defeated most authors. The publishing quarters of the *Udbodhan* were noisy, crowded, and bustling with activity, most of which required the swami's frequent supervision. But he sat writing at his tiny desk with the same concentration he gave to meditating on the Lord, and the first section of the book was published in the November 1909 issue of the *Udbodhan*; subsequent chapters continued to appear year after year as the book progressed. The magazine continued to require his articles. (These were later published in a book called *Bharati Shakti Puja*—in English, *The Worship of God as Mother in India*.) He also wrote articles for the Ramakrishna Mission's English journal, *Prabuddha Bharata* and assumed the responsibility of editing Swami Vivekananda's book *Jnana Yoga*. His duties as General Secretary of the Math and Mission constantly clamored for his time and energy. Meanwhile his work on these activities was often interrupted by the stream of devotees coming at all hours to see Holy Mother upstairs.

Swami Saradananda would often walk to Girish Chandra Ghosh's house in Bosepara Lane, close to the Udbodhan, and read him the chapter he had just finished writing. He would patiently wait for the playwright's opinion, for the swami considered Girish *Babu* (to use the Indian term of respect) an outstanding figure in Bengali literature. Girish Babu was delighted with the book and gave the swami tremendous encouragement in his work. In this way a friendship grew between the two very different personalities. Girish Ghosh was not only not a monastic, he had led a wild careening life in the Bohemian circles of Calcutta before meeting Sri Ramakrishna and becoming his disciple. Even then, his boisterous ways and carousing did not stop. Finally, as Swami Saradananda recorded in *Sri Ramakrishna, the Great Master* in his chapter on the attitude of the guru, Sri Ramakrishna persuaded Girish Ghosh to give him "the power of attorney" over all his activities. This famous incident began when

Sri Ramakrishna gave the dramatist a number of minimal religious disciplines to perform. But Ghosh, knowing his own fiery nature and profligate tendencies, doubted his ability to perform even these few basics. "Finding Girish silent," Swami Saradananda wrote, "the Master looked at him and, knowing his thoughts, said, 'Very well, if you cannot do that, remember Him (God) once before taking food and before going to bed.'"

Ghosh was in a terribly sorry plight and remained motionless and speechless, but there raged, as it were, a storm of anxiety, fear, and despair in his heart. The Master looked at Girish again and then said, smiling, "You will say, 'What if I cannot do even that?' Very well then, give me your power of attorney."

Power of attorney is a transference of responsibility to a trustworthy person who will execute all legal matters in court on behalf of the person who has signed such a deed.

Ghosh agreed at once, thinking he had found the lazy man's path to God. Having a person whom many noted religious figures regarded as a living incarnation of God, acting on one's behalf seemed a sure-fire path to success. But there is a deeper meaning to Sri Ramakrishna's offer; this meaning was revealed to Ghosh's mind as he began to associate with Sri Ramakrishna and learn from him over a period of several years. The dramatist found that his agreement required, among other things, thinking of Sri Ramakrishna with great frequency and as a result, his life was transformed.*

The public agreed with Girish Ghosh's opinion of the swami's writing. *Sri Ramakrishna Lilaprasanga* (in English, *Sri Ramakrishna, the Great Master*) quickly became a classic of Bengali literature and has been translated into many different languages.

Of all Sri Ramakrishna's monastic disciples, only Swami Saradananda kept a diary of day-to-day events, particularly those incidents that were connected with Holy Mother during her sojourn on earth. In Vedanta traditionally, there had been the feeling that spiritual aspirants should not pay much attention to time. They should practice constant remembrance of God

---

* For Girish Ghosh's reminisences of Sri Ramakrishna, translated from Bengali by Swami Aseshananda, see page 222.

with the purpose of realizing God, a timeless experience. History belongs to time. Samadhi, the experience of God, transcends time. All concepts and objects belonging to the world of change and relationship—to maya—are essentially distractions from the purpose of realizing God.

The advent of Sri Ramakrishna is intended to bring about a reconciliation between time and timelessness, reason and faith, action and contemplation. This is the reason that Swami Saradananda took great pains to record in his biography, *Sri Ramakrishna, the Great Master*, only those incidents that he could gather from actual eye witnesses. He always sifted facts from opinions. He would unceasingly encourage me to distinguish what I had seen from what I had heard from others and then to verify the truth of what I had heard. He was a staunch admirer and uncompromising advocate of truth—both historical (*vyavaharika*) and transcendental truth.

Here are some excerpts from his diary pertaining to Holy Mother's last days:

Friday, February 27, 1920	Sri Sri Ma reached here (from Jayrambati) at about 9 p.m. in Dr. Kanjilal's motor (car). (She had fallen ill and had been brought to Calcutta for treatment.)
Saturday, February 1920	H. M. under Dr. Kanjilal's treatment (Dr. Kanjilal was a homeopathic physician).
Monday, March 1, 1920	Sri Sri Ma better though suffering slight rise of temperature in the afternoon.
Wednesday, March 3	H. M. better and free from fever.
Friday, March 5	H. M. had gone up to 101° temperature in the afternoon.

Friday, March 12 — H. M.'s fever rose higher. Shyamadas Kaviraj's treatment began.

Thursday, April 8 — H. M. not better with Kaviraj's treatment so Dr. Bepin Ghosh took up her case from today.

Saturday, May 1 — Dr. P. D. Bose called for H. M.
(Dr. Bose was an Indian Christian. He was the chief physician of St. Paul's Cathedral Mission College, where I studied for my B.A. degree. On his first visit, he took the usual fee, but after hearing from Swami Saradananda that his patient was the wife of Sri Ramakrishna, whom he had come to respect from reading the Bengali version of the *Gospel of Sri Ramakrishna*, he refused to accept a fee in his subsequent visits. He continued to give his services freely and to visit Mother frequently until her *mahasamadhi*.)

Sunday, May 16 — Dr. P. D. Bose declared this case to be kalaazar (I believe kalaazar is a virulent disease characterized by high fever and a darkening of the skin that is said to be brought on by the darkening of the red blood corpuscles; in English it is called black fever. It is rarely found in the West. Dr. U.N. Brahmachari, who discovered "Soamin" as the antidote for the disease, was requested to give an injection. Swami Saradananda noted in his diary, "Dr. U.N. Brahmachari left, very sad and disappointed at the news. What to do next?")

Tuesday, June 1 — Doctors seem to have come to their tether's end with regard to the case of Holy Mother. So Kaviraj Rajenda Nath was called today and given charge of the case.

Thursday, June 17 — Sri Sri Ma very ill with indigestion and inflammatory pain in stomach. Very serious condition, but Kaviraj says it will pass over.

(Buddha says, "All compounded things must come under the law of decadence and decay. Therefore, Oh, Ananda, be a lamp unto yourself and work out your salvation with diligence.")

July 20, Tuesday	Holy Mother in peace and glory of *Mahasamadhi* at 1:30 a.m.
July 21, Wednesday	procession to Belur Math via Baranagore at about 10:30 a.m. and the *yajna* (oblation in fire) at about 3 p.m. A heavy shower ended the ceremony at about dusk.
August 1, Sunday	Special *puja* of the Ramakrishna Order at Belur and Calcutta Maths on account of the ascension of Holy Mother.
August 2, Monday	Special *puja* at the Nivedita Girls' School.

The direct disciples of Sri Ramakrishna alone knew the greatness of Holy Mother and recognized who she really was. Swami Shivananda, the President of our Order, wrote to a disciple of Holy Mother:

> The physical body of Holy Mother is no more visible to our mortal sight, it is true. There is no doubt that her passing away fills her devotees with pain. But they should take comfort in the thought that Holy Mother was not an ordinary woman. She was neither a seeker after truth nor an illumined soul. She is a special manifestation of the eternally free Universal Mother. She is one of the Divine Mother's beautiful expressions; she can be compared to the ten manifestations of the Divine Mother. In this age the Mother has

appeared in the world as Sri Saradamani Devi, her form made of the attributes of pure sattva, for the redemption of humanity and to help Sri Ramakrishna, the Avatara of our age, in his divine mission. Those that have received her grace have fulfilled the purpose of life. They are blessed. They will certainly be able to see her the moment they implore her with a longing heart to reveal herself to them by repeating the name, "Mother, Mother." I request you not to give way to depression. When the earthly mother dies, her children cannot see her in spite of their cries. But that is not true in the case of this mother, the Mother of the world, who has descended to the earth to lead her children to the abode of peace and freedom.

The Mother will grant her vision to a devotee if he cries to her in anguish. You are extremely fortunate because you have been initiated by her and received her grace. Whenever you pray to her with an importunate heart, being unable to bear the pang of separation, she will appear before you and console you. Believe me; it is true. The way you have expressed your sorrow to me, convey your sorrow to her and you will be comforted. This is not a human affair. It is a supernatural affair—an act of God as a token of God's love. Therefore, I advise you not to lose heart. Have firm and unwavering faith. Let not your faith be shaken even if the head be severed from the body and the world reduced to dust in the twinkling of an eye. Always cultivate constructive thoughts and say to yourself, "I am the Divine Mother's child. She has showered her grace upon me. What should I fear from the world? Why should I worry about my future? I am already free and my freedom cannot be taken away even by death." Keep faith and have absolute trust in the Mother. I am not telling you all this just to console you. These words are unquestionably true. They have come from my heart and from the depths of my soul. What more can I say? Accept my sincere blessing. That Holy Mother may keep you in peace and grant you your heart's desire—this is my prayer.

Before her passing, Holy Mother said to one of her disciples, "Don't worry when I am gone. There will be Sarat to look after you." The disciples of the Mother did indeed find a tower of strength in the swami. The privilege of attending him helped fill the void in my heart for the loss of the person who was both my spiritual mother and my guru. Many women disciples of Holy Mother would come to the swami in the late afternoon each day at the Udbodhan House for interviews and guidance. One woman devotee wrote, "Swami Saradananda has filled the void left by Holy Mother. We have lost a mother, but we have another mother in Swami Saradananda. Like Mother, he has been very compassionate to us and we feel very close to him."

Two verses of Shankara's *Crest Jewel of Discrimination* describe Swami Saradananda and his service to others:

> There are pure souls who have attained peace and greatness. They bring good to mankind, like the coming of spring. Having themselves crossed the dreadful ocean of this world, they help others to cross without any selfish motive. It is the very nature of these great souls to work of their own accord, to cure the troubles of others....

Sarala Devi wrote:

> After the passing away of Holy Mother, Swami Saradananda would rarely leave Udbodhan.... When the lady disciples of Holy Mother would come to Udbodhan, Swami Saradananda would feel a great joy. He would do everything in his power to make them feel comfortable, happy, and free, as Holy Mother used to do when she was alive. One day Swami Saradananda said to me when I went to see him in Udbodhan, "It is the Mother who has given all of these responsibilities to me. I am simply fulfilling her wish. Everything belongs to her. I take good care of Mother's children so that Mother will be happy."
>
> Again, I have seen when the swami would give initiation and his disciple would offer something substantial for the service of the guru. He would invariably use it for Mother's work. Before initiation if any student would ask about the things he should bring, the swami would plainly say, "Bring something for the worship of the Mother according to your means. That will be enough."
>
> Any money that his disciple would give as an honorarium to the guru, he would keep in the same box which he inherited from the Mother as a legacy, and which had

belonged to her, and use it for Mother's worship and service at Jayrambati. If he would receive cloth and other things, he would distribute it to the monks and to the brothers of Holy Mother, exactly as Holy Mother used to do.

If he received any money for his own personal needs, he would divide it in a threefold manner. One portion would be used for Sri Ramakrishna's service at Udbodhan, another portion would be for Holy Mother's worship at Jayrambati and the remaining balance would be used for his own personal needs. He would say, "I do this because the donors will be spiritually benefitted if I offer the major portion to our Master and Mother and leave a small amount for myself."

This attitude was reflected in whatever he did. When Sarala Devi wrote him from Comilla in East Bengal, where she had gone as a teacher for the Sister Nivedita Girls' School, asking for his blessings, the swami replied, "I have emptied my purse to you. You have served Holy Mother very faithfully. You have received her affection and many kindnesses. Now try to realize her true nature, for then you will achieve everything in life."

6

Western Visitors

DURING HIS PRESIDENCY of the Ramakrishna Order, Swami Brahmananda delegated the responsibility of receiving Western visitors to Swami Saradananda. Maharaj knew that Swami Saradananda would be the most capable person to make these guests comfortable and to communicate to them the ideals of the Ramakrishna Order.

The first visitor to Belur Math was the famous French singer, Madame Emma Calvé, who had been instrumental in arranging for the trip of Swami Vivekananda to the Far East and to Egypt.

Once Swamiji in a casual remark requested Madame Calvé to visit India. The pressing demands of her engagements in Europe and America prevented her from fulfilling his request during his lifetime. In 1911, deciding the time had come to make good her promise, Madame Calvé arrived at Belur Math with an interpreter. Swami Saradananda met with her immediately and took her to the small shrine built in memory of Swamiji on the actual spot where his body was cremated. Madame Calvé sat down in a meditation posture and prayed before the engraved emblem of Swami Vivekananda. Accompanied by the interpreter and a lay disciple of Swamiji, they walked across the spacious lawn to visit the temple Swamiji built in honor of Sri Ramakrishna. After Madame Calvé paid her respects to Sri Ramakrishna, she said to Swami Saradananda, "Swamiji used to repeat a nice chant which starts, 'Lead us from darkness to light.' Would you kindly repeat the whole chant if you know it. I am anxious to hear it."

Immediately, Swami Saradananda, with his sonorous voice,

chanted, "*Asato ma sadgamaya. Tamaso ma yotir gamaya. Mrityor ma amritam gamaya.*" (Lead me from the unreal to the real. Lead me from darkness to light. Lead me from death to immortality.) "Om, peace, peace, peace."

Swami Saradananda's chanting brought back memories of Swamiji to Madame Calvé. She saluted the Master, kneeling down with her head bent low as they do in a Catholic church; then she stood and was about to leave when Swamiji's disciple requested her to sing a song as an offering to the Master. Her magnificent voice charged the whole atmosphere with beauty.

On their way to the door, Madame Calvé caught sight of the picture of Holy Mother and asked, "Who is she?" Swami Saradananda said, "She is the wife and spiritual companion of Sri Ramakrishna. We lovingly call her Holy Mother, *Sangha-mata*, the Mother who supports and sustains our whole organization." At the request of Swamiji's disciple, Madame Calvé sang a rapturous song to please Holy Mother and win her grace.

In her book *My Life*,* Madame Calvé writes about her visit to Belur Math:

> Years later, when I was travelling in India, I wished to visit the convent where the Swami had spent his last days. His mother took me there. I saw the beautiful marble tomb that one of his American friends, Mrs. Leggett, had erected over his grave.... The monks of the Swami's brotherhood received us with simple, kindly hospitality. They offered us flowers and fruits, spreading a table for us on the lawn beneath a welcome shade. At our feet the mighty Ganga flowed. Musicians played tunes in strange instruments accompanying plaintive chants that touched the very heart. A poet improvised a melancholy recitative in praise of the departed Swami. The afternoon passed in a peaceful contemplative calm. The hours that I spent with these gentle philosophers have remained in my memory as a time apart. These beings, pure, beautiful, and remote, seemed to belong to another universe, a better and wiser world....

Lord Ronaldshay, the Governor of Bengal, came to visit Belur Math in 1919 on the public celebration of Sri Ramakrish-

---

* Nanda Mookerjee, ed., *Sri Ramakrishna in the Eyes of Brahmo and Christian Admirers* (Calcutta: Firma KLM Private, Ltd.).

na's birthday. Swami Saradananda received the governor with due courtesy and honor. The governor showed an interest not only in the Mission's secular activities, he asked to see the temple. When Swami Saradananda and the governor reached the temple door, the swami explained that devotees do not enter the temple wearing shoes out of respect to the deity. The governor genially acceded to the custom, but unused to taking off his shoes in public, soon blundered into difficulties. Swami Saradananda bent down and unloosed the shoelaces himself and helped the governor remove his shoes. Standing before the portrait of Ramakrishna in the shrine, Swami Saradananda explained to Lord Ronaldshay that the monks came to the temple three times a day for silent prayer and meditation and that the Master's influence extended outside the temple as the fountainhead of all their public works and the source of their personal dedication.

Then the governor asked to see the place where the rich and poor ate together without distinction of caste, creed, or color. (The Ramakrishna Mission's disregard of caste was a strong influence in freeing the country from bondage to superstitious practices.) The governor watched the preparation of the *khichuri* and a delicious sweet called *bunde* with interest; he inquired about everything he saw. Swami Saradananda explained that at the public celebration thousands of people would be fed; however, the people came not only for food but because they felt that Sri Ramakrishna would appear that day and accept their worship in his universal form of "Shiva as Jiva—God in Man."

The impression that visit made on Lord Ronaldshay was recorded in the anthology *Sri Ramakrishna in the Eyes of Brahmo and Christian Admirers*:*

> Associated with the monastic order which consists of sannyasins and brahmacharins is a mission, these twin organizations standing for renunciation and service respectively, declared by the late Swami Vivekananda to be the two national ideals of India. The mission undertakes service of all kinds, social, charitable, and educational. The monasteries are dedicated to the perpetuation through their spiritual culture of the great Ideal and Revelation which Sri

---

* For complete text see Letters.

Ramakrishna Paramahamsa embodied in his life. One of these branch monasteries, the Ashram of Mayavati hidden away from the world in the vast labyrinth of the Himalayas 50 miles northeast of Almora, is devoted exclusively to the study of advaita Vedanta, leading to knowledge of the Brahman proclaimed by Shankara, the absolute, impersonal and unconditional God—the material and efficient cause of the universe.

Some of these men I have met at the Belur Math. And having met them I know it is for no colorless abstraction that they have renounced the world. Whether known as saguna Brahman (God personal) or nirguna Brahman (God impersonal), it is to them the sole reality, the ultimate goal towards which sooner or later all mankind must direct its steps.

Another visitor was Mrs. Cook, an English woman from a good middle-class family. I never met Mr. Cook, a high official of the East Indian Railway Company in India, but I have seen Mrs. Cook several times in the Udbodhan. Whenever she would come, she would bring flowers, fruits, and candy in great abundance. Mrs. Cook was so charmed by the personality of Swami Saradananda that she wanted to take initiation from him. Seeing her earnestness mingled with sincerity, Swami Saradananda agreed to her request. An auspicious day was fixed and Swami Saradananda gave her initiation, after performing certain ritualistic ceremonies. Mrs. Cook loved and respected Swami Saradananda just as a daughter would adore her noble father; she would do anything to please him.

The Hindu idea of the motherhood of God appealed to her. Once she wrote a member of our Order, "I always call Sri Guru Maharaj *Mother*; it seems to be my national cry. I always addressed my Swami as that too. He has signed himself that. I know who he was and is. He could not hide from me."

Swami Saradananda was very fond of his Western disciple. He took special care not only of her spiritual well-being but also of her physical health. Seeing that the hot climate of Calcutta had enervated her, the swami advised her to go to Almora, a hill station in the Himalayas noted for its beautiful climate. She followed his advice and recovered her strength.

I have written letters to Mrs. Cook dictated by the swami

who used to address her as Beatrice. On 18 August 1925 Swami Saradananda wrote her:*

> The thing is, it is literally true and I am finding it to be so every day at present, that we cannot do anything however little or simple, unless the Divine Being wills it. So I will not try to explain matters. I have given you up entirely into the hands of the Master, and I am sure he will lead you safely and surely in his own time to truth, and peace everlasting. With my love and blessings to you always,
> Yours affectionately, Saradananda.

Mrs. Cook wrote the swami, asking for advice about the training of her daughter, Enid. The swami replied:

> We think we are loving without any selfish taint or hope of return, but deep within us there lurks the expectation that it should be returned and are quite at a loss when we find the case to be not exactly up to our inmost wishes. "To make our words move always in unison with our thoughts is the highest of all attainments," said Sri Ramakrishna; and Jesus said, "Be ye therefore perfect as your father in Heaven is perfect!" Remember always that children have brought their own karma with their birth and will develop accordingly in their own lines, and to hold before them the highest ideal by living the same is all that we can do to help them.
> Now for our belief in warnings, in a general way all of us believe in them. But in coming to practise it in our daily lives, we find it to be a very complex and puzzling affair. . . . So you see, it is not possible to lay a general rule of conduct. We shall have to adapt ourselves to each individual case in deciding. The best we can do under such complex cases is what our Holy Mother said and used to do herself—pray to the Lord and bring yourself to a perfectly unbiased mood and then, thinking over the question, decide to do what flashes in your mind after prayer.
> With my love and blessings to you and your children always, Yours affectionately, Saradananda.

---

* Translated by Rosamon Gilder, Appleton, N.Y., 1922

7

Caring for Others

SWAMI SARADANANDA WAS a wonderful nurse. He knew how to follow a doctor's instructions efficiently when caring for a patient. Just as important, he knew how to buoy up the spirits of those he cared for.

The swami sometimes sat up all night with sick patients who were hard to manage. He was always available for solving special problems such as convincing patients they must take their medicine. Swami Chidananda, one of Swami Brahmananda's attendants, was brought to the Udbodhan House for treatment when he fell ill. He refused his medicine, saying, "I will drink green coconut water and repeat the name of Hari." When Swami Saradananda heard that, he came to Chidananda's bedside and stroked his head gently. "Well, Chidananda," he said, "you can chant the name of Hari as much as you like, but coconut water you can't drink until your disease is cured. Now you will have to take medicine. Otherwise the doctor, who is giving free service, will not attend you." Chidananda took the medicine and was well in a few days.

No treatment was too difficult or too disgusting for the swami to attend to with his own hands. In the early days of the Alambazar monastery, when the disciples of Sri Ramakrishna were living together in great austerity, Swami Abhedananda had gone on a pilgrimage to northwestern India. He had followed the conservative north Indian sadhus' custom of walking barefoot to all the holy places and had returned to the Alambazar Math with a nasty wound on his right foot. A doctor diagnosed it as an infection caused by guinea worm. Proper nursing was vital if Swami Abhedananda were to get well; he could easily lose his leg and quite possibly his life.

For three months Swami Saradananda removed worms from the infection, washed the sore, applied ointment, and bandaged the foot. His unceasing care prevented the development of gangrene, and he kept Swami Abhedananda from becoming despondent by reminding him how Sri Ramakrishna maintained an inner calm despite the excruciating pain of his throat cancer. Years later, at the memorial held after Swami Saradananda had *mahasamadhi,* Swami Abhedananda said in his speech, "Brother Sarat, you are the giver of my life. How can I forget you? Please accept a few tears from my eyes in exchange for what you have done for me."

Swami Saradananda believed the mind as well as the body must be cared for. Despite the many demands on his time, he helped Margaret Nobel, the Irish devotee named Sister Nivedita by Swamiji, run a school for the education of Indian girls, which she founded in Calcutta with Holy Mother's blessings. He taught classes on the Bhagavad Gita and encouraged the school's teachers and students to come to Holy Mother for *darshan* and instruction and to gain the spiritual benefit from doing personal services for her.

The swami also encouraged Sarala Devi, who later became Bharatiprana, to attend the Lady Wellington Nursing School in Calcutta to become a qualified nurse. When Golap Ma, a companion of Holy Mother, objected that a Brahmin girl should not earn money, the swami pointed out that she was not going to nurse for the money but to be able to serve the Mother and her companions better. In her reminiscences Bharatiprana wrote:

> I used to go to Holy Mother's House almost every day from Sister Nivedita's Girls' School in Calcutta where I was staying.
>
> I had retired from teaching. Swami Saradananda had arranged for my board and lodging with his own funds. One day I heard from Swami Saradananda that Satadal, the wife of Sachin who was the grandson of the Rani of Punthia in Bengal, was very ill. Sachin and Satadal were both disciples of the swami.
>
> One evening Sachin came and said to the swami, "The illness has taken a very serious turn. I would appreciate it if you would kindly come to our house once and bless Satadal."

The next day when I went to see him, Swami Saradananda said to me, "Well, I believe Satadal will get well this time." I asked the swami, "Maharaj, how could you tell that Satadal will get well?" The swami replied, "When I went to see Satadal at her home, I saw Holy Mother (in a vision) placing Satadal's head on her lap and looking at her face with deep concern. Since Holy Mother was keeping Satadal's head on her lap and was anxious about her, I feel confident that Satadal will be cured through Mother's grace."

A day passed; the condition of Satadal became very grave. A medical doctor from Calcutta was called in. His judgment was, "The case is very serious and there is no hope."

At the Udbodhan, Swami Saradananda was rubbing some oil on his body and was about to take a bath when Sachin came in, caught hold of his feet and said in great despair, "The famous doctor, Nilratan Sarcar, has pronounced the case to be hopeless. I am in deep trouble. I have nowhere to go but to you. Please help me."

Hearing the words of Sachin, Swami Saradananda was deeply moved and looked at him compassionately. Sachin said, "Maharaj, you will have to come again to see Satadal."

At this Swami Saradananda replied, "What is the use of my going? Will it be of any avail? Please ask the priest to give you some holy water from the shrine. Call the ayurvedic physician, Shamadas Kaviraj, and ask him to see the patient and treat her."

Swami Saradananda quickly finished his bath. Before he sat for meditation, he said to his attendants, "It is my wish that none of you should call me until I finish my meditation and move from my seat of my own accord." Three hours passed. The swami remained absorbed in deep meditation. It is said that the prayer of an illumined soul never goes unanswered. After three hours the swami left his seat and attended to his normal business.

In a few days Satadal showed signs of improvement and was on her way to recovery. In a week she was her normal self again. Swami Saradananda remarked, "Some words of Sachin created a little doubt in my mind, but the Divine Mother has kindly removed that doubt in her own mysterious way. When Sachin came and, with tears in his eyes, said the case was hopeless, I did not know what to say to him. But now since the clouds have dispersed I am convinced that what the Divine Mother showed to me was absolutely true. All things are possible for her to accomplish. Glory be to her."

In contrast to his concern for the health of others, the swami bore his own illnesses with little fuss. In 1914 he was suffering greatly with kidney trouble, but he hardly mentioned his pain for fear Holy Mother, who was then in residence, would become worried. Neither did he permit the illnesses that plagued him increasingly as he grew older to deter him from devotional activities. Once his doctors ordered him to go to Puri in the hopes that regular bathing in the sea water would relieve his rheumatism. While he was there, he went to the temple of Jagannath every morning. Swami Gambhirananda recalled, "During the Car Festival it was a sight for the gods to see a fat person like the swami holding the rope of the car and pulling it with great enthusiasm and devotion."

Swami Saradananda was equally unsparing of himself in his work schedule; his daily life was lived with clocklike precision. He would rise at five in the morning and meditate in his room at the Udbodhan House. Then he would climb to the roof where he could see the Ganges and walk for half an hour. Coming down to his room, he would rub oil on his body and go to the Ganges for his bath. If he were too ill to go, he would ask me to use the hand pump to bring water to his bathroom on the second floor. Then he would put on a dry *dhoti* and take his breakfast of toast, cheese, orange marmalade, and tea. When he had completed his morning chores with his customary dispatch and orderliness, he would eat his mid-day meal in his room and rest for an hour or so.

After Swami Brahmananda's *mahasamadhi* in 1922 when Swami Saradananda began giving initiation to large numbers of people, he devoted the morning hours to *japa*, deep meditation, and praying for the good of all the people of the world. Occasionally, if the request were urgent, he would come downstairs and give spiritual instruction to devotees; otherwise the morning was given over to God, and his correspondence and other chores were crammed into the afternoon.

In the mid-afternoon he would read his mail and dictate. He always read what I had typed with great care before signing.

The swami reserved the hour between five and vespers for the women devotees who came for his blessings and spiritual advice and to talk about Holy Mother. When the vespers bell rang, the talk would cease, the women would go home, and the swami would disappear into his room to meditate. He came down after vespers to meet with the male devotees, who often had come from long distances to resolve their doubts and gain comfort and encouragement from the swami's words. Sometimes not a word was spoken; the swami would remain completely indrawn. But he radiated such serenity that the atmosphere was charged with the presence of God. Occasionally in the evening he would call for Swami Purnananda, whom he addressed as Doctor Maharaj.

"Well, Doctor," he would say, "what are you doing over there by yourself?"

"Maharaj," Swami Purnananda would ask in return, "how does one attain *asana-siddhi* (perfection while seated in an easy posture)?"

"Exactly as you are doing." And more than once Swami Saradananda would add, "You don't go out from your room— you're always sitting quietly behind closed doors. You get no exercise. I am afraid you will contract some disease. You should go out in the fresh air. Always take care of your health, for a sadhu's health is an asset. When his health is sound and his mind is cheerful, he can meditate well." This was a case of the "nurse" prescribing for the doctor. Swami Purnananda was an L.M.P. (Licensed Medical Practitioner) of the Calcutta Medical School, which awarded a diploma and not an M.D. degree. Swami Purnananda was skilled in the basics of western medicine; for that reason he had been sent to Mayavati to work in the Charitable Dispensary of the Advaita Ashrama. When Golap Ma had a heart attack, Swami Saradananda told me to bring Swami Purnananda. After he examined her, he assured us that the time had not come for her passing away. He was right.

Night offering was taken to the shrine at eight o'clock. The swami talked to the devotees until the offering came down from the shrine room. Then he would go upstairs to his room, eat a light supper, and go to bed around ten.

He was a talented cook. When he prepared meals, they were not only delicious, they satisfied the tastes of the different members of the monastic brotherhood. The swami was not a strict vegetarian like Swami Premananda. He used to eat the fish *prasad* from Sri Ramakrishna's shrine. Having been to America and Europe, he liked Western foods. He used to ask me to buy cheddar cheese, and orange marmalade, which were imported from London. Unlike most orthodox Hindus, Swami Saradananda did not shun bread that has been made with chicken eggs; sometimes he ate English cream cracker biscuits, too.

He used to tease me, saying, "You eat like a bird. How will you be able to do the Lord's work if you don't take care of your health? Eat well. Look at me and learn from me. Gather a few pounds of flesh and increase your weight. That will please me."

At that time I had the idea that the thinner you are, the more spiritual you are. It took me a long time to brush aside that idea. I learned to my surprise after coming to the West that I had to practice what I preached: "The Atman cannot be realized by a person who is weak. Strength alone is the medicine for all the ills of this life. Be strong, be fearless."

At one time I was very much disturbed over my health, which had remained poor since contracting malaria during the famine relief work in Khulna, Bengal. Swami Saradananda listened attentively when I brought the problem to him and chanted a line from a Bengali song, "Dangers of Himalayan magnitude will move away in a twinkling of an eye." Then he placed his hand on my head in blessing. I felt I was a new man. All my worries vanished. Since that day my faith in him has been absolute. I made up my mind that as long as he should live, I would stay with him and serve him.

Years later, he said to me affectionately, "All I could do, I have done for you. Still your health has not improved. If you go to America, your health will be all right." The wish of a perfected soul always comes true. I had never dreamed of coming to America, but destiny brought me here. Now I feel that it was to fulfill Swami Saradananda's desire that the Lord arranged to bring me here and grant me health so I might serve his devotees in the West.

In his dealings with us younger monks the swami's love and forgiveness were limitless. One day when I was with him at Puri, he told me he couldn't find the beads that he usually kept in a drawer. "They belonged to the Holy Mother and I kept them after her *mahasamadhi*," he said. "They were strung on a golden thread. Probably somebody came and took them on account of the golden thread while we were away seeing Lord Jagannath at his temple." I was concerned. I thought perhaps I had accidentally thrown the rosary into the sea along with the flowers after evening worship. I returned to the beach and searched for a long time but found nothing. The swami consoled me: "One by one everything is going away. This is the will of the Mother. What can be done? Don't worry."

As Swami Saradananda grew older, he could no longer personally look after the health of our sick monks and devotees, but he still gave his love and sympathy to the ill. One day when the temperature in Calcutta was over 100 degrees, Swami Purnananda called me and said, "Swami Saradananda has just left the house. It would be good if you would follow him and inquire where he is going."

Walking quickly, I reached the Baghbazar Street streetcar depot, where I spotted the swami. As soon as he saw me he said, "It is rather hot. You better go home and rest."

I told him I'd rather go with him. He gave me money and I bought two first-class tickets and we climbed aboard. "Where should we get down?" I asked. "Ezra Street," the swami replied. After five minutes we reached the street and I helped the swami off the car. We walked a few minutes in the stifling air and arrived at a building where a devotee was living on the second floor.

The devotee, named Khokani, was a Parsee who was suffering from advanced tuberculosis. He was overjoyed at the sight of Swami Saradananda. Khokani coughed almost continuously and was not careful about sanitary rules, using his hands instead of a handkerchief when he coughed. Nevertheless, the swami sat on his bed and comforted him by putting his hand on his head and massaging it gently.

Khokani asked his brother, who was caring for him, to go buy some fruits and sweets. Within minutes Khokani's brother returned. Without first washing his hands, Khokani peeled the fruits, sliced them and arranged the pieces in a dish with the sweets, offering them to the swami.

"Khokani," I protested, "Maharaj has just finished his meal. I don't think he will be able to take anything now."

But Khokani insisted. "Please take something, Swami," he begged. "It will make me happy."

Swami Saradananda took a few slices of fruit and a few sweets and gave the dish to me. I also took a little as the swami's *prasad*. The swami sat quietly and meditated a little and then took leave of Khokani, asking his brother to keep him informed of the sick man's condition.

On our way back to the Udbodhan, I said, "Maharaj, you should not have taken those fruits. I have heard that tuberculosis is very infectious. Your life is precious to all of us."

Swami Saradananda replied by quoting Sri Ramakrishna: "No harm will come if one accepts the food given with a loving heart."

After a few days, Khokani's brother reported that the sick man had passed away, comforted by his memory of the swami's visit and his love. I realized then that sanitary rules were not as important as fulfilling the wishes of a dying man. I recalled the words of a Hindu poet: "Who can fathom the depth of feeling in the hearts of great souls. They may do things mysterious to us, but their actions will always bear a deeper meaning in the eyes of God."

8

Swami Saradananda's Sense of Humor

HOLY MAN, WRITER, editor, nurse, lecturer, administrator, educator, Swami Saradananda was also a joyful man. No one could be around him long without becoming caught up in the fun he initiated or discovering his sense of humor.

I have seen Swami Saradananda happily romping with a little boy he had volunteered to care for. The incident happened when Harendranath, a close relative of Swamiji, adopted a little boy after his marriage. After serving for many years at our Vrindavan Sevashrama, Harendranath had to come to Calcutta to obtain treatment for tuberculosis. Swami Saradananda initiated his wife and arranged for her and the boy to stay at the Nivedita Girls' School, while Harendranath was being treated. The little boy, an excitable, restless child, created trouble both for his teacher and other children. Finally, the head mistress said to the swami, "Maharaj, during the recess period when the children are out to play, the boy fights with the children. I don't know what I should do to solve this matter."

Swami Saradananda said to her, "Please send the boy to the Udbodhan with the doorman of the school when it is time for recess, and I shall take care of him." Without taking his afternoon rest, the swami played with the boy in his room. One day the boy arrived as Swami Saradananda was finishing his midday meal, so the swami gave the boy a cup of rice mixed with milk, banana, and a little sugar. The boy said with a sigh, "I have not tasted milk for a long time. I wish I could get it every day." In those days if you did not have a cow, you did not have milk; at home in Vrindavan, Harendranath kept a cow to provide milk for the boy.) Hearing the boy's words, Swami Saradananda arranged for him to be given milk as long as he stayed at Nivedita's School; and every recess, the boy continued to play with the swami, whom he thought was his chum, not his babysitter.

Swami Brahmananda also loved to play with children. I have seen him put on a mask of a tiger and tease the grandchildren of Balaram Bose, a lay disciple of Sri Ramakrishna, stop to give them a handful of candies, and then go on with the play.

Sometimes Swami Brahmananda and Swami Saradananda would conspire to tease us young monks. When the time I hoped to be initiated into *brahmacharya* drew near, I received Swami Saradananda's permission to take a couple of days off from my work at the Udbodhan and go to Belur Math to formally ask for initiation of Maharaj, who was the President of the Math. When I arrived, Maharaj was seated in an easy chair on the porch overlooking the Ganges, a spot close to Swamiji's old room. He was relaxed, chatting with some of the younger monks, including a couple of young men who, like me, hoped to be initiated into *brahmacharya*. I saluted him and said, "Maharaj, I have come to receive your blessing. I will be ever grateful if you would kindly bless me with the vows of *brahmacharya* on Thakur's *tithi puja*" (his birthday).

Maharaj was quiet for a while. Finally he said, "Yes I will, but there is one condition. You must pay me 108 rupees in advance as *guru-dakshina* (honorarium for the guru). Otherwise I can't initiate you."

Stunned, I replied, "Maharaj, I have no money. It is impossible for me to pay such a large amount. If you don't bless me, I am lost."

Then Maharaj said gravely, "I have a suggestion that will solve your problem. "Swami Saradananda is very rich! He has all the money from the *Udbhodan*. You are his attendant. Go to Swami Saradananda and get him to pay that amount for you."

While I was standing there, speechless, Maharaj called another candidate over to him and said, "Govinda, you come from Midnapore. You will have to dance after the fashion that Orissa people are fond of, for me. If you do it well, I will give you *brahmacharya*." Without hesitation, Govinda performed the dance with suitable gestures of his hand to our great delight. Maharaj was pleased with his performance and laughed heartily.

Not knowing what else to do, I returned to the Udbodhan and narrated the whole story to Swami Saradananda with great seriousness. He nodded gravely. "Very well, you may return to Belur Math and tell Maharaj that I am his and everything in Udbodhan belongs to him as well. What he asks for will be given."

Relieved, I returned immediately to Belur Math, prostrated before Maharaj, and repeated Swami Saradananda's message.

But to my surprise and dismay, Maharaj shook his head. "Empty words!" he shouted. "How am I to know if he will do as he promises with nothing in writing? You are his secretary. Prepare something for him to sign. When I have his signature, then I will believe it."

Again I returned to Udbodhan, my mind in a turmoil. Swami Saradananda was at his meditation when I arrived. I sat and waited for him, none too patiently, and perhaps not as quietly as I might have. When his meditation was over, Swami Saradananda opened his eyes. "Well, I thought it might be you. Did Maharaj agree to give you your vows?"

Sadly, I told him this latest development, and gravely he listened to me. When I finished, he spoke without the slightest trace of emotion. "Very well, I shall do even better. I shall go to Belur Math with you."

The next day, we both went to Belur Math and approached Maharaj. After a few moments in his presence, Swami Saradananda suggested it would be better if I waited outside.

At length, Swami Saradananda came out of Maharaj's room and spoke to me, once again showing absolutely no emotion. "It has been arranged," he said. "You will have your *brahmacharya* vows with the others."

Even now, well over fifty years later, I can only speculate about what transpired between the two brother monks as they discussed "my case," and finally brought it to a conclusion.

And then, as with the children, after the teasing came Maharaj's generosity. Before the ceremony he said to me, "You have suffered from malaria. Your body is not strong. You need not bathe in the Ganges early in the morning before the *brahmacharya* ceremony. Simply sprinkle some Ganges water on your head. Again, neither should you go entirely without food for the whole day. Take some fruit and sweet as *prasad* after Thakur's midday worship from the *brahmachari* in charge of Thakur's *bhandar* (storeroom). That will be enough for you."

Following Maharaj's instructions, I had gone to Swami Suddhananda to learn the meaning of the mantras for the initiation. Night was still lingering when we gathered for the ceremony. The *homa* fire was ignited, and Swami Suddhanandaji solemnly recited the mantras. We repeated the mantras for the vows and offered out oblations into the holy fire, the symbol of Sri Ramakrishna. Maharaj was present throughout the ceremony. His face radiant, his mood was contemplative. After the ceremony, he gave us his blessing: "May Thakur give you the strength to fulfill the vows of *brahmacharya* in a manner that is as bright and shining, as pure and luminous as the sun. May he endow all of you, out of his abundant grace, with true love and with true devotion to his lotus feet."

At the end of the *homa* fire, we came to salute our guru. Maharaj stretched out his hand in benediction and put it on our heads. We felt the touch of the hand that protects and shields from all danger. He gave us new names; mine was Kalyana Chaitanya. I will treasure it always as a token of Maharaj's grace. That was the last *brahmacharya* vow that Maharaj gave while he was living in our midst.

In addition to teasing, Swami Saradananda loved a joke on himself. He used to tell the story of the time when he was living in the Barangore Monastery and had to go out begging for food, as was the custom in northern India after taking the vow of *sannyasa*. "I went to a house and chanted, '*Om nama Narayanaya*,' according to custom. A lady opened the door and looked at me with careful eyes and said, 'You have such a well-built, robust body. Are you not ashamed to come begging? Can't you get a job as a streetcar conductor and support yourself?' And immediately she banged the door shut in my face."

The sound of the swami's hearty laugh as he narrated that story still rings in my ears, bringing with it memories not of the grave, somber-looking man of his photographs but a face alight with fun and delight. Sometimes we young monks would say to a swami of our age who was robust in constitution, "Can't you get a job as a streetcar conductor and support yourself?" The young swami would understand our joke, for he had been present at the time of the narration, and there would be great fun among us.

What you learn in pain you teach in song: through fun and humor great souls teach us many things that abstract philosophies or sermons preached with great preparation cannot. We must trust in the permanence of the spirit and accept life as a great fun. Christ has said, "My burden is light, my yoke is easy." If we can cultivate a little humor in our dark days, we will find spiritual life neither boring nor dry but sweet and encouraging. Association with great souls helps us to do this through their precepts and through their art of spontaneous living.

Fun and spontaneity mixed in Swami Saradananda's nature with a generous portion of humility. He kept alive in his memory and in his actions the Master's teaching: "Have you seen those tiny crabs that are born in the Ganges just when the rains set in? In this big universe you are even less significant than one of those small creatures. How dare you talk of helping the world. Let a man get the authority from God and be endowed with His power; then and then alone may he think of doing good to others. A man must be freed of all egotism. Then alone will the Blissful Mother ask him to work for the world." Despite who he was and the experiences he had attained, for him greatness meant Sri Ramakrishna, Holy Mother, and his brother disciples. One morning after his bath in the Ganges, Maharaj said to the swami, who had recently arranged for Swami Turiyananda's joining them at Benares, "Brother Sarat, I am thinking of Swami Turiyananda. What an exalted state he is living in now. Such great souls can rarely be found in this world. Forgetful of his body and its intolerable pains, how he is dwelling in the realm of the spirit, being established in his true self. I would like very much to go to his room and salute him with all my heart's affection."

As soon as Swami Saradananda heard these words, he immediately left the Advaita Ashrama and walked to the Sevashrama, where Swami Turiyananda had been installed. It was summer. Swami Turiyananda had just finished his morning meal and was resting. His room was shaded with a screen to ward off radiation from the heat outside.

Swami Saradananda opened the screen gently so that Swami Turiyananda would not notice. Softly he approached, fell flat on the floor, and reverently touched the feet of Swami Turiyananda. Feeling his touch, Swami Turiyananda exclaimed, "Who is this that salutes me?"

"I am Sarat. Just now Maharaj mentioned your name when I was with him at the Advaita Ashrama. He wanted to visit you and salute you, for the state in which you are living is indescribable. Hearing his words, I was drawn to you. I could not resist the temptation of making good the words of Maharaj. Hence, I have come. Please accept my salutations."

Swami Turiyananda remained quiet a little while. Then he said, "Brother Sarat, do I not know who you are? I could not see properly as the room was dark. You have embarrassed me by doing such a thing. Shall I ever forget your spending the whole night in meditation on the rock in the mountain after we worshipped the Nilkantheswar Shiva together.*

The bond between the brother disciples of Sri Ramakrishna was indissoluble. Swamiji used to say, "The tie between us has been forged by our Master. He was truly the personification of love." That love was not the ordinary type of love that we know but the *agape* of the mystics that the saints knew through their experience of "beatific vision" granted them by the Divine Lord. The experience is ineffable, but its effects can be seen in their power to transform the lives of those who have had it.

Swami Saradananda and Swami Turiyananda were especially close. Whenever Turiyananda fell sick, whether he was in Puri or in Benares, Swami Saradananda would invariably come to his bedside. And how they would reminisce for hours about the Master and Swamiji to the delight of us younger monks.

Swami Brahmananda passed away in 1922. The trustees of Belur Math called a meeting to nominate the next president. Both

---

*See page 39.

Swami Saradananda and Swami Shivananda were nominated. It became clear that the majority of monks and ashram members favored Swami Saradananda, but he firmly declined, saying, "Swamiji made me Secretary of the Mission, and I don't want to relinquish that post." He used his influence to support Swami Shivananda for president.

Swami Shivananda was an ascetic of the ancient type—introspective, blunt, and not fond of social formalities. Moreover, he didn't feel at home in dealing with complex administrative problems. But Swami Saradananda assured him, "For those executive complexities, I am there always at your service." The trustees elected Swami Shivananda.

I believe that Swami Saradananda, in declining the presidency, sought the good of the Order and wanted to set an example for the younger monks. He wanted Swami Shivananda's spirituality harnessed for the betterment of the Mission and the good of humanity. He felt the responsibility of the presidency would bring Swami Shivananda down from his Himalayan heights of contemplation to tackle the problems of ordinary people with compassion and understanding.

10. *Dressed for Western audiences: Saradananda in New England*

11. On tour in America. Swami Saradananda seated, second from left.

12. *Saradananda*

13. *Brother Monks: Shivananda, Brahmananda, Saradananda*

14. *The Bengali playwright and poet: Girish Ghosh*

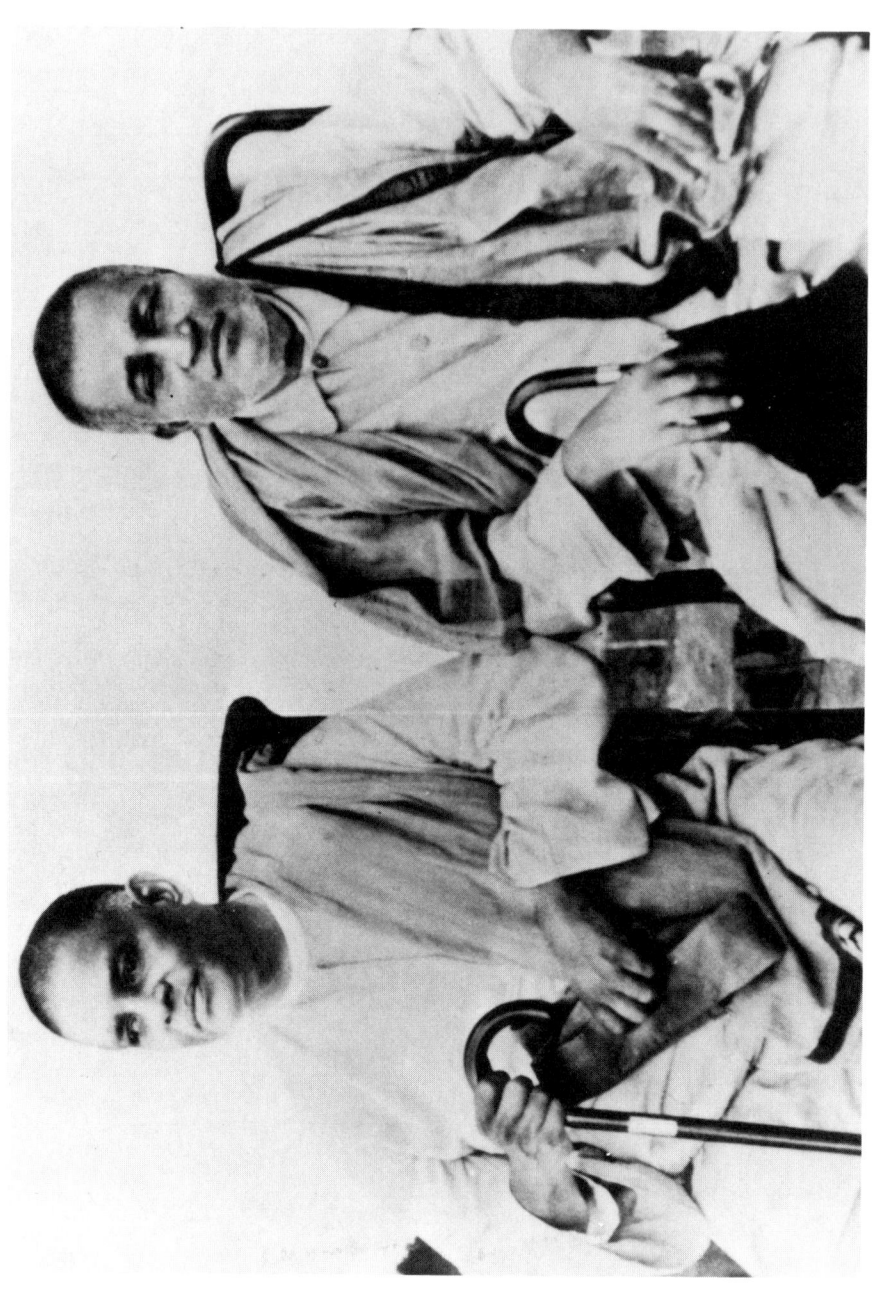

15. *Saradananda and Shivananda*

16. *Sarat Chandra Chakravarty: Swami Saradananda*

17. *Swami Aseshananda*

9

Samadhi and Mahasamadhi

ONE DAY AN attendant of Swami Saradananda worked up the courage to ask him if he had experienced *nirvikalpa* samadhi.

"Did I waste my time cutting grass when I lived in the company of Sri Ramakrishna?" he asked in reply.

When the attendant pressed him for details, the swami said, "Read the chapter on samadhi in *Sri Ramakrishna, the Great Master*. I have not written anything about samadhi without experiencing it myself."

He rarely mentioned his personal spiritual experiences and never described them in detail as Sri Ramakrishna had instructed his disciples not to reveal the secrets of their *sadhana* to anyone but their guru.

One of the few about which anything is known occurred in 1896 when the swami visited Rome on his way to London. The elaborate mass in St. Peter's Cathedral interested him but did not affect his mood. On his way out, he saw a statue of the Virgin Mary and stood in front of it for a long minute, then sat quietly nearby, meditating. He lost all outer consciousness: the world disappeared for him. His mind was filled with joy, and the radiance of love enveloped his being. In a vision, he saw the cathedral being supported, not by pillars, but by figures of saints shining with effulgent rays which penetrated to every corner of the building, filling it with holiness and spirituality. In the midst of the saints stood the Virgin Mary holding her divine Child in her arms. And as he looked at the Mother and Child, the swami felt the presence of Christ in his heart.

Once when Sri Ramakrishna had been talking to his devotees about Christ, the Messenger of Light, he went into an exalted state of consciousness. When he could speak, he said, "Sarat and Sashi (later Ramakrishnananda) in a former incarnation were disciples of Jesus Christ. They belonged to his very close and intimate family."

It is difficult for me to interpret the precise meaning of Sri Ramakrishna's words as I never asked Swami Saradananda about his relationship to Christ: We never asked certain questions of the direct disciples of the Master. The Bengali phrase that Sri Ramakrishna used was *Rishikrishna daler lok. Daler lok* can be translated as *follower*, but Swami Saradananda's experience in St. Peter's Cathedral suggests that he was very close to Christ because that experience was not of an ordinary type.

Ordinary love breaks because it is fastened to a finite soul, but when love is attached to the Infinite Spirit, it endures forever. Time and birth cannot sever that connection. Kalidas, the famous poet, said, "Love and friendship never die. They are renewed again and again from life to life. Such is the power of impression forged by love that time cannot change it and death cannot erase it. Perfect love is therefore established not in time but in eternity: deep calling unto the deep. . . ." Holy Mother put it more simply: *"Je yar Se Tar"*—he who belongs to Him will stay with Him from birth to birth.

It is interesting to note that, when Sri Ramakrishna met Swami Saradananda for the first time and wanted to call forth his spirit of renunciation, he quoted not from Hindu scriptures but from the Christian Bible.

We also know of a vision Swami Saradananda had at Dakshineswar when he happened upon Holy Mother as she came to bring Sri Ramakrishna a plate of rice, vegetables, and other dishes. She was wearing a thick red-bordered sari; her face was lit up with a smile, and the swami saw her as Annapurna, the embodiment of the abundance of nourishing food, an image that dazzled his eyes and left a deep impression on his mind. That vision may have been the reason he took the name Saradananda when he became a *sannyasin,* and it may also have prompted him to seize the opportunity to take the responsibility for caring for Holy Mother after Swami Yogananda's *mahasamadhi* in 1899. Holy Mother used to say, "Sarat and Yogin are my very own; they belong to my inner circle (*antaranga*)."

I believe Swami Saradananda's favorite deity was Mother Kali. When we went to Puri, I was privileged to gather flowers for his daily worship and remove them in the evening. At that time, I saw his album which contained pictures of Sri Ramakrishna, Holy Mother, and Mother Kali in her pose of great power (*mahashakti*). The swami wanted to worship the Divine Mother in all living beings. This is the goal of tantric worship, and in 1900 he undertook the discipline of tantric worship under the guidance of his uncle, Ishwar Chandra Chakravarty, a tantric adept.

The goal of *tantrikism* and of *advaita* Vedanta is the same—the attainment of freedom in this life through the realization of God. Only their methods differ. Vedanta uses a negative approach, teaching its followers that the objects, pleasures, and relationships of this world are fundamentally unreal: *neti, neti*—not this, not this—only God is real. The followers of tantra seek God not by avoiding the unreal but by looking for God the Mother—Shakti—in all things: Worship the Mother with all thy heart and soul. Liberation will come through Her grace. As the Durgasaptasati (the Chandi) says: "When the Divine Mother is pleased, all things are possible. She throws open the door to freedom and She bestows the boon of protection and fearlessness." In his *Life of Holy Mother,* Swami Tapasyananda wrote, "His (Swami Saradananda's) devotion has also received literary commemoration in his book *Mother Worship in India,* which he dedicated to her with the noble and significant words. 'By whose gracious look the author has been able to realize the revelation of Divine Motherhood in every female form—to the lotus feet of Her, this work is dedicated in all humility and devotion.'"

Worship of *Shakti* became the cornerstone of tantrikism. *Shakti* is God's creative aspect—the formless primal energy that is responsible for the manifested universe. The Divine Mother is both *Shakti*'s symbol and manifested subtle body.

Tantrikism has drawn its practices from two sources—Buddhism and Vedanta. In India many sadhus look down upon the Tantras, especially the Vamachara Tantra, which is called the left-handed method (traditionally, the left hand is used to cope with dirty objects, keeping the right hand clean and pure for eating and ritual worship) because Vamachara Tantra advocates the worship of the Divine Mother with items like wine and meat, which create *rajasik* tendencies. Instead of *rajasik* tendencies, spiritual aspirants should try to achieve *sattvik* tendencies, which come not from enjoyment of the senses but from renunciation of the senses. As the Vedas put it, "By renunciation alone, immortality can be reached. There is no other way to the attainment of freedom."

Nevertheless, we should not condemn a method due to its misuse and misinterpretation. The true goal of Vamachara is to awaken the supreme energy that in most people lies sleeping in a static coiled-up condition at the base of the spine. In order to spiritualize all six centers of human consciousness the energy's static state must be transformed to a dynamic state. The six centers of consciousness are called *muladhara, svadhisthana, manipura, anahata,* and *ajna*.

When the coiled-up energy is awakened, it travels from one center to another in a *vamamarga,* or left-handed or counter-clockwise direction, enlivening each center with tremendous power, which expands the individual's spiritual consciousness, until it reaches the center between the two eyebrows (the *ajna chakra*) and the *sadhaka* goes into samadhi. What happens then? If the *sadhaka* is earnest, the awakened energy will travel to the highest center of consciousness, the *sahasrara,* allowing the *sadhaka* to experience the awakened spiritual power, the Divine Mother, pervading the entire universe, within and without every particle of matter. The *sadhaka* feels *saham*: I am She: I am one with the Mother of the Universe, and, ultimately, I am Brahman, thus achieving the supreme unity.

Swami Saradananda translated the Devisukta of the Rig Veda that tells how Vak, the daughter of the sage Ambhrin reached this state, becoming a knower of Brahman. One of the verses attempts to describe her experience: "I spread the heavens over the earth. I am the energy of Brahman, the Mother of all. It is for me that Brahman resides in all the different intellects. It is I who have penetrated all the worlds with my power and it is I who am holding them in their places."

In *Sri Ramakrishna, the Great Master,* Swami Saradananda describes the experience Totapuri (the teacher of Sri Ramakrishna) had when he tried to cast off his body by consigning it to the Ganges:

> Tota almost reached the other bank but could not find deep enough water to drown himself. When the trees and houses on the other bank of the river gradually began to be visible, like shadows in the deep darkness of night, someone, as it were from within, pulled off the veil covering his intellect and Tota's mind was dazzled by a bright light and he saw Mother everywhere: Mother in the land, Mother in the water, Mother as life, Mother as death, Mother as the Supreme Fourth (*Turiya*) devoid of all attributes. That one whom Totapuri had so long been worshipping as Brahman was revealed to his inner eye as none other than this very Mother Herself—Brahman and Brahma-Shakti are one and the same.

Tota realized first the *Nirguna* aspect.

> Overwhelmed with the unprecedented joy arising from the experience of *bhava* samadhi, Tota went slowly to the *dhuni* (the holy fire of the sadhus) under the Panchavati and spent the rest of the night in meditation and repetition of the name of the Divine Mother, calling her, "Amba, Amba, Amba."

While coming down from Samadhi the *kundalini* takes the *dakshinachara*, or right-hand way. A *sadhaka* feels the *kundalini* is moving clockwise, encircling the different lotuses and absorbing the letters, or powers, into its own being and illumining them with the spirit of joy and self-fulfillment. Gradually it descends from center to center, coming to rest at last at the basic center called the *muladhara*. Thereafter the *sadhaka* remains ever-awake with the bliss of supreme attainment of oneness with Brahman.

Swami Saradananda once told Swami Vishweshwarananda that the Tantric awakening of the *kundalini* is the same as the Vedic mantra. *"Purnamadah Purnamidang"*—"the invisible world is infinite and this visible world is also infinite." The junior swami asked, "Would you kindly explain what you mean a little further?" But Swami Saradananda replied, "This is not a matter of discussion. It is a fact of experience. If you plunge into *sadhana* with determination and divine grace, you will know it for yourself."

Nonetheless, we need encouragement from one who has experienced the truth, during our rise and fall towards the goal from which there will be no return to *samsara,* or the world of ignorance.

What is the *sadhana* that an aspirant must practice? It is mantra *sadhana,* to repeat the name of your chosen aspect of God *(Ishta)* and to meditate on the *Ishta*'s divine form with deep interest and single-minded devotion. Steadfast, unwavering attachment to God is called *Ishtanishtha.* If you practice mantra *sadhana* for a long time, you will become one with your *Ishta* and realize your true nature to be the *Shakti* of Brahman. If you are fortunate and qualified, ultimately you will experience perfect union with Brahman in *nirvikalpa* samadhi. In that state you will know that your true state is not essentially different from Nirguna Brahman, the unconditional Absolute: "*pratyagatma* is verily one with *Paramatman.*" The awakening of the *kundalini* is intended to bring about that ultimate realization. That is why the Tantras speak highly of the efficacy of worshipping God as *Shakti* as a means to attaining that sublime realization.

Swami Saradananda says in his book *Worship of God as Mother in India* that India's special contribution to religion is to address God as Mother as a symbolic expression of the truth that the source of the manifestation of this world is the universal primal energy, which is intelligent and conscious as well as dynamic. The Tantras call this primal energy *(Shakti)* Mother, giving her the name of Kali. She is time and timelessness. She creates and dissolves what was created. In one hand she gives the boon of protection and with the other she dispels all fear from the heart of the devotee. This is her sweet and gentle aspect. But as the dissolver of creation, she also has a terrible or all-annihilating aspect. Artists portray this aspect by showing her with a sword in one hand and the skull of a beheaded person in the other, representing the Mother as the possessor of all opposing and contradictory forces in this world of manifestation.

A devotee must accept both in order to transcend the duality of *maya* and attain *jivanmukti.* A *sadhaka* practices self-control before worshipping the Mother with steadfast devotion and unalloyed faith. When the devotee's heart has become pure, he will reach the state of *bhava* samadhi: then the image that the devotee worships will not be an external statue made of clay nor even a subjective idea of the mind, but the image will be a solidified mass of consciousness, a tangible reality, radiant, living, pervading each person and object of the universe. When the *sadhaka* comes down a little to a lower samadhi that still maintains the consciousness of pure "I," he sees that the real nature of the vast manifested universe with its galaxies, stars, moons, worlds, oceans, and mountains are nothing but Shava and Shiva, the relative and the Absolute, change and changelessness—a blessed union of God the personal and God the impersonal—all in one. He sees that each individual and each object of the world is not separate and distinct but organically connected, living and conscious. Just as a human body with its head, feet, ears, eyes, and other parts is all connected by the principle of life, so all living beings and non-living objects are interconnected by the Divine Mother, the fountainhead of consciousness (*chinmayi*) and not an insentient mass of energy (*mrinmayi*), as preached by some scientists. She is indeed the principle of consciousness, living and sentient behind all the insentient objects of the universe, which science will never be able to discover through its objective methods of investigation. In great wonder and joy, the *sadhaka* pours forth his heart's ecstasy in a hymn such as the Dhyana mantram of Mother Kali: "*Karalavadanang ghorang*"—"I meditate on Kali who has four hands, dishevelled hair, a grim look, and terrifying face. She dwells in the cremation ground of my heart, which has renounced all desires of the world in order to adore the Mother as the one supreme principle of my life and the true essence of the universe."

The *rishis* of India discovered the dual form of the Mother through their experiences of samadhi. Her Absolute and relative aspects were revealed to them and in exalted states they discovered the different mantras and the various *dhyanas*. In his book on Mother worship Swami Saradananda commented, "There is not the slightest doubt in my mind about the authenticity of this truth." It was this positive, invigorating side of tantrikism that Swami Saradananda accepted and made known to the public in his own book on Mother worship and in his review of Sir John Woodroffe's *Principles of Tantra,* a review that was included in its second edition, a pamphlet that had been excerpted from the *Prabuddha Bharata.* He gave tantric *sannyasa* to some lay devotees as well as monastic members of our Order. The ceremony is called *purnabhiseka*; it entitles the recipient to perform *rahasva puja,* worship through symbols and ritualism pertaining to the deeper truths of the Divine Mother with the goal of winning her favor. When one of our monks wanted to perform tantric rituals, including the demanding *purascharana,* he would invariably approach the swami for advice. Swami Saradananda pointed out in his lecture on the "Worship of Shakti":

> The teachings of the Tantras are never at variance with those of the Vedanta; that this worship of Shakti has come down to us from the Vedic period there can be no doubt. In the Kena Upanishad we find the Devi (the Divine Mother) bringing the Devas—who grew arrogant by their victory over the Asuras—to their senses, and finally appearing before Indra in the form of a beautiful woman, Uma Haimavati, to offer him supreme knowledge. In the Chandogya Upanishad the Rishi Vamadeva advises a form of *homa* (the fire ceremony) for the purification of the household, and many have traced to that origin some of the symbology used in the Tantras.... Another great peculiarity of the Tantras is the higher standing in which they have raised womanhood—She should be worshipped as the special incarnation of divine energy, so the Tantriks bow down before every woman and look upon her as the manifestation of Shakti, the Mother of creation; nay, they offer their hearts' worship to the hallowed feet of all women and proclaim them to be special incarnations of the Shakti or the Devi herself.... None can worship the Devi except by being pure and holy, and by ordering one's life and worship in harmony with the holy will of the Divine Mother.

Traditionally Mother Kali is worshipped at night because night is the symbol of renunciation. In his spiritual training every *sadhaka* passes through the first "night," which is called *moharatri,* through pleasure and pain, through success and failure, through exaltation and despair, to the night of discrimination. Then he wakes from his dream and realizes that the experiences of everyday life will soon pass away: "Vanity of vanities, all this is vanity." The *sadhaka* becomes acutely aware of death—everything will be snatched away from him, including his favorite possession, his own body. He prepares to fight his most relentless enemy—*kalaratri*—the night of destruction. Following the instructions of his guru, he worships Mother Kali with rituals and ceremonies, with *japa* and meditation, chanting solemnly the verse from the Chandi: "*Saisha prasanna varada nrinang Bhavati muktaye.*" ("When the Divine Mother is pleased, she comforts and gives the boon of protection and grants freedom to mankind.") Pleased by this worship, the Divine Mother grants the *sadhaka* a boon, liberation. Then the night of worship becomes *maharatri,* the great night of enlightenment, absorbing both night and day into one moment of eternity. The Tantras say that this is *samvid,* the full knowledge of perfect wisdom in Brahman, which is the true face of the Deity or the *nirguna* aspect of the Divine Mother.

In the language of Kamalakanta "*Sakar akar nirakara*"—O Mother, thou hast taken a personal form to receive my worship, but thy true form is formlessness. Swami Saradananda wrote, "Oh, *Sadhaka,* if you worship the Divine Mother with the purity of your heart, fixing your gaze on the star of renunciation and meditate on Her effulgent form with steadfast devotion and intense faith, you too will in time be blessed with her vision; all your desires then will attain their supreme consummation. Sri Ramakrishna has given you the great assurance that the Mother comes to those who worship Her with childlike simplicity and have absolute trust in Her, waiting patiently for Her grace.... May she grant you your heart's desire is my prayer."

Mother had richly blessed Swami Saradananda with visions of Her during his lifetime. In keeping with his Master's teachings, he never discussed his visions, but after his *mahasamadhi,* a senior swami showed me his diary, for which I am grateful. These entries are written evidence from his own hand of the deep spiritual experiences which are timeless and transcendental but not irrational because they do not conflict with reason; mystic experiences can be achieved only by a strong mind, never by a weak mind.

Dec. 12, 1923	1st day of communion.
Jan. 4, 1924	2nd day of communion.
Jan. 17, 1924	3rd vision of Divine Mother.
Jan. 23, 1924	5th day of communion.
Jan 24, 1924	6th day of communion.
Jan. 25, 1924	7th day—special communion, repeating of *darshana*.
Jan. 31, 1924	communion poor.
Feb. 2	communion poor. (I believe it was for a short duration and therefore poor.)
Feb. 3, 1924	*Settled* non-communion. (Swami Saradananda had underlined the word *settled* with his own hand. Perhaps he did not desire to have any "*darshan*" for a definite reason.
Feb. 8, 1924	The circle of communion began again.
Feb. 9, 1924	2nd communion and massage.
Feb. 10, 1924	Intense communion touching center—massage. Repeated vision of the Divine Mother continues which culminated on Feb. 19.
Feb. 19, 1924	communion—"*you in me.*"

Repeated vision of the Divine Mother is not possible until the nerves are strong. I believe the word *massage* conveys the meaning that the Divine Mother herself touched the soul of Swami Saradananda and awakened the coiled-up energy called the *kundalini,* stimulating it to rise from center to center until it reached the sixth center (*ajna*) and enabled the swami to reach the Divine Mother. This exalted state of consciousness is called *samadhi* by the yogis and by the Christian mystics, beatific vision.

The nerves must be strong to have a spiritual vision because the impact of the vision would shatter unstrengthened nerves like the passage of a heavy surge of electricity through a flimsy wire. An instance of the terrible impact of a vision on the nervous system of one who has not properly prepared for the experience was recorded in the New Testament. When St. Paul had his vision of Christ on the road to Damascus, as the Book of Acts notes, "Blinded by the bright vision, Paul was led by the hand into Damascus, where for three days he could not see and neither ate nor drank. He believed that the resurrected Jesus had appeared to him." The vision transformed him from a persecutor of Christ and his followers to an admirer and a follower himself. That is why St. Paul says, "Be ye transformed by the renewal of your mind."

During his visions of February 9 and 10, the Divine Mother renewed Swami Saradananda's mind and nervous system, making his inner being fit to contain that deeper communion that every spiritual aspirant longs for with all his heart and soul.

In this age of materialism and scientific agnosticism, true visions and other valid spiritual experiences are rare. Swami Saradananda belongs to that group of valuable persons who tells us God is real because He can be realized: I have realized him; you too can find Him if your mind is one-pointed and your longing deep and intense.

Swami Saradananda had initiated a few students while he was in America, and he gave *brahmacharya* vows to Mr. Johnson, a young man Swamiji had sent to him. After returning to India, he gave initiation to a few ardent students—I have heard that Swami Mahimananda, one of our senior monks who became a trustee of Belur Math and another swami, Satchitananda "No 1," whom we used to call "Budo Baba" (Old Father) were his disciples from this period—but while Maharaj lived, Maharaj and Holy Mother were the official gurus who gave initiation to those who wanted to follow the teachings of Sri Ramakrishna.

After Swami Brahmananda passed away, Swami Saradananda began giving initiation and vows of *brahmacharya* and *sannyasa* to large numbers of people. Some days he would cut short his meditation in order to prepare himself to initiate disciples. Before giving *mantras,* he always did some simple worship to Sri Ramakrishna and Holy Mother, using flowers, sandal paste, leaves, and grass. He told us, "It is not easy to give initiation. You will have to work for your disciples. An illumined guru has to perform special *japa* for their inner growth and spiritual welfare. The relationship between the guru and disciple is established by God. The real guru has to take the burden of his disciples. He works for them through silent prayer and meditation. He has no rest until all of them have become illumined. It reminds me of the beautiful statement of Christ that a good shepherd has no rest until the last sheep has been brought to the fold."

I have seen on several occasions that before the swami would give initiation, he would prepare the mind of the student for the solemn ceremony. The swami used to say, "A good gardener always prepares the ground and makes the soil ready before he plants any seed." Once when an earnest devotee approached him for initiation, Swami Saradananda told him, "I am waiting for the command of our Lord. When I hear Him, I will initiate you. You will have to wait. If you are impatient, you may go to somebody else whom you like." The devotee wouldn't go elsewhere; he was adamant that he wanted Swami Saradananda and no other for his guru. He was prepared to wait indefinitely. After several months, he got his initiation. Later on, he asked the swami, "Did you hear the Lord's message in regard to me?" Swami Saradananda smiled and nodded.

By planting the seed, the swami meant the mantra, the holy word. A good teacher receives the mantra through deep meditation and charges it with power through the purity of his life and transmits it to his disciple.

Swami Saradananda told his disciples:

> Nothing can sever the spiritual relationship between the guru and his disciple. It is something eternal. But the disciple must listen to the words of the teacher and carry out his

instructions. If any impediment arises, the guru comes forward and removes it. Success depends on the sincerity and effort on the part of the disciple. What an amount of labor boys put forth in order to pass an examination! It is like that. If one is earnest, one need not struggle so much. It is a pity that man does not want God from the bottom of his heart. If he really wants him, he will surely find him. Work hard. Repeat the mantra with unwavering devotion. Seed has been sown. Now you must water it with unfailing faith. You may use your beads as a help in concentration. The need for not letting the beads "go hungry" is for the purpose of getting into the habit and lessening the distraction of the mind while counting them. All this is necessary to create yearning for God. When yearning comes, the vision of God will not be far off. He will reveal himself to you and fill your heart with infinite joy and bliss.

Although he had the right to command, he always gave his views in the form of suggestions, advice, and encouragement. He was more than a teacher, he was a counselor and friend.

At Bhubaneswar Math my duty was to draw water from the well and pour it into the "kunjo," a porous mud vessel, for the swami's drinking purposes. One day, while I was carrying the vessel by its slender elongated neck, the vessel slipped from my hand, broke, the bottom falling out and spilling the water. It was a real mess. The water soaked the white linen sheet and the mattress on which the swami was seated, reading his correspondence. I was very much afraid, thinking that perhaps he would be so angry that he wouldn't allow me to serve him anymore. It would have been a great blow to my heart to be denied that privilege. I prayed to Sri Ramakrishna to forgive me and to intercede in this matter.

Seeing my gloomy face, Swami Saradananda said, "Why are you so sad? This water pot will go on its way alone; it will not have cholera or typhoid. Don't worry. I am going for a walk. You take the mattress upstairs and put it in the sun on the roof of the porch. The sun is bright and scorching today; within half an hour the mattress will be dry. You bring it back to my room and all will be well."

My heart brightened; I followed the swami's instructions meticulously, and everything was perfect. Even today his teaching that all compounded things are bound to decay is fresh in my mind.

Another time, we were walking together on Baghbazar Street in Calcutta when he stopped suddenly and said to me, "Be not like a creeper on a tree. Stand on your own feet. Depend on no one. Depend on your own self and bend all your efforts toward realizing the goal."

During these last years he was in poor health; he began to withdraw his mind from work and, despite his failing strength, spend long hours in meditation. When he did so, he sat like a rock, immovable, completely oblivious to the outside world, his face radiating serenity.

Doctor D.P. Ghosh, who was treating the swami for diabetes, rheumatism, and high blood pressure, told one devotee, "It alarms me to see the swami spending so much time in meditation without paying any heed to his health. It will be good if you ask him to reduce his period of meditation." The swami replied, when he heard what Dr. Ghosh had said, "What am I to do in old age? Here sitting quietly I repeat the name of the Lord. Nobody will do anything. At least by seeing me they may be inclined to do something."

When one of his attendants asked him what need there was for a man like him to meditate so long, impairing his health, he said, "The call has come. I am preparing for the great journey. Now meditation is the food of my life, and chanting His name, the source of my delight."

In those days he would always remind us of the purpose of our lives, of the vows we had taken. He would constantly emphasize one direction—to dive deep in spiritual practice and never be content until the direct vision of God was attained. It is said that holiness is contagious. If one goes near the fire, he is sure to get warm. I found this to be true. Whenever I sat in meditation with Swami Saradananda, time passed unnoticed and my mind was raised to a plane of peace and tranquility. To convince and quicken others as he did—that is the function of true holiness.

The one task that still could capture his painstaking attention was the building of a temple in Holy Mother's memory at Jayrambati. Holy Mother had said to her devoted attendant in Jayrambati, Swami Parameswarananda, "My child, after I leave this body, many devotees of our Master will come here. You should all do something so that they are properly taken care of. It will hurt me to see them go elsewhere for food and shelter during my absence. It will be good if a temple is built and an accommodation for monks and devotees is arranged, where they will meditate and think of God with simple living and high devotion, away from the noise and cares of the world. That will please me immensely."

From the day that Swami Saradananda had heard of the Mother's wish from Swami Parameswarananda, he resolved to see her wish fulfilled. His dream was realized on Akshaya Tritiya day (a very sacred day to the Hindus) May 1923, when the temple was consecrated with a formal ritualistic worship, including the *homa* ceremony, performed by Swami Visweswarananda. Monks, devotees, and villagers from a dozen miles distance were fed sumptuously with *prasad*, or sanctified food. Everyone's heart was filled with joy, feeling the living presence of the Mother in the temple that was dedicated to her memory.

After vespers, a large crowd gathered in the living room of Holy Mother's house. I was seated very close to Swami Saradananda. Suddenly his eyes fell on me and he said, "Kiran, would you tell us how you joined our monastic order." I felt a little trepidation; then I thought, "The swami is my very own. Why should I be afraid to speak before him?" My fear left, and I said, "Maharaj, I was studying for the M.A. degree at the University of Calcutta in 1921. Mahatma Gandhi's non-cooperation movement was going on in full swing. While I was walking toward the University to attend my lectures, I saw students, who had been picketing, lying flat on the ground to bar entrance to the University. I could not bring myself to trample over their bodies, and for a few seconds I didn't know what to do. Suddenly I thought, Why non-cooperation with the British government? Why not non-cooperation with the world? So I came to Belur Math to join the Order.

"Mahapurush Maharaj was kind and allowed me to stay. He gave me the duty of serving the Daridra Naraya next day, which was Swamiji's public celebration day. The monks liked me and I stayed on. After a few days my mother came looking for me. One of the swamis took her upstairs to see Mahapurush Maharaj. I was called. My mother said, 'Maharaj, you are Ghosal.* I am also Ghosal. You are my spiritual father. Please send my boy home. I will be grateful to you.'

"Mahapurush Maharaj ordered me to return with my mother. I stayed home for a few days; then I received a letter written in Sanskrit from Swami Omkarananda, one of the monks at Belur. Its substance was—He who runs away is saved from the bewitching spell of *maya*. I felt it a warning from God not to stay long. So, when the family went to the dining room for supper, I mentally said goodbye to my mother and came to the railroad station, boarding a train for Calcutta. Arriving at the Belur Math the next day, I went straight to the shrine and then went to Mahapurush Maharaj's room and bowed down at his feet. He said, 'You can stay, but if your mother comes, you will have to go back. I cannot see her weep.'

"I wrote my Mother, 'Please do not come. If you come again, I will go to the Himalayas and you will not be able to trace me or have any contact with me at all. If you do not come, I will go and see you whenever you need me with the permission of Mahapurushji.' My mother was reconciled, and I continued to stay at the Math. Years later, whenever I would go from the Udbodhan, Mahapurush Maharaj would smilingly say, 'My grandson has come. Shankar, feed him well. Give him some good *sandesh*.' To me he would say, 'Write to my daughter that she will always have my blessings. Let her pray to *Thakur*. All will be well through his grace.'"

Swami Saradananda listened to my story with joyful attention. Then a bell rang for supper. One by one, everyone came and prostrated before him. He blessed each one by placing his hand on the person's head. When I felt his hand on my head, blessing me, I knew the meaning of the song—"All my sorrow thou hast lifted by the magic touch of thy hand. All my pain thou hast removed by the soothing charm of thy blessing!"

---

* A fairly common family name.

Swami Saradananda would not permit his ill health to stop him from giving initiations. Sometimes he would initiate several people on one day; then he would not be able to eat his lunch until very late. Out of curiosity, a close devotee asked him, "Maharaj, why do you take so much time giving initiation? I have seen Holy Mother give initiation. She would finish within a short time."

The swami remained silent for a while, and then he replied, "Well, Holy Mother had tremendous power. If she would simply touch a person, he would achieve everything. But I cannot do that. I have to meditate and pray to the Lord with great earnestness and I have to wait patiently and see that the Master has accepted the children that I have brought him. I have no rest until I feel it and know it decisively. I have no peace of mind until I see that the Master has accepted the students and has taken responsibility for their future growth and spiritual development."

Swami Saradananda said to one of his disciples, "The Chosen Ideal and the indivisible soul, both are emanations of the same light manifesting in two forms. It is from the individual light of consciousness that the Chosen Ideal is made. Again, it is from the same light of pure consciousness that the form of the individual soul is fashioned."

He initiated about 150 disciples in all, showering his blessings on them and transforming their lives. Two of his disciples, Miss Sarah Fox and Miss Rebecca Fox, were high school teachers from Oakland, California. They wanted Sanskrit names, so he named Sarah Fox *Premika* and Rebecca Fox *Radhika*. After their initiation, the sisters lived in India for some time before returning home to their teaching jobs. After several months Rebecca fell ill and died. Sarah, a member of the Vedanta Society of nearby Berkeley, lived a few years more. In her will she bequeathed some money to the Berkeley Center. Swami Ashokananda, who headed the center then, used the funds to build the Swami Saradananda library. I remember when the Fox sisters were staying in the Sister Nivedita Girls School near the Udbodhan House. On his birthday, Swami Saradananda dispatched me with fruits and beautiful roses to give to the sisters.

They were delighted to receive a present from their beloved guru.

His last major work was the holding of the Ramakrishna Mission Convention at Belur Math in 1926. Though not well, he worked hard to make it a success. Monks from 100 Math and Mission Centers from India to California came to Belur to compare notes and make future plans.

Even that late in his life his eyes were on the future. In his Address of Welcome he warned against the danger that can result from public acceptance of the Ramakrishna movement: "For security brings a relaxation of spirit and energy, and a sudden growth of extensity quickly lessens the intensity and unity of purpose that were found among the promoters of the movement."

On 6 August 1927 the swami followed his usual routine of taking his bath, meditating three hours in his room, and then going to the shrine to prostrate before the pictures of Sri Ramakrishna and Holy Mother. This morning after emerging from the shrine, he went back in again, repeating this unusual behavior a few times. Finally he emerged, his face shining, and went to his room.

I went to his room in the late afternoon and he dictated letters to me for one and a half hours. The bell for vespers rang and I was about to go to the shrine to join my brother monks in singing "Breaker of the World's Chains We Adore Thee" when the swami asked me to wait and finish all the letters before leaving. He read each letter carefully and signed it. I took the letters and mailed them.

After vespers, Swami Haripremananda and I went to the swami's room and found him half reclining on his bed, struggling to get up, but unable to do so. He said to us, "Don't tell anybody. Make no noise. I will go downstairs to meet the devotees soon."

Vaikuntha Nath Sannyal, who had also come into the room, asked me to call Dr. Ghosh. When the doctor arrived, he told us to put an ice bag on the swami's head and change it every five minutes. I went by streetcar to buy new icebags; by the time I had returned, the Udbodhan House was crowded with monks from

Belur Math who had come to render service to their beloved swami.

We learned that he had suffered a stroke and that there had been damage to his brain. He retained consciousness, but his speech was impaired. A few days later the swami could only smile in response to Dr. Ghosh's question, "Sarat, do you want to drink tea?" Another day he had to use his left hand to drink holy water from a spoon.

All three systems of medication—Western, homeopathic, and ayurvedic—were tried with no visible results.

Even without speech Swami Saradananda continued to transform the lives of those who came to see him. When the homeopathic doctor came to treat the swami for the first time, the swami looked at him and the doctor's agnosticism vanished. He became an ardent devotee of the Ramakrishna Order.

It was the anniversary of Krishna's birthday, 19 August 1927. The swami's condition was rapidly worsening. All hope was gone. About 1 p.m. we began to chant, "Hari Om Ramakrishna." In the midst of our chanting, the swami drew his last breath. We all chanted:

> That invisible is infinite.
> This visible is also infinite.
> This Infinite has been projected from that Infinite.
> When this Infinite merges into that Infinite,
> All that remains is also Infinite.
> Om peace, peace, peace.

Epilogue

After his death we read his diary and saw how many times he had recorded communion with the Divine Mother.

The great ones have gone from this world of illusion, but they are not gone beyond our reach. Swami Saradananda told one of the disciples of Holy Mother, while we were traveling together by train on our way to Puri, that Sri Ramakrishna blessed him with a vision near Sakshigopal, which is close by Puri, pointing out the exact spot where he saw his Master's face lit with a heavenly smile. He had received the vision at a time when he was grief-stricken at the loss of Sri Ramakrishna and his heart was longing for a vision. When we want to see them as deeply as the swami wanted to see his Master, they will be there for us. They lived to show us the way. The rest is up to us.

Swami Saradananda once said to me, "You have made such a big prostration; what do you want?"

"Please give me special instructions besides what Holy Mother has given me," I said.

"That cannot be done," the swami replied. "What Holy Mother has given you is the last word in spiritual life. You will achieve everything by chanting that holy name. Our Mother is the Divine Mother herself. Have faith. Cling to her, and whatever is needed she will do for you."

Swami Saradananda's Writings

Letters from Saradananda to Holy Mother

Sasi-Niketan, Puri
2nd Ashwin, 1329

May Sri Ramakrishna be my refuge.
To the Lotus Feet of the Most Revered Holy Mother:

Please accept my thousands of *shastanga pranams* (humble salutations). Sannyal (Vaikuntha Natu) and I left Calcutta last Tuesday and arrived here the following day—Wednesday morning. The reason for my coming is to see Hari Maharaj (Swami Turiyananda), who is seriously ill. Before coming, I wrote a letter conveying the news and seeking your permission. I hope you have received that letter which was mailed to Jayrambati via a post office at Deshra.

After my arrival, I saw Hari Maharaj. I found him a little better, but the condition is still serious. The doctors say that, if no complication arises, after ten or twelve days the swami could be taken to Calcutta.

Hari Maharaj is now completely bed-ridden. Surgical operations were performed in three places—left hand, left foot, and right foot—to remove the pus due to infection. As a consequence he is unable to move from one side to the other. He is lying flat on his back by day as well as at night. Sri Ramakrishna graciously has endowed him with wonderful patience. That is why he is lying calmly, enduring everything with absolute resignation to the will of the Divine Master and the Mother. He is in good spirits. He is spending the time talking cheerfully to people, narrating stories, singing songs, and entering into conversations in order to make people happy. Please bless Hari so that he may recover and be strong enough to go with us to Calcutta. Hari sends his *shastanga pranams* to your holy feet.

Revered Rakhal Maharaj is doing well. He was deeply worried about Hari Maharaj's serious ailment. At first, he was very much afraid. But now since our coming and hearing the good report of the doctors, his fear has abated a little. Amalya and the others who are here as well as Sannya send their respectful loving *pranams* to you.

Your letter of 30th Ashwin was received today. It was redirected from Calcutta. I learned from your letter that the cook has left. It worries me a great deal. This is the time of year—the season of malaria—when help with cooking is urgently needed.

I am sorry to know that you would not be able to come to Calcutta even after the celebration of Jagaddhatri (an aspect of the Mother of the Universe) is over. Since you are not coming to Calcutta, what good will our going to Jayrambati during the worship of Jagaddhatri do? If we go and suffer from an attack of malaria, will it not give you trouble by making you anxious?

By the will of Sri Ramakrishna it is ordained that you will come to Calcutta in the month of Magha. We will go then to Jayrambati to bring you with us to Calcutta.

Please write how much I should send for the Jagaddhatri puja. As soon as I reach Calcutta, I shall immediately send the money. All the items that you have written for in your letter as well as those suggested by Jogin Ma will be sent at the earliest opportunity after my arrival at Calcutta.

Most obediently, your servant and son,
Sri Sharat

Calcutta
20th, Chaitra, 1325

May Sri Ramakrishna be my refuge.
Salutations to Thy Lotus Feet, Most Revered Mother:

We have decided to send Sarala to Jayrambati by the morning train next Saturday. She will be accompanied by Ruma Devi, who comes from the Himalayan region in Mayavati. The two will be escorted by Dr. Mati. Ruma Devi's home is in a village close to Mayavati and is along the way of the pilgrimage to Kailash. She comes from a respectable family. She is an extraordinarily religious person. She became deeply interested in our order after many years of hearing about you and Sri Ramakrishna from the swamis of the Mayavati Advaita Ashrama. She came down to Calcutta about a month ago for the sole purpose of meeting you and being initiated by you through your grace. She has been living with Sudhira and the others at the Nivedita School since that time. She comes from a cold country. Seeing her discomfort from the heat of Calcutta, which is too much for her, I am sending her to you. Be pleased to initiate her through your grace. After initiation she will return with Dr. Mati to Mayavati and then proceed to her own home.

Please keep well by having your bath and meals at the regular times. If you fall sick through irregular habits, there will be distress in the hearts of us all. I hear that you suffered terrible pain twice this past week. How do you feel now?

The daughter of your western disciple will get married in two months. Through your grace she has found a very good husband. Her mother has written to me and requested me to convey her news to you and to give her loving greetings to you. From Sarala you will hear more about your English disciple.

We are all doing well. Please accept our *shastanga pranams*.
Yours devotedly,
Sarat

Calcutta
16 Vaisaka, 1326

May Sri Ramakrishna be my refuge.
Salutations to the Most Revered Mother.
Dear Mother:

Please accept my *shastanga pranams* as well as those of the others who live here. We are all shocked by the sad news from Jayrambati of Nyada's death. I can imagine how painful the loss must be to you. This is the play of Sri Ramakrishna. He alone knows the meaning of the play. How can we understand it? Because we do not know his purpose, we suffer. Even the fact that we suffer because we don't know his purpose is due to his grace.

Through your blessings, all of us are doing well here.
Yours devotedly,
Sarat

This essay appeared in the book Stray Thoughts (The Literature and Religion of India) *by Swami Saradananda, published by the Ramakrishna Mission, Mylapore, Madras, apparently around the turn of the century. A preface to the essay states that it was originally "read at a miniature kind of Parliament of Religions held in 1897 at Nashville, Tenn." The September 18, 1897 issue of* Brahmavadin *states that the swami read the essay "before the Free Religious Association of America."*

The Harmony of All Religions

The peculiar feature of India is the all-embracing quality of her religion. Long before the Sun of Nazareth had risen on the horizon of Palestine, long before the mighty Buddha had sent his disciples all over Asia to preach the doctrine of sympathy and compassion—with special instructions not to revile any religion (for whoever reviles one religion injures all religions)—India had heard the words of one who preached with a voice of thunder the principle that all religions lead to the same goal. In the Bhagavad-Gita the divine Krishna said: "Whosoever comes to me through whatsoever way, I reach him. Know that all men are coming along the ways which in the end reach me." India's history demonstrates that this principle can be put into practice. Never has the religion of India encouraged religious persecution, and Hindu civil government has never limited individual liberty in the field of religion.

Vedanta promotes an attitude of active sympathy of all religions for one another. By sympathy the Vedantist does not mean a kind of dull indifference or haughty toleration which seems to say, "I know you are wrong and my religion is the only true one, yet I will allow you to follow your religion and perhaps one day your eyes will be opened." Vedanta's sympathy is not patronizing but of a direct positive nature. Vedanta says that all religions are true—they all have the same goal. They are, as it were, parallel lines proceeding from the same point or the radii from a common center. Or, as a Vedantic poet expressed it, "Like the waters of different rivers following through straight or winding paths and mingling with the ocean, losing all name and form, they all meet in Him, who is the one ocean of light and love."

Why should we quarrel then? Why may I not follow my own path and at the same time actively help you to make the conditions of your traveling your own path easier? This is the one great truth that Vedanta has to give to the world. Vedanta has never proselytized, never attempted to break the wonderful harmony of the religious symphony of the universe by bringing it down to monotones. The mission of Vedanta in the West is not to make Hindus of the Christians but to make the Christians better Christians, the Hindus better Hindus, and the Muslims better Muslims; to convince people that in and through all these various religions, there runs one common thread of truth—whatever way you go, you cannot but reach God. "He is the mover, the sustainer, the Lord, the witness, the stay, the refuge, the friend of this universe," or as St. Paul says, "in Him we live and move and have our being." The Infinite is the beginning of this evolution, and He is the end of it. Vedanta, therefore, recognizes the one great fact that there is unity in variety in nature's plan; however much variety there may be on any plane of existence—the physical, the mental, or the spiritual—yet in and through it there is unity.

The second great fact on which Vedanta builds its universal sympathy for all religions is that variation is necessary to evolution. What does evolution mean but the unfolding, the changing from one form to another—hence, the variation? Destroy variation, bring sameness to any field of nature, and you destroy evolution. The universe is so interrelated and nature is so uniform throughout that this is true not only in the physical and mental planes but also in the spiritual. Destroy variation in the religious field—try to make everyone think alike, try to subjugate all religions to any one religion—and you will find that you have destroyed religion itself.

Fortunately, attempts to make everyone think alike will invariably fail, so it is impossible to replace the many religions with one religion. Give every religion its proper place and know that they are all ways of attaining the Truth. The Truth will never change. It is beyond the changes of nature, beyond the realm of law and causation. Truth is manifested in law and causation; yet each manifestation is always partial and limited, and so the manifestations will always vary. Different ways will be discovered in different times to reach that Truth, and the religions to come will be just as true as those that exist in the present day.

From ancient times many have tried to find a common ground on which all religions could meet. Attempts have been made in Alexandria, in Greece, and in many other places to extract the truths from every religion and combine them into a new universal religion. They have failed miserably because they never recognized the fact that variation is necessary to evolution. They never saw that all religions are true and effective at different stages of the soul's evolution. They never understood that all religions point toward one great truth—that the goal of evolution is to make human beings perfect by leading them into the superconscious state. Religions which seem diametrically opposite in their rites and ceremonies and doctrines are in agreement here. In the symbolic meaning of ceremony and mythology or in the clear-cut language of philosophy, they all speak the same truth—that every person's real nature is perfect, that the little personalities grow and expand until they find themselves to be the one universal Being, infinite and perfect. This heritage is not extraneous to the individual or the exclusive property of one person or some people, but it is the essence of everyone; it is the gradual unfolding of what is within us all.

We in our ignorance think that the statement of Jesus, "I and my Father are one," was true of him alone, or that his injunction "Be ye therefore perfect as the Father in heaven is perfect" should not be taken literally. In our foolishness we think that the superconscious state, which transcends the realm of speech and thought, is a lower stage, a stage brought about by the mind's constant focusing on one subject. If the mind can become hypnotized by concentrating on an object, we are already hypnotized by sex, money, and power. Going beyond the obsession with these trifles that are here today and gone tomorrow by concentrating on God will develop our faculties to their highest potential. It is worse than hypnotism to think in the face of naked facts to the contrary that we are free or that whatever our senses report or our brain thinks is true.

Shake off such foolish ideas, and follow your own religion. Know that nothing can destroy you. You create your own heaven and hell. "The kingdom of heaven is within you," and you will find it as soon as you wish. See that the universe is God's playground, that he has not left the management of it in the hands of anybody, and that we human beings, whatever we are doing, are coming nearer and nearer to the Deity.

Some people say that preaching the universal sympathy of all religions will destroy religion entirely, that it will lessen religious belief which is based on the recognition that there is only one true religion. Shall we, then, let people continue to believe in the infallibility of their own religion? Will it not be better to open our eyes to the knowledge that the students of logic, of history, of science, and of religion itself are bringing to us every day? Vedanta tells us, follow the truth wherever it leads you. Truth will never conform to the individual or to society, but the individual and society must conform to it. Faith and belief gain their strength by being based on Truth; no amount of belief in untruth will strengthen one's life.

It is unreasonable and false to say that the sympathy you extend toward other religions would be at the expense of the intensity of faith in your own. Believe as intensely as you can in the infallibility of your own religion; follow it in your daily life. At the same time know that other religions are also means of reaching God for minds that think differently from you. In society there must be united action in conformity with social laws and also liberty for individual action; in religion, every group must have perfect individual freedom and yet there must be active sympathy for all the others. Active sympathy and toleration are possible only when we look upon other religions in the same light as we look upon our own, when we believe in the infallibility of all religions. We will have to learn the one great fact that if one religion is false, the others are false as well, and if one is true, the others are true too. For if religion and revelation come through the process of evolution, it cannot be the exclusive property of any one sect or any one individual. It is as common as God's wind and rain, which come both to the just and the unjust; it is like universal space, embracing everything that is sentient and insentient.

This lecture was written at the request of the Ethical Association of Brooklyn, N.Y. in 1896. Originally titled The Vedanta: Its Theory and Practice, *it was later published in Swami Saradananda's book, Stray Thoughts.*

Individuality and the Philosophy of Vedanta

The philosophy of Vedanta evolved in India thousands of years ago; the precise date is unknown. It existed long before Buddhism, long before the age of the Ramayana and the Mahabharata—the two great pre-Buddhistic epics of India. The principles of Vedanta underlie all the different religions and sects that exist in India. Moreover, the *rishis*, or seers of thought who were the fathers of Vedanta, claim that its principles underlie all the different religions that exist on the face of the earth and all that will come in the future. Vedanta's goal is that same goal that all religions, society itself, humanity are rushing toward, either consciously or unconsciously through the process of evolution.

One great peculiarity of this philosophy is that it is not built around one person or prophet. It is founded on the latter portion—the knowledge portion—of the Vedas, as the term *Vedanta* suggests. The word *Vedas* comes from the Sanskrit root *vid*, to know; according to the oldest Hindu commentator, it implies all the supersensuous knowledge that has been revealed to human beings up to the present and that which will be revealed in the future. The word *Vedas* later became applied to the book that kept the record of this knowledge. The Vedic commentator went on to say that this supersensuous knowledge might be revealed not only to Hindus but to other people, and their revelations should be regarded as part of the Vedas.

The Vedas are divided into two great parts. The work portion teaches us how to reach heaven by performing our duty, being moral, and doing good deeds. The knowledge portion teaches us that not even heaven should be our aim; its enjoyments are too fleeting and transitory. Our aim should be beyond relativity—to merge with the Divine, that center of all knowledge and power.

This system of philosophy took ages to evolve, and note that it never went against religion in India. They always went hand in hand. In order to satisfy the whole person religion must appeal not only to the heart but also to the mind. Therefore, it must have a sound foundation of metaphysics. Are we not complex beings, a combination of reason and emotion and will? Can any religion satisfy us that does not fulfill our highest aspirations in all three aspects of our being?

The rapid march of science and the wonderful discoveries it is making every day strike terror in the hearts of many people. They seem to think that the foundation of religion is being undermined and, consequently, our whole social fabric is in imminent danger. But the seers of old (who by their study of the internal world found the source of religion, of morality, of duty, in short of everything that forms the basis of our being—that ocean of knowledge and bliss absolute out of which the universe has come) if they were here today, they would rejoice at the discoveries of science. Instead of undermining religion, science is making the foundation of religion stronger than ever inasmuch as its exploration of the material universe is discovering the same unity that the *rishis* discovered in the spiritual world. And it must be so, for is not the universe one connected whole? Can we ever know the external universe without the internal? Internal, external, spiritual, material—they are only words. We speak of natural laws that govern the external—the material—universe; but are these laws anything else than the means by which our mind connects a series of phenomena?

This universe according to Vedanta is one connected mass. Start from the external and you come to the internal. The external universe has come out of the infinite ocean of knowledge and bliss and will go back into it again. It is evolving and involving throughout all eternity. Viewed as one unit, it has no change or motion. Change and motion are possible only when there is a comparison, and a comparison can be made only between two or more things. All change is within it. It is perfect.

This chain of evolution and involution, this progression from the unmanifested—the seed form of nature—to the manifested, and the repetition of the cycle can have no beginning in time. To admit a beginning would be to admit a beginning to the Creator. No, Vedanta says, creation is eternal as the Creator is eternal: sometimes it is manifested and sometimes it remains unmanifested.

What is the purpose of creation, the motive behind this eternal flow of evolution and involution? The answer that Vedanta gives is that there is no purpose; it is the play of the Infinite. You cannot ascribe motive to the perfect without implying that it is imperfect. The Infinite, the Absolute, the Perfect, has no necessity to create. The Infinite is absolutely free and independent. And the Absolute is the only real existence.

The universe is but a speck in that infinite ocean of knowledge and bliss. The Absolute plays, projecting this world of phenomena, wearing masks of imperfection while remaining one, perfect, in all splendor and glory. "He vibrates and he does not vibrate. He is far and he is near. He is within all and he is without all this world of phenomena." "As the webwombed spider projects and takes back its thread, . . . so this universe comes out of that ocean of knowledge and bliss and goes back into it again."

Science, by tracing evolution to its cause, has arrived at the laws of the survival of the fittest and sexual selection as factors behind the change of one species into another. Vedanta concurs with regard to the dynamics of evolution, but Vedanta adds, the true cause of the change of one species into another is the struggle of the Divine within every form to manifest itself more perfectly. As one of our great philosophers has said, when irrigating a field from a tank placed above ground, the water seeks to rush into the field, but it is barred by the gate. Open the gate and the water will rush out into the field by its own nature. The struggle of the Divine to manifest itself more perfectly has produced higher and higher forms. The struggle is still going on and will cease only when the Divine manifests itself perfectly without any bars or bolts to hinder its expression.

The highest point of evolution transcends conscious existence, and so we call it superconscious existence. Some individuals have reached that point long ago. Christ and Buddha and all the great teachers attained that state. The whole of humanity is struggling towards superconscious existence, without being aware of their goal.

Can evolution become complete? Vedanta says that it can.

Evolution presupposes involution. To admit an unending chain of evolution would be to conceive of motion in a straight line, which modern science has proved to be impossible. But what will take society ages and ages to reach, individuals can attain in this lifetime; as the religious history of the world demonstrates, some have already attained it. What are the holy books of all religions but records of the experiences of those who attained that stage?

Examine those books, read between the lines, and you will find that what Vedanta expresses in the famous aphorism, "Thou art that infinite ocean of knowledge and bliss"—*Tat twan asi*—was called *nirvana* (the perfected state) by Buddha. It was the goal of Christ's injunction to be perfect even as the Father in heaven is perfect and of the Muslim sufis' striving to become one with the Truth. Vedanta claims that this idea of oneness with the Divine, this conviction that our real nature is infinite and perfect, lies at the heart of every religion; only in some the idea is expressed symbolically through myth and ritual. Vedanta claims that what a few persons have attained long ago is the natural inheritance of all. Sooner or later everyone will attain it. Therefore, according to Vedanta, each of us is divine and everything that is strong and good and powerful in human nature is the expression of the divinity within.

The basis of ethics and morality lies in our superconscious existence. Contemporary attempts to find a permanent basis of morality in the relative world have been worthless. Everyone of us feels that without morality and unselfishness neither the individual nor the nation can develop. Even those standing outside the pale of religion advance ideas of morality and unselfishness on utilitarian grounds—that we must conduct ourselves in a way that brings the greatest amount of good to the greatest number of people. But if I ask these pragmatists why I should look upon my brother as myself or why I should not try to secure the greatest good for myself alone, no plausible answer is given. The answer that Vedanta gives is that you and I are not separate from each other or the rest of this universe. It is a mistake to think ourselves distinct and unconnected entities. Both history and science shows just the opposite: we are not independent from each other; this universe is one connected whole. There is no break in the ocean of matter in which our bodies represent but so many different points. Behind the external there is that one vast ocean of mind in which our minds represent so many different whirlpools. And behind that is the Soul, the Self, the Absolute, the Perfect.

Everything in human life points toward this oneness. Our love, our sympathy, our kindness, our doing good to others—all are expressions, conscious or unconscious, of this oneness with the universe. Consciously or unconsciously each of us feels it; consciously or unconsciously each of us tries to express it. We are one with the universal Being and as such all souls and all entities are one: by injuring others we injure ourselves and by loving others we love ourselves.

This statement gives rise to a subtle question: Shall we lose our individuality when we attain the superconscious stage? Vedanta turns the question around. Are we now individuals in the proper sense of the term? Does individuality refer to the ephemeral elements in us, or does it refer to our unchangeable essence? Do you apply the term individuality to the body and the mind which are changing every minute? If so, there is no need to ask if we are losing our individuality inasmuch as we are losing or changing these elements every minute of our existence. Think what great changes we have, each of us, undergone since we were born. Think of the changes required for a wicked person to become a good member of society or for the protohumans, through the process of evolution, to become the builders of great civilizations. Is the change of individuality lamentable in these cases?

Vedanta says by developing your individuality, you become a perfect individual. You change your apparent present individuality for the real one. The process of evolution is from lawlessness through law to the state that is beyond law; from the unconscious through the conscious to the state that is beyond the conscious. Our conscious existence, where every action is accompanied by the feeling of ego, does not cover the whole of our existence. During sleep or when we perform automatic actions, there is no feeling of ego. Superficially the highest and lowest stages of consciousness seem to be one, but there is as much difference between them as between darkness produced by want of light and darkness produced by an excess of light, or to use the scientific term, the polarization of light. An illiterate, ignorant person enters the superconscious state and comes out a sage, a prophet, a great seer. He has discovered in himself the eternal fountainhead of all knowledge and power; he has found the kingdom of heaven within. "For him," say the Vedas, "all doubts (and hankerings) vanish forever and all selfish knots of the heart are cut asunder; the endless chain of cause and effect fades and dies for him who attains the highest."

Attaining superconscious existence has been described as seeing and feeling—realizing—God. But what is God? Logic coupled to science has proved without a doubt that our ideas of God are anthropomorphic. We create and worship God in our own image, our own mental representation. What, then, is the necessity of worshiping God? Why worship a mental creation? The history of religion shows that the idea of God has grown and developed along with human development. From fetishism and animism we came to polytheism and then to monotheism. Perhaps their dreams or the love of dead ancestors or the stupendous forces of nature around them suggested the possibility of an existence beyond the death of the body to those protohumans and early humans and they tried to peep beyond the screen of their senses. Searching for the superconscious, they refined their beliefs gradually through the stages of ancestor worship and nature worship to the recognition of gods or spirits behind the forces of nature. Eventually they developed the concept of a supreme God. Some will say that, although worshiping this progression of concepts helped to develop human intellect, now that we have become more sophisticated we ought to discard every concept of God because they are all necessarily anthropomorphic. Vedanta does not deny the anthropomorphism of the different concepts of God but asks, are not all our ideas of the external universe anthropomorphic? Has not science already demonstrated that the senses are deceptive and that we can never know things as they truly are? If it is reasonable to reject our ideas of God because they are anthropomorphic, it is reasonable to throw away all our other ideas as well. Yet how many of us are willing to do so or have the power to do so? Although all we know about the external universe is what our minds represent it to be, these anthropomorphic ideas have been responsible for our personal growth and the survival and development of the human race.

Vedanta says that it is neither wrong nor foolish to worship God, whatever the concept. Human groping toward the truth is a progression not from error to truth but from lower to higher truth. Even truth is relative. What is the truth for one state of being is not true for another state. The different ideas of God are nothing less than different views of the Absolute, the Infinite, as seen from different planes of the relative. Supposing we were to journey to the sun: our view of the sun would change every minute along the way. With each million miles we see different visions of the same sun. What was at first a bright little disc grows larger and brighter and hotter until at last we experience the sun in its entirety. All this time the sun has not changed, but our view of it has. This is the pattern of man's progress toward the Infinite. Through the limitations of his senses and his intellect, he sees only a distorted glimpse of the Infinite. As he grows spiritually, his supersensuous perception grows and his glimpses of the Infinite become less and less distorted until at last he perceives the Infinite in its entirety: He discovers in himself the infinite ocean of knowledge and bliss.

Vedanta has no quarrel with any religion. It sees all religions as so many different ways of attaining that one, indivisible ocean of knowledge and bliss. "As the different rivers, having their source in different mountains, roll down through crooked or straight paths to come at last into the ocean—so all these various creeds and religions, starting from different positions and running through roundabout or straight courses, at last come to Thee, O Lord." Vedanta condemns nobody; it looks upon all human beings not as they appear to be at the moment but as they really are. It teaches that sooner or later all of us will discover our real nature and will know ourselves to be the One source of knowledge, power, and bliss. Each of us is advancing toward that moment of discovery. The worker by doing good to others, the philosopher by developing his reason, the lover of God by focusing his emotions—all, all will attain the superconscious plane, the pinnacle of evolution. What if some are agnostics or atheists? The question is, are they sincere? Are they ready to sacrifice themselves for the good of others and for truth as they know it?

Vedanta says there is no fear for them. They will come to higher and higher truths and ultimately they will reach the highest Truth. Allow infinite variation in religious thought. Follow your own ideal—but do not try to bring everybody to your opinion. It never can be. Unity in diversity is the law of nature. Do not try to make yourself the standard for all, but know that unity forms the background of this diverse universe, and whatever way we travel, all of us at last will arrive at the Truth.

These spiritual teachings appeared in The Apostles of Sri Ramakrishna, *compiled and edited by Swami Gambhirananda, published by Advaita Ashrama, Mayavati in 1972.*

The Spiritual Teachings of Swami Saradananda

No special time and place are necessary to repeat the Lord's name and worship him. You can repeat his name wherever you are.

The mind gets purified through selfless work. And when the mind becomes pure, knowledge and devotion are manifested in it. Knowledge is the very nature of the Self, but being covered with ignorance, it is not manifest. The object of selfless work is to remove this ignorance.

First you have to attain knowledge. When you return to this world of diversity after attaining knowledge, you will see everything as before, but you will no longer be attached to what you see. After you realize God, the world seems to be like a mirage. There is nothing in it that can attract you.

What really comes through spiritual practice is unswerving faith—faith in the words of the guru, in the Lord, in the scriptures.

No one is wholly without defects. But some try to get rid of them, while others do not feel the need for that. Since you have taken refuge at the Lord's feet, you certainly feel the need of eliminating your faults. You also have the will to do so, and the Lord will grant you the strength to succeed. We too have taken shelter under him and are trying to free ourselves from all shortcomings. What power have we to help others? Nevertheless, I always pray wholeheartedly for your good and for the good of all the others, and I do so now.

Whatever work increases your discontent and stands in the way of God realization is bad. You should discard it.

All souls are forever free; that is why every mind hankers for freedom. A true leader never hampers that craving for freedom. His only concern is to see to it that when a person gets liberty, he does not misuse it.

Brahman and Brahman's power are not different, like fire and its power to burn. The scriptures speak of Brahman as the Cosmic Person (*Virat*) and of the power associated with Brahman as the Mother of the Universe (*Shakti*). That is why the presiding deity of the *Gayatri* mantra is sometimes spoken of as the Cosmic Person and sometimes as the Mother of the Universe. There is no contradiction in imagining the presiding deity either way.

You complain that thoughts of your duties sometimes intrude when you sit for meditation. We are all in the same predicament. You cannot escape wandering thoughts even if you leave work and retire to a forest. But, if through God's grace, it becomes firmly impressed on your mind that the world is impermanent and if you become gripped by the feeling that God alone is your true goal, then this unsteadiness of the mind will be greatly eliminated. To have a strong longing for God and to feel ill at ease because God has not been realized comes from the grace of God. Pray to him for this with all earnestness.

You need not meditate long on your guru, but remember to salute him and then spend most of the time in meditation on your Chosen Deity. Meditate on the deity as you go on repeating his name. Since past mental tendencies cannot assert themselves while you are hard at work, you should apply your whole mind to it. Selfless work is the best means of winning a victory over past tendencies.

You must have faith in the enlightened souls and carry on your religious practices accordingly. Trying to understand the pros and cons of their teachings with our impure minds—occupied as they are with thoughts of the world—leads nowhere. Give up the attempt to understand everything and start your spiritual practices by relying on what the Master has taught.

When you sit down for meditation, say to yourself: This is my own Chosen Deity, who like an eternally pure and indivisible ocean of Existence-Knowledge-Bliss, pervades everything. I exist within Him. It is He who exists everywhere inside and outside myself. After meditating on this for a while, start your *japa* and meditate as usual. This will remove the unsteadiness of the mind.

If the mind continues to be unsteady, pray to the Lord, "Lord, kindly make my mind steady!" Know this for certain—He hears whatever you say and knows whatever passes through your mind.

Both peace and peacelessness come to us for the sake of our own experience, according to God's will, but we have to remain steady under all circumstances by holding on to Him. From one point of view, peacelessness appears to be preferable for then one calls on the Lord with greater earnestness.

The greatest sin is to think oneself weak and sinful. If you have to believe anything, believe that you are His children, the heirs to His infinite strength and bliss.

Nowadays there are many religious societies, but after a few days flurry, people seem to lose interest in them. What is the reason for this? The reason is our words are not in accord with our thoughts. The first step in religion is to be sincere to the core.

Our scriptures say, and so do we, that all men are images of the Lord. But what do we do in practice? We despise sweepers and other low caste people. We treat our women—those in whom lies dormant the wonderful strength of the Mother of the Universe—as slaves. Only at the time of worship do we utter the words that all women are images of the Divine Mother!

The four kinds of spiritual practices—jnana, yoga (raja), karma, and bhakti—are meant for four types of people. But the aim is the same—to kill the lower self. Think deeply and you will find there is hardly any difference among them. In fact, there is none. Kill the self and you will be free.

Comments on Karma Yoga

Vedanta says that the goal of life is to obtain freedom, to unite with the Supreme. Vedanta has four methods of accomplishing this, the four yogas. The aim of all four yogas is the same, but everyone cannot attain this one end by the same method. Some people have mystic tendencies; they must realize God by means of meditation and inner searching. Some are strongly emotional; they must center their emotions on a personal God and use the discipline of devotion. Others are philosophers, pure and simple; to them the idea of dependence on a Being outside themselves is not appealing; reason and sheer force of will alone can help them. And there are those who require activity in order to make progress; they do best with the science of karma yoga, the path of work.

Karma yoga is based on the law of *karma*; it achieves its goal by the effect of work rather than by the work itself. The law of karma points out that a person's character and tendencies are determined by past actions. If you do good deeds, your character and desires will reflect that goodness. If your actions have been evil, your tendencies will become more evil. Good deeds are the only remedy for past misdeeds, and karma yoga shows you how to work to achieve this result.

It divides work into two categories, work with motive (that is, with the hope of a reward for your labors) and work without motive. Work with motive is subdivided into work done for name, fame, and material reward and work done for the benefit of others.

Vedanta tells us that we are what we have made of ourselves. And if we work with any of these motives, we shall be bound to that motive: the law of cause and effect will bind us to it. Freedom is the aim of religion—freedom from life's dualities, even freedom from happiness because happiness entails a corresponding unhappiness. To be rid of the effect (that is, the bondage) we must first remove the cause. As long as there is motive behind our work, that work is selfish and will keep us in bondage.

Some say that Vedanta is selfish because it focuses on freedom for the soul. Vedanta does focus on freedom for the soul, but we must never lose sight of two important factors—the ego is not the soul, and in the final reality there is only one Soul. Therefore in freeing the Soul, we must first destroy the ego which holds the Soul in bondage; and when we release the Soul—that reality which we do not at present know—we are to all intents and purposes working for one another.

For work to be unselfish it is essential that we be unattached. If we work for another because we have feelings of particular regard for that person, there is motive in our work. Instead, we must fill ourselves with the feeling that we are one with the universe. Those who believe in God should try to see God in everything. If we can put this approach into practice, it will be impossible to become attached to our work. Our work will be without motive and therefore, it will not be limited by the law of cause and effect. Work as masters, not as servants. Care not for the results, for that also is a motive.

Of course, the majority of us are unable to work without motive. Fortunately karma yoga can teach us to improve and purify our motives, to work for others rather than ourselves and persistently to increase the circle of those for whom we work until we attain our goal of embracing all and everything.

Duty is not to be despised. We must, indeed, fulfill our duty. But duty is not the end, the aim of life. And this is of great importance, duty varies according to nationality and creed. The highest point of duty is reached when we recognize the truth and justice of the customs of those around us and suit ourselves to the customs of those among whom we are placed rather than try to make them subservient to our own preconceived notion of what customs and habits should be.

As Swami Vivekananda once said, "We should always try to see the duty of others through their own eyes, never want to judge the customs of other races or other peoples by our own standard." The only way to do duty is to fulfill that which comes to hand. The nature of the work is not its test, but the manner in which it is done. "To work you have the right, but not to the fruits thereof," and karma yoga says that it is possible to work without motive. It has been done in the past and you can begin to do it now.

These spiritual precepts have been taken from the collected letters and transcripts of conversations of Swami Saradananda. In preparing these selections I have made use of several volumes in Bengali, published by the Udbodhan Office, Calcutta. The letters were written by Swami Saradananda to his disciples and to several lay and monastic followers of Sri Ramakrishna. The major portions were composed during the latter part of the swami's life, between 1917 and 1927. A remarkable feature of the originals is their brevity and lucidity. The conversations were set down during the same period. My plan has been to translate only those portions which are of universal appeal and throw light on problems of spiritual life. I have inserted topical headings for an easy grasp of the subject matter; these are not in the original.

Spiritual Precepts

Need for Spiritual Practice

You have read in books how Sri Ramakrishna awakened the spiritual consciousness of Swami Vivekananda and other disciples by a wish or a single touch. You might have thought within yourself that you too would get such an awakening from your guru at the time of initiation. You have had no peace of mind because you were disappointed. The scriptures say, "Nothing can sever the spiritual relationship which grows between the guru and the disciple; it is something eternal." Have faith in the words of the guru and practice hard. Restlessness arises because of the outgoing tendency of the mind. As the mind becomes more and more indrawn, more and more concentrated, the wild roamings of the mind will cease and you will experience inner joy and ineffable bliss. Let your heart overflow with pure love for God and you will gain that by which man becomes immortal in this very life.

Supreme Knowledge

What is known as the destruction of the mind in Vedantic literature is not a state of vacuum. It is a state of deep concentration. The mind is to be made absolutely one-pointed through meditation on God. Then alone this condition will arise. Gradually the mind will become steady, like an unflickering flame, and be fully absorbed in Brahman. All the tumult and noise of the external world will be silenced. The individual soul will cast off the limitations of a conditioned existence and be united with the Absolute, that sea of calm bliss. The scriptures call this experience establishment in the truth, or attainment of the supreme knowledge.

Perfect peace will not come until the mind is fully concentrated. You must dwell on God uninterruptedly and be absorbed in the contemplation of His true nature. There must be no slackening of efforts until the goal is reached, until samadhi is attained. Continue whatever spiritual disciplines you are doing. Through steady practice the mind will gradually be absorbed in samadhi. Mental worship of the guru and the Chosen Ideal is to be carried on as before. Then you are to think that your Chosen Ideal has become the inmost Self of all living beings and the very principle of consciousness. You are to calm your mind by single-minded devotion to God and by reflecting on the ultimate Reality as the foundation of all existence. You may recite the *Gayatri* at the end of your meditation. It is a Vedic prayer, meaning: "I meditate, with an unwavering mind on the effulgent light of that Absolute Being from whom the universe has sprung. May He illumine our consciousness so that we may cross the ocean of worldliness and see His blissful form throughout eternity."

Resignation to God

The Lord is making you His own. He will not allow even the slightest ego to remain within you. The sufferings and difficulties you are undergoing are intended to make you realize that you have no independent will of your own. It is all given over to the Lord. Therefore, be contented with what He does and wherever He keeps you. Never allow any doubts to cross your mind. The moment doubt arises, immediately think of the Lord and be convinced that whatever takes place by His will is always for your good. Whatever is happening is happening at His command and, if He wills, the situation will change. With this attitude resign yourself to the Lord and be happy and free from cares.

Need for Meditation

If the mind is engaged in different kinds of activities, it is natural that it will be restless. It is foolishness to expect calmness all of a sudden and an unobstructed vision of the Chosen Ideal during contemplation. It is for this reason that you must set apart a definite time and sit for meditation regularly. However busy you may be, you must not forget to sit twice every day, in the morning and in the evening. You may begin with a period of fifteen minutes each time, but gradually you should increase the period up to an hour, if not more. If you practice *japa* and meditation regularly, without break for some years, you will see for yourself what result comes to pass. Your mind will become pure and you will be absorbed in the thought of God. Then you will be reluctant to leave off meditation even for a single day. There will come an inner tranquility which will fill your heart with joy. Fasten your mind to the Lord and always hold your *Ishta* in front of you. You have come to the world to realize God. That is the sole purpose of life. It has no other end. Forgetfulness of the *Ishta* is as good as death. Strive hard, for through struggle alone one attains the grace of his own mind and yearns for God. When the yearning comes, the vision of God will become a realized fact.

You have asked why in spite of your sincere efforts the mind is so unruly that it refuses to come under control and you are not able to fix it on God. The reason is that the mind is not yet pure. Have you not heard that Sri Ramakrishna used to say that the image of the moon is not clearly reflected in a pool that is agitated and muddy? When the water is steady and transparent the image is visible; then the image is not broken up into fragments. Remember that the same is true of the mind. The reflection of God is always in the mind, but until the mind becomes tranquil and pure, the image of God cannot be observed. In other words, God is always present within us. But we will not be aware of that presence until the mirror of the heart is clear. Through *japa* and meditation you can purify the heart and then the true nature of God will be revealed to you. Then you will experience that blessed state in which all doubts vanish and the heart overflows with pure love and joy of His presence. This has been beautifully put in the Upanishads: "The knots of the heart, which are ignorance, become loosened, all doubts are dissolved, and all evil effects of deeds are destroyed when He who is both personal and impersonal is realized."

Power of Faith

You feel depressed because your faith is lukewarm. You must cultivate self-confidence. Without *shraddha,* or firm faith in oneself, man is no man; he is a bundle of negatives. He accomplishes nothing. Believe that you have the power to achieve anything that your heart sets itself upon. Instead of doubting yourself, feel that you are the possessor of infinite strength and have the might to overcome all difficulties. It is the strong, the heroic, who do noble deeds and become great. Those who are weak and vacillating are lost like broken clouds in the sky. Keep your faith firm and repeat the name of the Lord. You will know everything from within yourself. Your mind will become your guru. It will show you what to do, what not to do, and point the way to truth. By and by you will realize everything. Do not be in a hurry. Impatience is the greatest obstacle in spiritual life.

The Lord has made you an instrument of his work and you have been doing some wonderful things. In spite of that, you are saying, "I have no peace of mind. I have no end of worries. Life is not worth living. Everything seems to be slipping through my fingers." When I hear such statements, I say to myself, "Oh Lord, shall I laugh or cry?" If you ask my advice, I can only repeat what I have said before, "Oh fool, he who has taken refuge in the Lord, has he anything to complain of or worry about?" He knows that he has surrendered himself to Him and the Lord has accepted him. This is all that he need be aware of. He need know nothing else. Like the kitten, he knows only his mother. Wherever his mother places him, he is contented. Whatever may be the circumstances, good or bad, pleasing or unpleasing, he does not care. He is happy, he does not grumble. He never stops repeating the name of Mother and looking up to her for comfort and consideration. If it is the will of Mother, do you think that it will take time to grant the vision and fulfill the desire of your heart? When you belong to her, there is no question that visions and experiences will be yours some day in your life.

If She does not come now, She will surely appear before you at the time of death and free you from all the cares of the world.

For the present, forget yourself completely, wipe out the sense of "me and mine" and you will enjoy supreme happiness. Without doing that, if you go on calculating like a shopkeeper, "I have not gained this," you will never be happy. This will lead you from misery to greater misery and ultimately draw you into a sea of despair. Until a man gives up shopkeeping and rids himself of the spirit of bargaining, no peace will reign in his soul. The Master, while lying ill at Cossipore Garden, used to say, "Those who came to me expecting some earthly gain have deserted me, saying, 'Ah, if he is an incarnation of God, why should he fall sick? If sick, why can he not cure himself by his will power?' But those who are my own have stayed with me. They are serving me day and night and are suffering a great deal in seeing this misery."

Have faith in Sri Ramakrishna. You have the blessings of Holy Mother. She has taken responsibility for you. Why worry? Whenever negative thoughts arise, remembering the Lord drives them away. In good time you will be able to realize that all you have done for the Lord has not been in vain. Mother's protecting hand has been always upon you. By her grace you will be able to see her, talk to her, and hear her message. All will come to you when the time is ripe. Do not the scriptures say, "One realizes the Atman within oneself in time"?

Marriage or Renunciation

Whether you are to marry and live in the world or to become a monk and renounce the world—this is a very intricate question. You alone are the fittest person to decide. None can do it for you. If your devotion to God increases and your mind is drawn toward his lotus feet, He will provide you with the opportunity and everything will be favorable and all your problems will be overcome in an unexpected manner. By His grace the world will drop off like the water from the feathers of a duck. So, depending upon Him, resign yourself to His care. Let Him decide what is best for you. But one thing you must strive for without letup: You are to work unceasingly so that your love for God, without growing dim, becomes more and more intense and your relationship with Him becomes more and more intimate. If you can make Him your very own, He will see to your welfare and never let you down.

It is not necessary that everyone become a monk. Nor has everybody the aptitude and necessary prerequisites for leading a monastic life. If you have no obligations to your family and you feel a strong urge to renounce the world for the sake of God, you are free to do so. But you must watch carefully and see whether it is a passing emotion or a genuine desire. Very often one does not know the subtle desires that lie hidden below the surface consciousness which create trouble in later years.

What you have written does not seem to be sound to me. None can become a monk by making plans ahead of time. You have said in so many words, "Let me now enjoy working and earning money. When I am through, I will join the monastery." We may make plans, but there is another power which turns them into ashes or converts them into success. If you ask my opinion, my advice is that you lead a good life—no matter where you live—in the world or out of the world. It does not make any difference where you are led; try always to be His. Make Him the goal of your life. Give your mind to God and to none else. This much I can say: "He who dwells in God has nothing to fear from the world. He will be protected from all dangers and difficulties." I always wish good things for you. May Sri Ramakrishna guide you and show you the path of truth and light.

The Power of the Divine Name

I am pleased to learn that a group of devotees are assembling every week in your home for study, discussion, and singing of devotional songs. This is very good. To sing the glory of the Lord in the company of devotees is a means to devotion, if the right mood and proper atmosphere is kept up. But along with singing you should also spend some time in repetition of His name in silence. The scriptures say that the name can be repeated audibly, semi-audibly, or mentally. Of the three, mental repetition is the best. It will purify your mind and help you to keep your thoughts in God. "The name of God is identical with the Lord," says Sri Ramakrishna. Every word is the symbol of an idea. Every thought has its counterpart in words. We cannot think without using words mentally. When you are alone, instead of thinking idle, useless things why not think of the Lord? And the easiest way to remember God is to repeat his name. Sri Krishna says in the Gita: "Of vows, I am the vow of *japa*."

But mechanical, parrot-like repetition will do you no good. You must utter His name with feeling and devotion. If instead of thinking of the Lord your mind wanders while you chant his name, how can you expect the desired result? It will be just like rowing a boat without pulling up the anchor. So you must repeat the name and meditate on its meaning so that your mind may be withdrawn from sense objects and fastened on God. This is what Sri Ramakrishna asks us to do in his precept: "Make mind and mouth one. Harmonize your words and thoughts. If they are united, success is bound to come." Patanjali says the same thing in his aphorism, "One must repeat Om and reflect on its meaning." One can meditate on Om as well as on divine forms. But you are to follow the instructions of your teacher and repeat the name given by him.

On *Japa*

The name of the Lord you receive at the time of initiation is sacred to you. It is your mantra. You must not speak of it to anybody except your guru. The purpose of keeping it secret is not for any occult reason but in order to let it sink into your deeper consciousness and reveal to you the truth, the knowledge of which will make you free. Constant repetition of the mantra is keeping good company. It must be natural, like breathing. The repetition of the divine name will bring into your mind holy associations, the blessed qualities of God, and take away all the blemishes of the heart. The disciple must practice hard, with patience and determination, until he attains the direct vision of God within the sanctuary of his heart.

The power of the mantra is tremendous. As a living seed holds the potential of a tree and is able to yield fruits and flowers in season, so the mantra has the power to bring spiritual progress and ultimately liberation from the world of suffering and death. The scriptures say that when the spiritual power is awakened, the mantra is seen in golden letters and sometimes is heard as clearly as a human voice. All these things are matters of experience. They cannot be known through intellectual understanding or mere discussion. One has to practice spiritual discipline for many years. In time, everything will be revealed from within oneself. Then the aspirant realizes God in and through the mantra which appears as the visible form of the Infinite Being, which is formless and nameless.

The main thing is the one-pointedness of the mind. It is the nature of the mind to flit from object to object. It does not remain steady. Even in sleep it wanders about and conjures up fantastic dreams. Diverse thoughts will distract your mind and you will feel exasperated. But do not give up the spiritual struggle. It is hard to control the mind; but it must be done. There is no other way. The more you think of the Lord, the more other thoughts decrease. There must be a continuous flow of one thought—the thought of God—during the period of wakefulness. Then, at the time of meditation or in sleep, unbecoming thoughts will not find any peephole to enter. Through ceaseless effort one must bring the mind back if it wanders away and fix it on the Chosen Ideal. This is what you read in the Gita. But mere reading is not enough. Unless you practice, you will not assimilate the teachings.

So without losing heart, carry on. Let your mind flow toward God as the river flows toward the ocean. As Sri Krishna says in the Gita: "Patiently, little by little, a man must free himself from all mental distractions, with the aid of the intelligent will. He must fix his mind upon the Atman and never think of anything else. No matter where the restless and unquiet mind wanders, it must be drawn back and made to submit to the Atman only."

Directions for Meditation

Plunge yourself into spiritual disciplines with all your heart and soul. That will give real satisfaction. Why for a few days? A whole life is to be spent for that purpose. Nothing can be achieved speedily. One who is prepared to persevere to the end receives the grace of the Lord. I pray that you may have unwavering devotion and abiding faith in Him.

With regard to spiritual practices, the general rule is wise discernment and moderation in everything. You may have read in the Gita: "Yoga is not for him who sleeps too much or for the keeper of exaggerated vigils. Let a man be moderate in his eating and recreation, moderately active, moderate in sleep and in wakefulness. He will find that yoga takes away all his unhappiness."

Do not strain yourself; do as much as you can. Indeed, you must get sufficient rest and maintain good health. But at the same time you must not give way to lukewarmness and become lax in your struggle. There is no hard and fast rule regarding the number of hours to be spent in study and meditation. Everything is to be done according to one's convenience and capacity. Gradually you should increase *japa,* the repetition of the name of the Lord, and the period of your meditation. Regularity is very important in spiritual life. Therefore you must try to keep the same hours as far as possible. At other times, keep a watch over your mind and see that recollectedness continues throughout the day. There is no need to observe the vow of silence. One can practice recollectedness without it. What you should avoid is gossip and worldly talk.

Wherever you are, you must obey the orders of your superiors and perform your duties to the best of your ability. There is no need to ask me about such matters. Use your discretion and act accordingly. If there is any problem pertaining to your spiritual life, you may ask me and I shall be glad to answer your question. For the rest, you must think for yourself and stand on your own feet.

If you carry on your spiritual practices with implicit faith in the Lord—who is your own—you will understand everything in due time. It will gradually be revealed to you how you can cultivate absolute reliance on God while performing your duties. If you are sincere and have the attitude that it is His work that you are doing, He will show you the way.

Remember these things: (1) An impure person can never be a good worker. (2) A true worker works with skill and efficiency but will at the same time maintain inner peace and tranquility. However arduous his task may be, he will not grumble. He will avoid all misunderstanding and quarrels and be tolerant of other people's viewpoints. (3) In the midst of all kinds of work you must allot some time for *japa* and meditation for they are the means to self-knowledge. Jesus Christ said to his disciples: "Ye are the salt of the earth." It seems to me *japa* and meditation are, as it were, the salt of work. In all religious organizations whenever the observance of spiritual practices slackens, work becomes saltless, and the members drift without knowing where they are going or where their work is leading them.

Follow the instructions of your teacher and meditate regularly. Meditate on the guru, seated on a white lotus with twelve petals. This center is situated in the brain above the eyebrows. Before performing *japa* and meditation, recite the hymn to the guru mentally:

"I meditate on the guru, whose nature is that of Absolute Reality, who is beyond good and evil, pleasure and pain, life and death, and all the pairs of opposites and who is the constant witness of the changing phenomena of the universe. I seek refuge in Him, who is the embodiment of knowledge and liberation, who is pure, stainless, and all-pervading like the ether and through His grace removes the darkness of my heart. May He awaken my consciousness and grant me freedom and bliss."

When you meditate on the guru, you are to think that it is the Lord who has taken the effulgent form of the guru and who, with a smiling face, is showering His blessings on you.

You have written that at the time of meditation you find it difficult to think of the lotus. While meditating on your Chosen Ideal if you are able to visualize the form, it does not matter whether you visualize the lotus or not. Again, if you cannot bring before your vision the luminous form of your guru, think of him as you have seen him with your eyes. All these devices have been prescribed in the scriptures only as aids to the concentration of the mind. The main thing is to turn your mind toward God. Sri Krishna says in the Gita:

> Give me your whole heart,
> Love and adore me,
> Worship me always,
> Bow to me only,
> And you shall find me:
> This is my promise
> Who love you dearly.

You seem to think that meditation is not possible unless one is aware of the true nature of God. That is not correct. If you have perfect knowledge of God, you are already illumined. To say that you will practice spiritual disciplines only after you have attained full conviction and knowledge of His Being is tantamount to saying: "I will enter the water only after I have learned to swim." In that case you will never learn. It is only through *japa* and meditation that one removes all obstacles, attains purity of heart and finally arrives at the full consciousness of God.

A Sanskrit verse says, "He who wishes to meditate on the Lord after all his problems are solved is like the fool who wishes to bathe in the sea after the waves have subsided." That moment will never come. The sea will always have waves. Similarly, favorable opportunities are hard to find in this world. Therefore do not wait for propitious moments. Every moment is propitious when you use it properly. If you call on Him with a yearning heart, He will surely respond. Create an intense dissatisfaction for the things of the world. Cultivate a longing for holy company and the desire to know God, by knowing whom all our wants are satisfied.

Sri Ramakrishna used to inspire his listeners with this song:

> Dive deep, O mind, dive deep
> in the ocean of God's beauty,
> Descend to the uttermost depths
> And you will find the gem of love.
> Light up, O mind, light up wisdom's shining lamp,
> And let it burn with steady flame
> Filling your heart with unceasing joy.

Freedom Through Desirelessness

To attain peace one has to practice control of the senses and the mind. Conflicting desires arise in the mind. Because of those desires the mind is constantly lashed into waves. As long as these waves form, the mind is restless. In order to control these waves which give rise to thoughts of a worldly and distracting nature, one must live a life of self-discipline. Of all disciplines chastity is the foremost. It is fundamental; all other disciplines will follow naturally if one practices this primary virtue. Those who lead an unregulated life and think impure thoughts lose their powers and strength of mind. They are at the mercy of passing desires and the feverish cravings of the senses and are slaves.

The mind has tremendous potentialities. It is the storehouse of infinite energy. Through control and inner check we can unfold these potentialities and gradually develop the power to work toward good. Each one of us is a repository of infinite power. If we can manifest our latent capacities, we will become almost all-powerful. Prophets and incarnations who have come and gone have shown us one thing, that we too can become heirs of knowledge and power like themselves—if we only have the will. If we struggle, walking the path taken by them, we too will reach that goal one day. If it were not so, the life of an avatar would have no meaning. The great teachers and incarnations of God verify the truth that "life is worth living." They set before us a goal and show us how to realize that goal. They point out methods of discipline suited to the age and to people of diverse moods and temperaments. Their one message is the call to spiritual awakening, for who knows when the Atman, the Self, will be awakened from Its slumber? Sri Ramakrishna used to say, "If the soul hungers for God, Self-knowledge may come in three years or in three months. If the desire is intense, it may come even in three days." Rightly does the Gita say:

> When can a man be said to have achieved union with Brahman? When his mind is under perfect control and freed from all desires, so that he becomes absorbed in the Atman and nothing else. "The light of the lamp does not flicker in a windless place:" that is the simile which describes a yogi of one-pointed mind, who meditates upon the Atman. When, through practice of yoga, the mind ceases its restless movements, and becomes still, he realizes the Atman. It satisfies him entirely. Then he knows the purified heart but is beyond the grasp of the senses. He stands firm in this realization. Because of it, he can never wander from the inmost truth of his being.

Is it possible to realize this truth living the life of a householder? Many people think that if one gets married and has a family, it is almost impossible for him to practice self-control. This is utterly wrong. What stands in the way of a householder controlling his senses? Sri Ramakrishna used to say: "Make your mind and speech one and you will attain everything. Do not limit it to restraining the senses: Many other excellent qualities will be reflected in your life."

Forgetting the true nature of the Atman, which is eternally free, man seeks worldly objects for the enjoyment of his senses. He considers pleasures derived from external things sweet and enchanting. How many people realize that every pleasure is invariably mixed with some measure of pain? Accepting the one, necessarily involves the other. Swami Vivekananda would often say, "Joy comes to man wearing a crown of sorrow on its head." Ordinarily man is so engrossed in the joyful side of the picture that he finds no time to think of the crown of sorrow. He forgets that if he accepts the one, he must take the other with it. Hence our scriptures warn us: "Beware O man! think not that the enjoyment of the senses is the goal of life, for suffering is its inseparable companion. Look upon both pleasure and pain as your teachers. Enlarge your vision and accept that as your goal which will free you from the bonds of Maya."

The aim of the scriptures is to teach people how to develop

the spirit of renunciation in married life. Through worldly experience, with its joys and sorrows, they will come to know the value of detachment, without which no happiness is born. Gradually they will understand that the pleasures of the world are short-lived and unreal and that the only reality is God. To know Him, to be united with Him by prayer and meditation, is the noblest aim and aspiration of life.

It is an undeniable fact, proven by experience, that the mind will not pursue an object of enjoyment for long if it is enjoyed with proper discrimination. Sri Ramakrishna repeatedly said that discrimination between the real and the unreal was imperative for a spiritual aspirant. A seeker of God should always discriminate in this manner: "Well, my mind, you hanker after this food and that dress and you are never satisfied. But don't you see that all kinds of food, whether they are quite ordinary or the finest delicacies, are the same? They are nothing but modifications of the five elements of matter. Similarly, the same components of blood and flesh, of bone and marrow, which are the products of those elements, form those who are beautiful as well as any others. Why should you then have preferences and liking for special objects? Will they ever help you to attain that which is the abode of supreme bliss?"

What should one do if in spite of these arguments the mind refuses to listen? In that case you should enjoy the object of desire once or twice, while discriminating between the real and the unreal. Small desires, such as sweets, can be renounced in this way after enjoying them with proper discrimination. But it is dangerous to apply this same method to major desires. The moment an aspirant begins to gratify them, he becomes so involved that he cannot extricate himself. Therefore these major desires have to be renounced and uprooted completely from the mind by realizing the danger and the defects inherent in them. If they are given free rein, they will stifle the power of discrimination.

Sri Ramakrishna used to say that all his spiritual attainments were for the sake of others. If people would do one-sixteenth of what he did, they would be blessed. That is why he assumed the responsibilities of married life and exemplified the noble ideal of the hearth. Had not Sri Ramakrishna married, some of his critics would probably have remarked that he talked so vehemently against lust and gold and preached the ideal of renunciation so eloquently because he himself had not married.

The marriage of Sri Ramakrishna has a deep meaning. He entered into it with the idea that people might learn from his example that marriage is a sacrament and has an ideal much higher than the gratification of the senses. This ideal was not exemplified in the lives of Rama, Krishna, Buddha, Jesus, Shankara, and the other *avatars*. It was demonstrated in the life of Ramakrishna to fulfill a great need. For the first time in the history of the world an absolutely pure married life was expressed through lifelong spiritual practices and austere disciplines. Sri Ramakrishna would say, "Let men cast their own lives in this mold and fashion an image of purity and perfect beauty."

Preparing the Ground

Instead of sitting idly, waiting for an illumined soul to become your guru, make an effort to do these three things which are necessary for spiritual life: contemplate God, study the scriptures, and associate with the holy. First prepare the ground by digging, removing the weeds, and watering the soil with earnest care. One of the secrets of life, which will be revealed to you if you study nature intelligently, is that as soon as the soil is ready the sower of the seeds inevitably comes. Wherever there is want, there is also fulfillment. Where there is demand, there is also supply. Whenever an aspirant longs intensely for God, he finds the way toward the fulfillment of his desire. Sri Ramakrishna often said: "The Mother will not allow any of her children to go hungry. He who is hungry in the morning will be fed in the morning. He whose appetite is aroused late in the evening will be fed in the evening." Every sincere wish of man will be fulfilled. This truth has been corroborated by saints and seers all over the world throughout the ages. We too have experienced it in our own lives to a greater or lesser degree.

An illumined teacher is a great spiritual power because he has entered into the heart of Reality. His perception is not clouded by the fog of ignorance. He has free access to supersensuous knowledge, which is a sealed book to the ordinary person. Sri Krishna says in the Gita:

> The recollected mind is awake
> In the knowledge of the Atman
> Which is dark night to the ignorant:
> The ignorant are awake to their sense-life
> which they think is daylight:
> To the seer it is darkness.

You have asked how an illumined soul knows the past and the future of his disciples. I should say that this is to be understood in a spiritual sense. A good teacher sees through the subtle body of his disciple and imparts his teaching according to the past and future impressions that are revealed to him in the depth of meditation. An enlightened soul does not use occult powers nor does he take recourse to astrology, for astrological calculations are in many cases unreliable.

When you feel depressed, you must drive away that feeling by saying, "I belong to the Lord, He is my very own. I am His child. He is holding me by the hand and will surely do what is good for me." These thoughts will bring strength to your nerves and faith in your heart. When you are not able to fix your mind on God, pray earnestly to him, "O, Lord, please make my mind steady since I am not able to do it myself. Helpless as I am, I seek refuge at your feet."

Know for certain that the Lord hears everything and knows everything. He listens to your least whisper. He is aware of every thought that arises in your mind. Whatever you ask of Him with a yearning heart will be granted. Do not be too inquisitive. It is not possible to understand the deeper truths of spiritual life with an impure mind attached to sense-objects. Trying to practice religion according to the directions of such a mind only leads to a maze which goes round and round without an escape. Therefore give up all attempts to understand spiritual truths with your limited intellect. Have absolute faith in the Lord; rely on Him and practice spiritual disciplines. Cry unto Him with a longing heart. He will reveal Himself to you when the time is ripe. Listen to a song which Swamiji used to sing before Sri Ramakrishna:

O Lord, must all my days be spent
So utterly in vain?
Down the path of hope
I gaze with longing, day and night.
My poor heart's humble cottage door
Is standing open wide;
Be gracious Lord, and enter there
But once and quench my thirst.

The Concept of Maya (the Dynamic Power of God)

The universe as perceived by us has no independent and absolute existence. It has an empirical reality only as long as it is perceived as real by the mind through the doors of the five senses. Suppose we had a sixth sense, the universe would seem different. World-appearance has no real existence of its own. It is neither unconditional nor unchangeable. Time, space, and causality are mere concepts of the mind, and through these categories of the mind we see this world-appearance.

The indivisible Brahman, by contrast, is beyond the ignorant mind; there is neither time, nor space, nor causality in the Absolute. He, the unchangeable Reality, is one without a second. How can He, therefore, be the cause of the universe? This universe is a superimposition upon Brahman. It is a creation of our own mind. Whatever, therefore, is seen or sensed or perceived through the instrumentality of our ignorant, unregenerate mind is said to be Maya. As long as the mind remains unregenerate, it is not possible to go beyond Maya. That this world-appearance is illusory is not realized until one goes beyond Maya by attaining Brahman. But again, the finite, impure mind cannot reach the pure, infinite Brahman. By the purified mind alone He becomes known, and the knower of Brahman becomes Brahman. When one is thus established in the knowledge of his true being, Maya bids him goodbye. Then he does not make the mistake of seeing the snake in the rope. The world-appearance vanishes for him. Only Brahman remains, shining in self-effulgent glory.

The Balance of the Yogas

A full life cannot be one-sided; it needs proper balance. If you want to achieve perfection, you must harmonize the three paths of knowledge, action, and devotion. They are not antagonistic but complementary. The truth of this statement can be verified in the lives of the great spiritual teachers of the past. According to the place, time, and circumstances of their age, some may have shown a preponderance of knowledge; some may have revealed intensity of love, and some may have exhibited wonderful enthusiasm and a great passion for work. Seen superficially, these paths seem to be mutually exclusive. But if we probe deeply into their lives and study their conduct carefully, we will find a perfect blending of these three approaches to Reality. Behind the shining wisdom of such souls lay unity. Their spirituality was built on the rock of harmony. The goal of all these three paths is the same. Each path is equally powerful. But none should be undertaken to the exclusion of the others: Knowledge must unite with devotion. And this unity must be expressed through action. Knowledge without love is dry. Love without service is pure sentimentalism.

The Ideal and Application of Modern Vedanta

The present Vedanta movement is characterized by two currents—the harmony of all religions and all religious moods and the service of man as God. In the past, the highest ideal was to remain absorbed in samadhi. But the present ideal is to forego that bliss, forcibly to drag down the mind from the transcendental plane of consciousness, and to plunge into activities for the good of the many. In order to do this one has to merge one's will into the Divine Will. Being established in the plane of consciousness that is beyond the realm of duality and nonduality and at the same time living a life of self-dedication and service is considered the highest ideal of our age.

How is this ideal to be translated into practice? Through purification. There are different states of consciousness. From the study of psychology we know that every thought and feeling affects the body. As we develop our consciousness, simultaneously we will feel different physical reactions. Both body and mind are being purified. When intellect, egoism—all the aspects of the mind—have passed through the process of cleansing, there arises unbroken recollectedness of God. The more one purifies these internal organs, the more one is able to detect and interpret correctly the will of the Universal Mind. This knowledge has a transforming effect on the life and character of the individual. His unripe ego dies forever. Like a machine moved by the operator, he is a tool in the hand of God. He becomes incapable of doing anything wrong. He does not take a false step nor do his feet slip from the path.

As long as there is a tinge of lust, as long as there is awareness of the distinction between man and woman, it is not right to say, "I am working under divine inspiration. I do everything He makes me do." Religious life has not begun until one has completely effaced the idea of sex and of all carnal desires. To carry this ideal into practice is difficult no doubt, but it is not impossible. Saints and divine incarnations have demonstrated the truth of this principle in their own lives. They are our exemplars.

Religion is not in temples or in churches. It is not in holy places or in scriptures. Religion is a matter of realization. Therefore, one must not search for it in external things. The kernel of religion lies in practice. Religion has to be practiced every day, in every act and in every phase of life. It is to be firmly established in our character so that the divinity within may be manifested in all its beauty and grandeur.

Meditate regularly. Sri Ramakrishna used to say, "Don't forget to call on God. Meditate every day twice—in the morning as well as in the evening. This will quicken your spiritual progress and lead you to the goal."

Paths of Affirmation and Negation

You have quoted a passage from the scriptures. It is true, without renunciation immortality cannot be attained. But the sages have prescribed two paths for arriving at the goal of renunciation. Those who have known the transiency of the world and are free from all physical cravings give up everything and embrace the life of monasticism. This is the path of negation. In this path the spiritual aspirant is aware of his goal from the very beginning and consequently renounces the popular view of the world and life that makes one forget the reality. But there is the other path that is equally true and equally helpful in leading aspirants to the highest goal. This is known as the path of affirmation. Those who follow this path do not have to renounce everything from the very start. The mind is attached to various objects of the senses. It refuses to come under control. What will mere restraint do? These spiritual aspirants may enjoy a few things of the world, slowly learn to become detached, and gradually rise up to the height of complete renunciation. This is the religion of the householders.

Those who are attracted to objects of the senses have to learn detachment through experience and for them the scriptures have advocated the second course of living in the world but not being of the world. In every religion you will find mention of these two paths. According to their nature and tendencies, people choose the one or the other. For example, in Christianity you will read of St. Paul who said, "I say therefore to the unmarried and widows, it is good for them if they abide, even as I. But if they cannot contain, let them marry; for it is better to marry than to burn." But whichever path you follow, guided by your innate tendencies, ultimately you have to renounce everything for God. Let this truth be firmly rooted in your mind and press you onward toward the realization of the goal. The Upanishads rightly say: "Hear, all ye children of immortal bliss, also ye gods who dwell in the high heavens. Follow only in the footsteps of the illumined ones, and by continuous meditation merge both mind and intellect in the eternal Brahman. The glorious Lord will be revealed to you."

Control of Lust

Why do you magnify a small matter into a big thing? You are wasting your time thinking about the origin and effect of lustful thoughts in your mind. Instead of doing that, try to cultivate a positive attitude and think day and night how far you have been able to love God and how much devotion you have toward Him. You should analyze your mind and see whether you have been able to cover every bit of work with the spirit of God and judge whether the duties you are performing are for His sake or for the propitiation of your spurious self. It should be your stern endeavor to see the manifestation of God in everyone especially in your wife and children. You have written that there have been lapses ten times before in the past. If there be ten times more in the future, you should not be dejected. Constantly brooding about things over which you now have no control will cause more harm than good. This will surely jeopardize your spiritual life. Dirt cannot be washed by dirt. Even charcoal looses its blackness when it comes in contact with fire. Similarly, lust cannot remain when the image of God pervades the mind.

You should drive away all depressive thoughts, telling yourself that it is the nature of the mind to have passions and they arise due to past habit. Fix your mind on God and they will leave you alone. As it is natural for the body to crave food and rest, so it is natural for the mind to crave the objects of the senses. Sri Ramakrishna used to say the sin of the mind is no sin. Free your mind of all anxieties on that score. Bestow no thought on what is past. If negative thoughts arise, pay no attention; consider them as insignificant things, beneath your notice.

But you must remember that if one stays in a room full of soot, it is inevitable that a few dark spots will rub off on his garment. Why should you worry on that account? Follow the example of St. Durgacharan Nag, who used to say, "There is the guru to take care of me. Like the holy river Ganges, the guru will wash away all my sins and make me pure."

One thing you must bear in mind is that nobody has been able to conquer lust by his own effort. You can overcome lust only if the grace of God descends on you. Pray sincerely to Him for guidance. By touching the feet of Holy Mother you have certainly attained a different position and a higher state than most, but you have not yet realized that the things of the world are paltry and not worth striving for. In time you will understand the vanity of all earthly things and long for God in a more intense way. No sooner does the spirit of longing enter your heart than you will be blessed with the vision of His continuous presence and be totally absorbed in Him. If you ask why the Lord does not remove all desires from your mind, the answer is that He knows, but none else. Probably He knows that you will be free from the bondages of the world after some years so there is no necessity to forcibly drive them away. So you must review in your mind whether you have been able to pray to Him with all sincerity every day. You are to watch whether your love for God is increasing day by day. This must be your aspiration and aim. The only means by which we can overcome lust is through constant repetition of His name and not through privations and austerities. Has not the Gita said: "The abstinent run away from what they desire but carry their desires with them. When a man enters Reality, he leaves his desires behind him."

PRANAYAMA

Try to cultivate pure and whole-hearted love for God. That should be the aim of your life. Without love, spiritual exercise in the form of posture and rhythmical breathing are of no avail. If you think that posture and purification of the nerves will be helpful in fostering the spirit of devotion in your mind, you may do them. If you want to know the exercises that are to be performed for the purification of the nerves, here is the procedure: First close your right nostril and inhale slowly through the left. Then close the left nostril and exhale slowly through the right. Immediately after exhalation, start inhaling through the right nostril, close it and then exhale through the left. In this manner you may do five or six breathing exercises as an aid to concentration. You need not worry about awakening the spiritual power called the *kundalini*. If you can chant the name of the Lord with a steadfast mind and meditate on His blissful form, you need not bother about anything else. In time meditation will automatically lead you to the blessed experience known in the scriptures as awakening of the *kundalini*. The only method by which this can be done is by developing intense love of God and not by breathing exercises. The great teacher Shankara rightly said: "Certain knowledge of the Reality is gained through meditation upon right teaching and not by sacred oblations or almsgiving or by the practice of hundreds of breathing exercises."

Our Master, Sri Ramakrishna, has warned against depending upon such external means as *pranayama* and other hatha yoga exercises. He has told us repeatedly not to pay much attention to them. When over-zealously done, they may upset the brain or lead to some dangerous results. He has advised us especially to meditate. He was insistent on it. All his emphasis was laid on prayer and meditation. But since you are anxious to do a few breathing exercises, you may do them as a preliminary step to meditation. At present you are to do the exercises for the purification of the nerves for a couple of months and then, when you write me next, I shall teach you a simple *pranayama*. But always bear in mind that your main objective is not the control of breath, but the control of mind through meditation and to be absorbed from day to day in the awareness of God.

Rules About Food

You have asked me whether vegetarianism is absolutely necessary for leading a spiritual life. My answer is that no hard and fast rule can be made with regard to food. Can we live without doing harm to some form of life? Do you think plants and vegetables have no life? Our scriptures say they have; science has proven it. If you can preserve the strength and vigor of your body and mind while living on vegetarian food, you are at liberty to do so. But if, while foregoing fish and meat, your health deteriorates, you must give up such ideas and take a more moderate stand. As a general rule, when the body becomes weak, the mind is weakened also. A weak mind is unfit for meditation. When a man with such a mind tries to meditate, his mind runs away. It is only a strong person with sufficient will power who can concentrate and fix his mind on God. Therefore, you must not do anything that will impair your spiritual life.

Whatever you eat, make it an offering to the Lord. You are to think that God resides in the body in the form of fire and that the food you eat is given as an oblation to the fire. At His command you are performing an internal sacrifice ceremony. By these thoughts the physical act of eating will be consecrated into a ritual and your scruples about injury to animals will be avoided. But to keep this attitude in the mind is not an easy matter. It needs regular practice and right-mindedness.

It is for this reason that monks in India make a firm resolve not to take meals without reciting the following verse from the Gita:

> Brahman is the ritual,
> Brahman is the offering,
> Brahman is he who offers
> To the fire that is Brahman.
> If a man sees Brahman
> In every action,
> He will find Brahman.

SELF-EFFORT AND SELF-SURRENDER

There is no contradiction in the teachings of Sri Ramakrishna. He did not make one rule for all. He used to see the inner tendency of the person and then advise him accordingly. His instructions were addressed to different people in a different manner because of their temperament and their ability to apply his principles to life. To those who were young, energetic, intense with a fiery enthusiasm and in whom he saw the potential for becoming a monk, his inspiring words were: "Now overlook all desires for name and fame and plunge headlong into spiritual disciplines; never rest content until the realization of God has become an accomplished fact." He would brighten smoldering fire in their hearts saying: "Is it possible to realize God without renunciation? Renunciation of lust and greed is the most essential prerequisite for entering into spiritual life. What is there in the world except anguish, misery, and trouble? Tell me, who is happy in the world? If you seek the world and long for sense objects, the world will drag you down. But if you seek God and renounce everything for Him, God will lift you up and your consciousness will be filled with unending bliss."

To those who were encumbered with life's heavy responsibilities, who were enmeshed in the net of *samsara* and had become old, his advice was: "I have cooked the food and placed it on the plate. Your task is simply to sit and eat. You will not have to do anything. You are merely to lift it up to your mouth and enjoy. I have taken the responsibility. You will not have to do any spiritual disciplines. I have already done it for you. It will be enough if you give me the power of attorney and be at ease." He knew that conditions were not favorable for them to do spiritual practice, and if asked, it would not be in their power to follow his instructions. And so he would advise them to rely on him and take refuge in the Lord. But the difficulty in observing complete self-surrender and giving your power of attorney to the Lord is shown in the story of G.C. Ghosh and Sri Ramakrishna. In later years, when questioned, G.C. Ghosh would say, "Did I then ever dream that self-surrender meant so much? Now I find ordinary spiritual discipline has an end, at a certain point in time, but this business of self-surrender has no end. One has to be watchful and be always on guard. One must scrutinize at every moment, whether even the minutest thought and action arise and are accomplished at the prompting of the Lord or of one's own ego."

You have asked me what you should do under your present circumstances. My advice is: Perform spiritual disciplines. Do *japa* and meditate to the best of your ability. You are young. You have many years ahead of you. If you struggle, you will be able to achieve. This is the time for you to be up and doing. So waste no moment. Let not this golden opportunity pass by. If you neglect it now, much will be your repentance in later years. Remember what the Lord says in the Gita:

> What is man's will
> And how shall he use it?
> Let him put forth its power
> To uncover the Atman
> Not hide the Atman:
> Man's will is the only
> Friend of the Atman:
> His will also
> The Atman's enemy

Action and Contemplation

Always try to be busy and keep yourself engaged in good works and in good thoughts. When the mind is idle, all kinds of negative thoughts arise and create trouble. There is an old saying that an idle brain is the devil's workshop. It is too true. The mind abhors a vacuum. It needs to be filled. However, it is necessary to devote some time to silence and contemplation. Repeat His name and meditate in the early hours of the morning, when nature is calm and the stillness can be imperceptibly felt. Do the same thing in the evening at the auspicious moment when the day disappears and the night comes to call all aspiring souls to turn within for prayer and contemplation. The rest of the time you must spend in some kind of activity. The work that you do is to be performed with a right attitude. You must feel that the duties that you are discharging have been entrusted to you by the Lord. You are doing them only to satisfy Him and not to satisfy your selfish will. No work is menial. Even scrubbing the floor may be turned into worship if there is the remembrance of the Lord within. He looks into our hearts and judges our actions accordingly. Done sacramentally, every work is an offering to the Lord, He accepts it as He accepts a flower placed at the altar with devotion. There is nothing so powerful to purify the mind as work done unselfishly with a spirit of dedication and service. That is the only way by which you can rid yourself of bad thoughts. Don't you remember the words of Sri Ramakrishna? "The more you go toward the East, the more will the West be left behind."

I am grieved to learn that you want to retire from your work and go to a quiet place. It seems work has become a hindrance to your spiritual life and is causing you trouble. During meditation instead of thinking of the Lord, you think of persons you have met or plan different things that you will have to do in the course of the day. You want a drastic remedy. But remember, you may leave work and go into a forest and still your mind will trouble you. Even there thoughts of the world will haunt you and will not permit any peace. It is the very nature of the mind to call up impressions that are buried within and to think of pleasant thoughts pertaining to sense objects. To control the mind, to focus your attention to a point on God is an uphill task. It cannot be done in a day. It needs vigilant care and persistent effort. Until you have fully grasped the truth of the statement, "The world is unsubstantial and illusory as a dream," the restlessness of the mind is bound to recur. The mind is unsteady because it clings to objects of desire. Desire is like a fire which always craves new sensations. If you ignore its demand, it will burn itself out and be extinguished. Therefore, carry on your meditations without paying any notice to the intrusion of distracting thoughts. Try to impress on your mind that you have no one in the world except the Lord as your companion and refuge. Try to deepen this consciousness by struggle and patient endeavor and you will find unbecoming thoughts will gradually disappear.

If there is a strong attachment for God and a burning desire to realize Him, all other attractions will drop off. In the life of everyone there comes a time when he feels completely satisfied after prolonged enjoyment of sense objects. At that time, if one comes into contact with a holy man, he feels blessed and prompted to lead a life of spirituality. One becomes dispassionate toward the world by seeing the emptiness of chasing mundane pleasures and clinging to transitory things. Until a man is ready and sees through the appearance of the world, no spiritual instruction will be of any avail. First the ground is to be prepared, then alone will the seeds take root and grow into beautiful plants.

Make Him the ruler of your heart and be completely His. Offer up your body, mind, and soul at His lotus feet. Be convinced that the sole objective of life is to have the direct vision of God. Let not your mind be moved from the ideal by name or fame or any of the other glittering toys of life. Do not repent the past. Past mistakes have taught you some lessons. Never mind the failures. Be up and doing and strive on toward the goal. By constantly thinking of sin one aggravates sinful tendencies all the more. Sri Ramakrishna was averse to all negative ideas. He would say, "If a man boldly says there is no poison, even the poison of a snake bite disappears." Repeat unto yourself the idea that you are a child of God and have become pure since the moment you first uttered the name of God. Know for certain that none is completely free from the fetters of lust and greed until he has seen God. Rightly does the Gita say:

> Water flows continually into the ocean
> But the ocean is never disturbed.
> Desire flows into the mind of the seer
> But he is never disturbed.
> The seer knows peace:
> The man who stirs up his own lusts
> Can never know peace.
> He knows peace who has forgotten desire.
> He lives without craving:
> Free from ego, free from pride.

Patience in Suffering

I am sorry to learn that you are suffering from a lot of troubles. Everything happens by the will of the Lord. Happiness and unhappiness, both come to us through divine will for our education. One thing we have to learn is that we are to cling to Him for support and remain unperturbed in the midst of all circumstances. If we view life from another angle, we will notice that it is unhappiness that teaches us more than happiness; it is misery that cleanses our hearts more than enjoyment. In the days of adversity the mind is naturally inclined toward God more than in the days of prosperity. You must have read in the Mahabharata that Kunti, the mother of the Pandavas, said to Krishna, "Oh Lord, let there be misery, trouble, and misfortune for me always, for I can remember you with constancy of heart when I am in trouble. Weak as I am, I am prone to forget you when I am basking in the sunshine of comfort and pleasure." Sri Ramakrishna used to sing a song describing the anguish of the heart of a devotee when he forgets God. This is one of the beautiful songs of Ramprasad which Sri Ramakrishna liked very much:

> Mother, this is the grief that sorely grieves my heart,
> That even with Thee for Mother, and though I am wide awake
> There should be robbery in my house.
> Many and many a time I vow to call on Thee
> Yet when the time for prayer comes round,
> I have forgotten....

> Glory and shame, bitter and sweet, are Thine alone;
> This world is nothing but Thy play.
> Then why, O Blissful One, dost Thou cause a
> rift in it?

Whenever you feel miserable and spiritual life seems dry, you must drive these feelings away by thinking that you are His servant, His child, part of Himself and that your Chosen Ideal is always there holding you by His hand. You are safe in His care, and nothing but good will come to you in the end. Remembering this, you must pick up strength and banish from your heart all depressing thoughts. Despondency is the greatest obstacle in spiritual life. It saps energy and destroys your ability to struggle. Repeat your mantra several thousand times a day. That will give you strength. If evil thoughts appear, be indifferent to them. They come due to the impressions of previous lives and it is good that they rise to the conscious plane; it will be easier for you to control them. If your mind is unsteady and you cannot fix it on the Lord, pray to Him with a yearning heart, "O Lord, I have no one in the world. Thou alone art my own. Please make my mind steady for I cannot do it myself. Helpless as I am, I take shelter at Thy feet."

Remember, the Lord listens to every word that you utter, every thought that you think. Whatever you ask of Him with sincerity will be fulfilled. If you can surrender yourself to Him, you will be at peace. Let Him do what He thinks best. True resignation comes only after hard struggle. Only when the wings are tired, does a bird sit on the mast of a ship to rest. Have faith in Him who never forgets His devotees, even though they forget Him. Listen to what Sri Krishna says in the Gita: "The Lord lives in the heart of every creature. He turns them round and round upon the wheel of His Maya. Take refuge utterly in Him. By His grace you will find supreme peace, the state which is beyond all change."

Work As A Means to Perfection

You have quoted two verses from the Bhagavad-Gita in order to substantiate your point, but there is no logical connection between them. Sri Krishna is speaking of two different things and their contexts are not the same. The text of the nineteenth verse of the third chapter states:

> Do your duty, always, but without attachment.
> That is how a man reaches the ultimate truth;
>   by working without anxiety about results.

Here Sri Krishna speaks of his special message—the message of karma yoga. If a worker performs his duties properly and his life embodies the spirit of detachment throughout, he will ultimately attain the highest goal. In other words, he will see God in everything and attain pure knowledge, which will burn all the seeds of karma. He will not be born again, and his soul will merge itself into Brahman at the dissolution of his body.

Now let us examine the nineteenth verse of the eighth chapter of the Gita, the meaning of which you seem to have totally misunderstood:

> Thus they are seen, O Prince, and appear unceasingly,
>   Dissolving with the dark, and with the day returning
>   Back to the new birth, new death;
>   All helpless, they do what they must.

Here the Lord is speaking of the worker who dies in the period of smoke, night, the dark half of the month, and the six months of southward course of the sun. He will go to the "lunar light," [chandraloka] and after staying for some time, he will come back into the world to be reborn. From this we can understand that the worker who has not been able to work unselfishly and consequently could not attain illumination through karma yoga will die in the period mentioned above and will return for rebirth. There are two paths for the journey of the soul after death, which are known in the scriptures as "the path of the bright ones" and "the path of the fathers." By the former, the yogi goes to *Brahmaloka*, remains absorbed in contemplation of Brahman, and attains final liberation at the end of the cycle.

An embodied being does not have the right to choose at the last moment which path he is to take. This is decided by the Lord, who has the sole prerogative in this regard. But the Lord is not whimsical. He decides through the law of karma. The cumulative effect of the karmas of the individual's entire life will be the guiding factor in forming the Lord's decision to shape the destiny of the soul for its sojourn through the path of light or the path of darkness. But the *karmayogi* who has worked with the attitude of seeing "inaction in action" will attain knowledge that will cut all his bonds and make him free. By the grace of the Lord he will know that his soul will not go to any place but will enter into the realm of bliss when the flame of life is extinguished.

What is this knowledge? It is the experience of unity, the one ultimate Reality that alone exists. Perception of multiplicity is ignorance. Because we have alienated ourselves from Him, we are suffering. All troubles will cease when we go back to the center and rest in Him. Are you really separate from Him? You feel yourself separate because you think so; else you are always connected with Him in all the three states of consciousness. But mere talking about it will not do. You must realize it. Swamiji used to say: "We know so much that it would have been better had we known a little less." You are to work hard. If you are hungry and someone else eats for you, your hunger will not be satisfied. How hard we worked when we lived in the Baranagore Monastery soon after the passing away of Sri Ramakrishna. Many days went by when we had only one meal a day and that consisted of rice and salt. There were days when we could not even procure salt, not to speak of vegetables. But we had one single idea: We must realize God. We practiced severe austerities in those days. The impressions left by those austerities are so deep that, at will, we can become absorbed in meditation and forget the world, by His grace. You too can do that if you struggle with unremitting zeal and continue it for some years. Now, my advice is: Depend upon God and stand on your own feet. Remember the words of the Upanishads and dive deep into spiritual practice, never be contented until the goal is reached.

"By the pure in heart He is known. The Self in man, within the lotus of the heart, is the master of his life and his body. With mind illumined by the power of meditation, the wise know Him, the blissful, the immortal. The knot of the heart, which is ignorance, is loosed, all doubts are dissolved, all effects of deeds are destroyed, when He, who is both personal and impersonal is realized."

Spiritual Consolation

I am glad to know that you are keeping well. But I do not like the tone of despair in your letter. Please tell me why you are so depressed, my child. You have seen Holy Mother. You have received her blessings. Why should you feel motherless? Why should your heart be dry? Why should you be melancholy? Her grace, her compassion must have removed all your wants and filled your heart with the fragrance of her love. The Mother has shown you the way to liberation. Follow the path she has chosen. There will not remain the slightest void in your heart. True, Mother is gone. We will not be able to see her again with these eyes. That is the nature of all physical forms. The human body is bound to decay. Today or tomorrow, it will surely die. But have no fear, my child. Our master and Holy Mother have given you refuge. Their spirit is undying, their presence everlasting. Believe in the reality of their presence and give up the faintest sigh of doubt and despair. Surrender yourself completely to their care and you will see in time all difficult problems will be solved, the hardness of the road will be smoothed. My child, why do you bemoan your lot? You have Mother's love. You have the affection of Maharaj. They have showered their kindness on you in abundance. Still you complain. What had we when Sri Ramakrishna, the only support of our life, left us? Holy Mother was young then. We, a handful of boys, were launched into a world of many critics and few sympathizers. From that day on, what was our support? What did we hold to as our prop in life? Who has guided us all these years? None but He to whom we belong. It is He who has led us, guided us, and held us by the hand, through thick and thin, like the mother bird holding her fledgling under the wings of her protection and love. He alone is the protector of His children in their sorrows and grief. He alone is their savior in their trials and troubles. He alone is their comforter in their dark days of loneliness and scorn. Leave all your worries behind and take refuge in our compassionate Lord. Know for certain that He will not leave you. He will never fail you when you cry His name with a longing heart.

Inscrutable are His ways. We do not know how he works. He

does everything. We are mere tools in His hands.

Let me tell you a story which I heard from a lady* in America, whose guest I was for sometime. She said to me that one night she saw in a dream a luminous figure, full of love and compassion. He was looking at her steadfastly and was about to say something. Then her dream was interrupted. She was at that time passing through a terrible crisis. The vision filled her with inexpressible joy and removed all her agony. She thought to herself, "Who is this man? The figure must be a Hindu. He must be a holy man, a saint, far above the type of man we come across in everyday life. His gentle eyes radiated purity and love. They have given comfort to my weary heart."

That vision created a deep impression in her mind and changed her inner life tremendously. Whenever she heard that a Hindu had come to New York, she would leave her home in New Jersey and visit him, expecting to find the person she had seen in her dream. She came to that great city several times with this desire, but she had to go back disappointed. When I came to New York, she heard my lecture and was impressed. She invited me to her home and requested me to conduct a class on Vedanta philosophy so that she might introduce me to her friends. I agreed. I gave several talks on Vedanta. One day I spoke at length on Sri Ramakrishna. After hearing my lecture, my hostess became interested and wanted to know more about Ramakrishna. She asked me whether any picture of Sri Ramakrishna was available. Seeing her interest, I showed her my album containing the picture of the Master. She exclaimed with a choking voice, "This is the man I have been searching for all these years. It is he who came to me in my dream and blessed me with his gracious presence. His eyes showered benediction on me and removed the agony of my soul. I shall eternally be grateful to him."

Hence my advice to you is to cast off all depression and live contentedly in whatever condition the Master places you. Surrender your body, mind, and soul to him and you will find infinite joy and a source of perennial inspiration.

The letters of Swami Saradananda that are collected here were written over a thirty-year period. Almost invariably the words Sri Sri Rama-

---

*Mrs. Wheeler of Montclair, New Jersey. See page 23.

krishnah Saranam *headed his letters, and usually he signed them Sri Saradananda. For the sake of space both the heading and the signature have been omitted here except in those cases when he used his personal name, Sarat. Most of them were written in Bengali.*

The Letters of Swami Saradananda

REPORT OF SWAMI SARADANANDA TO THE EDITOR OF BRAHMAVADIN, MADRAS, INDIA WRITTEN IN A LETTER ON JUNE 6, 1896 FROM LONDON, ENGLAND

Swami Vivekananda has made a good beginning here. A large number of people attend his classes regularly and the lectures are most interesting. Canon Howeis, one of the leaders of the Anglican Church, came the other day and was much interested. He saw the swami before, at the Chicago Fair, and loved him from that time. On Tuesday last the swami lectured on education at the Sesame Club. It is an important club got up by the ladies for diffusing female education. In this he dealt with the old educational systems of India, pointing out clearly and impressively that the sole aim of the system was man-making, and not cramming, and comparing it with the present system. He held that the mind of man is a reservoir of knowledge and that all knowledge present, past, or future is within man, manifested or non-manifested, and the object of every system of education should be to help the mind to manifest it. For instance, the law of gravitation was within man, and the fall of the apple helped Newton to think about it and bring it out from within his mind.

LETTER WRITTEN TO DR. LOGAN, PRESIDENT OF THE VEDANTA SOCIETY OF SAN FRANCISCO, CALIFORNIA ON JULY 24, 1902 AFTER THE PASSING AWAY OF SWAMI VIVEKANANDA AT BELUR MATH, INDIA

... We sent a cable to the New York Vedanta Society with directions to communicate to you and to all[the] friends in the United

States about the nirvana of our beloved Swami Vivekananda. He entered into the life eternal on July 4, Friday evening at ten minutes past nine.

It came upon us so suddenly that even the swamis in the other rooms of the Math had not the slightest intimation of it.

The swami was meditating in his own room at seven p.m., leaving word that no one was to come to him until called for. An hour after he called one of us and requested him to fan him on the head. He lay down on his bed quietly and the one tending him thought he was either sleeping or meditating. An hour after, his hands trembled a little and he breathed once very deeply. Then all was quiet for a minute or two. Again he breathed in the same manner, his eyes getting fixed in the centre of his eyebrows and his face assuming a divine expression and all was over.

All through the day he felt as free and easy as possible, nay, freer than he had felt for the last six months. He meditated in the morning for three hours together, took his meals with a perfect appetite, gave talks on Sanskrit grammar, philosophy, and on the Vedas to the swamis at the Math for more than two hours and discoursed on the yoga philosophy. He walked in the afternoon for about two miles and, on returning, enquired after everyone very tenderly. While resting for a time, he conversed on the rise and fall of nations with his companions and then went into his own room to meditate—you know the rest....

Sri Sri Ramakrishnah Saranam

Udbodhan Office
Baghbazar, Calcutta
October 5, 1920

Sriman A.,

Sri Sri Maharajji (Swami Brahmananda) is at the Bhubaneswar Math. Sometime ago there was talk of his coming here, but he did not come. The climate of Bhubaneswar is almost always good in winter. For this reason, I think he will be there for quite a while. So, if you come to Calcutta during the *puja* holidays, you will not be able to meet him. Inquire now and then and try to come here when Sri Sri Maharajji comes.

Instead of confining yourself to waiting for a true guru, try as far as possible to think of the Lord, keep company with *sadhus*, and read good books. If the field is ready, a good crop grows when the seed is sown. And it is a secret of nature that, when the field is ready, the seed comes of itself. When a want is felt, it is fulfilled. If there is real feeling of want, there will come the means of getting the needed object—this truth was corroborated by the *sadhus* and the *sastras* (verses from the scriptures); we have also realized its validity, more or less, in our own lives.

A true guru has supersensuous powers. He visualizes the inner body of the disciple and instructs him in accordance with his past and future impressions. This is what seeing the past and the future means. Telling the past and the future by divination with numbers or by the use of astrology is not infallible in most cases.

He will arrange everything in time if you try to call on Him with a sincere mind. Accept my blessings.

Wishing you well,
Sri Saradananda

Calcutta
April 9, 1921

Sriman A.,

Received your letters. This much I can tell you—Sri Ramakrishna has come as the spiritual teacher of the world and whoever will have faith in him and take his name need not worry about salvation. His name itself is the grand mantra; take it daily as many times as possible. If you would like to take initiation of any other type and you feel that the name itself is not enough, instead of writing me again, write to Sri Maharaj at Sri Ramakrishna Math, Bhubaneswar, Puri, and do as he instructs.

Wishing you well,

Calcutta
November 27, 1921

Received your letter. By consulting the readings of the horoscope, people always lose faith in their own capacity and become weak-minded. Readings of the horoscope are made from the movements of the planets and stars, but from those movements nobody can say how far a man's capacity will be manifested. For that reason, self-effort can change the readings of the horoscope this way or that.

Practice and detachment are necessary to bring one-pointedness to the naturally restless and out-going mind. It seems to me that you could not have been calling on Thakur regularly every day as I asked you to. Sit by yourself, take the name of God, morning and evening, and think about the transitoriness of all things of the world. Then alone the mind will gradually become one-pointed. Of course complete one-pointedness takes many years of practice. Accept my blessings.
Sri Saradananda

Calcutta
February 4, 1923

Received your letter. Accept my blessings.

Japa is to be counted on the fingers of the left hand.

In answer to your second question: Only when the intrinsic, real form of Holy Mother is seen can the *jiva* (individual soul) attain knowledge, devotion, and liberation. You have not yet seen or realized her real form. You have seen her only as your guru. By practicing the instruction she gave you during initiation, you will know her *swarupa* (true form) and your desire will be fulfilled.

In answer to your third question: In Jayrambati there will be the consecration ceremony of the temple; it (the initiation) will take place then.

I am anxious to receive news of K.'s illness from B. of your Math. Tell B. that, when I receive his letter, I will write to K. what is necessary. Convey my blessings to B.

Wishing you well,

Bhubaneswar Math
November 28, 1924

Happy to receive your letter. I have written with my hand below the answer, as far as I know it, to each question. Accept my blessings always and convey them to all in both the Ashramas. I heard that C.'s health has become very bad. Please let me know how he is doing. I have not been well since coming here. Possibly it will be all right after I have been here for some time. All are well here.

Wishing you well,

(the questioner:) ... I want to know many things about samadhi, but that desire cannot be fulfilled here as there is nobody I know of who has experienced samadhi. The amount of personal experience that you have had and the detailed description that is given in *Sri Sri Ramakrishna Lilaprasanga* is not given in greater detail in any other book. I want to learn about the following things. I hope you will remove my ignorance by instructing me.

1. In which place or *chakra* does the *kundalini* rise up when the forms of God are seen in meditation?

Answer: Possibly in the *anahata chakra*.

2. During the awakening of the *kundalini* do the lotuses in the *chakras* bloom for only the yogis and not for the devotees?

Answer: For the devotees also.

3. Does the *kundalini* rise up as light, and as it rises to each *chakra*, does the lotus described in that *chakra* blossom?

Answer: Yes, that is what the scriptures say.

4. Cannot the man stand during samadhi, or does he lie down?

Answer: Samadhi can take place under all conditions, while walking, sitting, or lying down.

5. When can one have the vision of the Master?

Answer: It is achieved by intense yearning, devotion, and one-pointedness of the mind.

6. The body becomes exhausted after *japa* and meditation. Is it good to sleep at that time? I have heard that sleeping at that time is injurious to the chest.

Answer: I cannot say whether sleeping at that time is injurious to the chest. Possibly not.

7. In raja yoga one learns that by practicing *pranayama* a kind of vibration is generated. I think such vibrations come while making *japa* with meditation also.

Answer: Some experience that.

8. Why do a slight fever and other obstacles come while making *japa* and meditating?

Answer: *Prarabda karma* seems to be the reason.

Calcutta
May 4, 1925

Received your letter of May 2. That is natural for youth, more so if bad company is added to it. In that case it becomes impossible to put up a barrier of self-control. Once the bad habits become strong, it takes much pain and many years to get rid of them. So from now onwards, practice daily, keep holy company, have good thoughts, pray with great yearning to Sri Sri Thakur, and read good books. If you follow these instructions with a whole heart for a year or two, you will be able to see the result. Those who fail to benefit by then should marry and lead a good life.

Accept my blessings.

Calcutta
May 21, 1925

Happy to receive your letter dated May 16. I am glad to know that you like Swargashram. Devote yourself to spiritual practices with a whole heart. That will make me happy. Why for some time? You should practice throughout your whole life. I pray to the feet of the Master that you may have devotion and faith. Make *japa* and meditate as much as you can bear, but don't go beyond your capacity. Needless to say, you should keep an eye on your health so that you keep fit. There is no rule that so many hours of study and so many hours of *japa* and meditation should be done, but try to increase your *japa* and meditation by degrees. Try to remember to think of the Lord always. Of course you are to take your bath, food, rest, and exercise. There is no need to observe silence; it is enough not to talk idly. It is not necessary to do *puruscharana* from sunrise to sunset or throughout the whole of one *tithi* (lunar day). Do the daily *puruscharana* as I told you.

Don't get disheartened if you do not have the results of your spiritual practices in the beginning. You will surely see the results in due time if you practice with patience and perseverance. Afterwards, when you progress more, you will understand everything yourself.

What more is there to write? We are all well. Accept my blessings and convey them to B. and to all the others.

Wishing you well,

Sasi Niketan, Puri
June 26, 1925

Happy to receive your letter dated June 22. The mind will become calm if you call on Sri Sri Thakur daily. Never forget to do that. Of course during examinations, you should study as much as possible so you will pass. I bless you and pray that you should do well in the examination. Write to me again after the examination. Most probably I shall be here at that time as I was ill for about a month previously and I feel mostly well since coming here. I shall tell you what you should do when you write me after your examination. Do not be eager to serve the people now. Sri Sri Thakur selects those who can give the whole of their minds to his lotus feet to serve the people. Otherwise, despite the best intentions, the work will not get done properly. Therefore keep your attention on him first of all. Accept my blessings always. Belong completely to God and put your personal interests at His feet. The only purpose of life is to have a direct vision of Him—try to know this. Then, the mind will never again be shaken by the glamour of name, fame, and power; only then the mind will be safe from the clutches of lust and gold. What more to write? Become His through and through.

Sasi Niketan, Puri
June 29, 1925

Received your letter dated *Ashad* 10. I did not answer the two letters you wrote to me while I was at Kasi as I could not decide what to write. Moreover after coming to Calcutta, I had to settle a great deal of the Math's business in meetings with Shivananda Swamiji and the others and I had to arrange many other projects. And after that I suffered more than a fortnight of fever. As a result there was a shortage of time. As soon as I was a little better, I came here and now I feel almost well. Accept my blessings always and convey them to all the others in the two Ashramas.

Sorry to learn that the condition of your mind and body is not good. With the coming of age, the body declines and one cannot hope to get back the health of youth. So attend to the body just enough to struggle on and try hard to get peace of mind. Peace of mind can be had by spending more time in meditation and other spiritual practices and by depending on the Lord. Therefore, call on Sri Ramakrishna and Mother as much as you can and pray to them with great yearning. I am also passing my days in semi-retirement. The main purpose of human life is the realization of God. What is broken cannot be made new again, and Holy Mother has done this [to you] so that you might see your mind clearly. But this is certain, Holy Mother will never forsake you and will do whatever is good for you in the long run.

The two *slokas* (verses) you quoted from the third and the eighth chapters of the *Gita* have no relation or sequence. In the third chapter one thing is being told and in the eighth, another. The meaning of the nineteenth *sloka* of the third chapter is that the *karmayogin* who spends his life working yet always remains unattached will, at the end, obtain the *parama,* i.e., the highest refuge. That is, he will realize Sri Bhagavan in everything and, achieving pure knowledge [of God], he will merge with Brahman. In the twentieth *sloka* of the eighth chapter, Sri Kirshna says that the *karmayogin* who dies at the time of the "smoky' night, "krishnapaksha, daksinayana..." will live in the *chandraloka* for some time and then will come back to the world. This means that the *karmayogin* who could not always work without attachment and so did not attain success in his path will die at the time of the "smoky" night etc., and will come back to the world. Although the *jiva* has not the power to decide to go to the *devayana* or *pitriyana,* still his course is determined by the work he has done throughout his whole life, and the *karmayogin* who was successful in his karma yoga and obtained pure knowledge [of God] will know through God's grace which course he will have when the body dies.

Wishing you well,

P.S. When I return to Calcutta, remind me to send you a good copy of the *Gita,* one that has been translated by a friend of ours. You will learn many things from that.

Calcutta
October 30, 1925

Glad to receive your letter dated October 23. I had already learned of the passing away of Muktananda. He has found refuge at the lotus feet of Sri Ramakrishna and Holy Mother; he is in great peace. You are also their children. The purpose of your life will surely be fulfilled.

The state that comes during meditation etc., of which you have written, is very good. Thus the *kundalini* wakes up, and when fully awake, it endows the *yogi* with pure knowledge [of God] and pure devotion. To have the anxiety that "God is not yet realized" is very good. I bless that your yearning should increase much more and that you may have the vision of Sri Sri Thakur in a short time.

My health is all right. There is no certainty of my going to Kasi. Convey my blessings to K. and the others.

Wishing you well,

Calcutta
November 1, 1925

Glad to receive your letter of October 28. Accept my blessings always. I am well. Here are the answers to your questions:

1. The Vedas are the words of those who have realized God. They are called *apta purushas* (realized souls) and the Vedas are called *aptavakya* (revealed word). Rely on their teachings for your spiritual practice. It is not possible to understand with our clouded intellect, which is attached to worldly things, so spiritual practices that are directed by the intellect do not have good results. Give up trying to understand everything and proceed with your *sadhana,* having faith in the words of Sri Ramakrishna. He used to say that there is *prarabda* (unavoidable karma) as well as *kripa* (God's grace). Through his grace karma can be overcome by experience.

2. If drowsiness comes while concentrating on the object of

meditation but joy persists, then it cannot be called lethargy or sloth. It is not a high state of mind, but still it is good, and by daily practice it will go away.

3. If by doing *japa* the mind becomes calm and the desire for meditation comes, then meditate. The means of subjugating the restless mind are *vairagya* (renunciation) and practice—this is written in the Gita. There are no other means.

4. There is no necessity of doing *pranayama*. At least, Sri Ramakrishna did not ask us to do it. Control of the breath comes of itself when the mind is concentrated through love of the Chosen Ideal.

There is no necessity of your solving these questions, nor do I have the time. Make *japa* and meditate daily and remain pure in body, mind, and speech—by that alone you will achieve your life's goal. Faith, strong faith, in the words of the Master—that is necessary, you must know that.

Pay a little attention to your studies. Know that is also a part of religious life. For if you do not complete the education necessary for earning money for simple food and clothing, it will be impossible to meditate and think of Him.

Wishing you well,

Calcutta
November 1, 1925

Received your letter. My health is all right. I bathe in the Ganges now and then and also take a walk. All are well in the Boarding House. Hope R. has become healthy and strong by now. Accept my blessings always.

It is true the mind becomes distracted if one takes the remains of food from a man of worldly temperament, but there are other reasons as well. Take Sri Sri Jagannath Deva's rice *prasad* every day for a few days; and when sitting for meditation, at the very beginning think: My Chosen Ideal is everywhere, covering everything like the unbroken sea of Satchidananda, and I am always in Him. He is everywhere, within me and outside of me." Concentrate on this thought for some time, meditate, and make *japa* as usual. Then the distractions of the mind will go away.

All are well here. Give us your news, now and then. My blessings to N.

Wishing you well,

Calcutta
June 3, 1926

Received your letter of May 21. I could not answer as I was not well and also for other reasons. My health is better than before. Hope through the grace of the Lord your health is all right by now.... Accept my blessings always and convey them to all the others there.

It is impossible to give detailed answers to your questions in this small letter, so I am answering them in brief.

1. As Sri Sri Thakur practiced all types of *sadhana,* it can be inferred that he practiced hatha yoga a little also. The bleeding from the roots of his teeth while he performed the *puja,* as was recorded in the *Lilaprasanga* and by the comments at that time gives the inference added weight. However, he never asked us to practice *pranayama.* As to his not doing hatha yoga later on, it may be concluded that, when he saw that God cannot be realized by it, that it only strengthens the body, and that it increases body consciousness, he gave it up.

2. I have heard from Swamiji that he (Swami Vivekananda) practiced a little *pranayama* at home. But he was essentially a *rajayogi* and an adept in meditation. While meditating, his breath would automatically stop and there would be no consciousness of the body. I know he did not make any special practice of hatha yoga. And he observed that unless a competent instructor is found, in many cases *pranayama,* etc., can cause harm. That is why he has advised others to take the path of devotion coupled to knowledge. Of course, he instructed many of his disciples to do a little purification of the *nadis,* i.e., to breathe in slowly and then breathe out slowly five or seven times. And in his English book, *Raja Yoga,* he has explained many aspects of *pranayama* and has told of their benefits, but at the end he said not to practice it without a competent instructor. Actually, his opinion was identical with Thakur's, i.e., since God cannot be realized by practicing hatha yoga, *pranayama,* etc., it is not necessary to do them. *Japa,*

meditation, study of the scriptures, discrimination between the real and the unreal—all these he emphasized with great stress.

3. Jnana, karma, bhakti, and yoga are what Swamiji has taught; there the meaning of yoga is raja yoga, i.e., to try for *dhyanasamadhi,* etc.

4. If a student does a little *pranayama,* say one or two *pranayama* before sitting for *japa*—that can be allowed. That will do no harm.

5. The Mission does not say anything for or against taking part in politics. Thakur did not ask us to do anything regarding that. Swamiji asked the Mission to avoid those endeavors. That is why up until now the Mission confines itself to religion and service to the people.

6. As all things change, so India's state of subjugation will also change one day and political independence will come. The Mission does not know, nor does it try to know, how long that will take. The Mission wants people to become stronger in spirituality and character. After they develop character and strength, they will discover how to manage society and administrate the country.

7. The Mission has started a *vidyapitha* (school), etc., with the idea of helping the boys and girls to learn through their student life to develop character and to structure their life with high ideals. At the end I want to say that as much as you yourself progress in spiritual practice and become meditative, so much will you be able to solve these problems automatically. So keep your attention on that.

Your well-wisher,

Calcutta
June 29, 1926

Happy to receive your letter. My health is better nowadays. Accept my blessings always.

When hopelessness overcomes you, drive it away by thinking, "I am His servant, His daughter, His partner; my guru and my *Ishta* are always holding me by the hand and are watching over me." This thought will strengthen the mind. Repeat your mantra daily for as many times as you can and, while you make *japa,* visualize the Master. If the mind does not become steady, pray to him fervently, "Lord, make my mind calm." Know that the Master hears your words and understands your feelings. Whatever you ask of him earnestly, you will get.

Wishing you well,

Calcutta
November 16, 1926

Received all the news from your letter of 24 Karik. I pray to Sri Ramakrishna that you be well and strong again and have pure devotion at his lotus feet.

It is good that you are having the *ayurvedic* treatment. Take care and take your medicine regularly. I am well. All are doing well here. Now and then write about yourselves and make us happy. Glad to know that a special arrangement has been made in the Ashrama for your stay and your diet. Whenever you require anything, tell A. or S.; hope they will make arrangements for that as much as possible.

The answers to your questions:

1. You may take the name [of God] in the way you like.

2. It is better to make *japa* by keeping the rosary down by the breast. Some say that the rosary should not be lowered down to the navel. If that is inconvenient for you, you may spread the edge of your *chadar* or some other thing [over your hand] and then do it. The main object is to take the name of Sri Ramakrishna; so do it in whatever way is convenient for you.

3. Do not practice the *pranayama* you read about in the book on raja yoga. Do exactly as the doctor says. Possibly he will ask you to breathe freely once or twice and hold your breath and then let it go out slowly. Ask him about this and do as he instructs.

Wishing you well,

Calcutta
November 23, 1926

Dear B.,

Since your letter, I am anxious to know about the illness of your mother. Through the will of the Master, let her be well quickly—that is my prayer. Your father's health is also not at all good. Serve them as much as you can and earnestly pray to the Master and the Mother. One cannot see Holy Mother without her grace; so open your whole heart to her with simplicity. My blessings to you that you may have pure devotion at her lotus feet and be blessed by having a vision of her.

I am well as usual. All the others are well here. Convey my blessings and good wishes to your mother, your father, and L. I shall be glad to receive news from you now and then.

Wishing you well,

Calcutta
December 21, 1926

Just received your letter of the 17th instant. My body is all right. Accept my blessings and good wishes always and convey them to C. and the others of the Ashrama.

Glad to know all about Bhagavanananda from the letters written by you and him. It is good that he wants to stay at Kasi and do spiritual practices. Tell C. and make arrangements for his stay in the Advaita Ashrama. He has written that he will have *Bhiksha* (alms) from the almshouse. Help him as much as possible with that as well.

Glad to know that you like the picture of Holy Mother. It is almost time for her birthday festival. Hope you and all the others where you live are doing well. All are well here and in the Math. It is getting colder and colder nowadays. Make us happy by sending us your news now and then.

Wishing you well,

Sri Sri Ramakrishnah Saranam

Dear Bhagavanananda,

Received your letter. It is good that you want to stay at Kasi and engage in spiritual practices. My blessings to you so that, through the grace of the Lord, you may realize the Self and live in peace and happiness. Tell C. that you may stay in the Advaita Ashrama at night; hope he will make all the arrangements regarding this.

My body is all right. Make us happy by sending us your news now and then.

Wishing you well,

Calcutta
January 12, 1927

Glad to learn from your letter of December 28 that the birthday festival of Holy Mother went nicely. Accept my blessings and good wishes always and convey them to N., A., and the others.

Go on calling on Sri Sri Thakur as you are doing and everything will come through his grace. We, of course, always bless you so that you may have pure devotion. Is it a matter of little fortune that you are having joy in calling on him and are in good health and spirits? Rest at his feet; depend on him; whatever is needed, he will do for you—you need not worry about that. As your circumstances at Rajpur are good, stay there for some time. I am well. All are well here. K. is here; he will write to you after a while. He has received all your previous letters. Convey my blessings to S. and tell him that I was glad to receive his letter. Let him write now and then about himself to make us happy and free from anxiety.

Wishing you well,

Calcutta
March 29, 1927

Received your letter. Be content in what the Master wills. There is no use in becoming restless. As I wrote to you previously, stay where you are and depend on him. There is no point in worrying: if he wills it, you will meet me. I cannot go anywhere without the approval of the doctors. But they will not agree to my going to Kashi now, for I cannot bear the heat. Do not think that you can have more of your guru's grace by staying with him. Those who call on the Lord with sincerity and simplicity will receive his grace wherever they stay.

Know my blessings and good wishes always and convey them to G., B., and all the others there. I am well.

Wishing you well,

Calcutta
May 4, 1927

Received your letter dated April 24. Glad to know that you had your bath safely during the *Kumbha* and that you have obtained a *kuti* (hut) to your liking on the Ganga near the Swargashrama. I pray that you think about Sri Sri Thakur and get much peace and joy.

It is a matter of great sorrow that Swami Tattwananda (Govinda), the *pujari* of Sri Sri Thakur here died yesterday of the smallpox. Everything happens through the will of the Lord. He died at such a tender age! All the others are doing well, more or less. I am well. Accept my blessings and good wishes always and convey them to the others. Tell Chaitanya that I have received his letter and send my blessings. Revered Mahapurushji and the other *sadhus* of the Math are doing well. May Sri Sri Thakur keep you well and give you pure devotion—that is my prayer.

Calcutta
June 17

Received your letter dated June 13. Glad to know that you are thinking of God and reading the scriptures during your stay in that lonely place. I pray to Sri Sri Thakur that you may have pure devotion at his feet and progress toward peace and joy by remembering the Lord and meditating on Him.

Accept my blessings and good wishes and convey them to your mother and to K., S., and all the others there. I am well. Mahapurush Maharaj is doing well. All are well here and in the Math. The heat has lessened a little because of the recent rains. Hope all of you are well.

Wishing you well,

Calcutta
July 8, 1927

Received your letter dated 20 *Ashad*. We also knew that Simla is a very cold place. Anyway, we hope that after staying there for some time, you will become completely well. Let us know now and then how you are managing. Accept my blessings and good wishes always. You may go to Hardwar if convenient, in the month of *Aswin* . . . I am well. All are well here and in the

Math. I have received the letter of Srimati R. The news from Kasi is good as before.

If you get joy from meditating on the *bija* (seed word) of your mantra, then do that. You wanted to know how to meditate on the name. Try to concentrate on the sound produced by the name. Then the mind will become calm and peaceful. "The name [of your *Ishta*] is Brahman," say the scriptures. Bliss will come only by taking the name.

Wishing you well,

Calcutta
July 8, 1927

Received your letter dated 20 *Ashad*. Accept my blessings. My health is all right. It is hot here, too, but it rains now and then. I have received the letter saying that G. has arrived safely.

Now I know about your dream and the violations of religious observances by other people in the kitchen of your present house. If like the Hindustanis you make a square fence on four sides of the oven while cooking and bring your own water and cook inside the fence and then offer the food to the Lord, I think there will be no defilement. Of course, nobody should enter the fenced area while you are cooking and offering. As this house is convenient in every way, it would be foolish to give it up hastily and go to some other place.

Hope you are doing well. Convey my blessings to L., M., and the others.

Wishing you well,

Calcutta
July 18, 1927

After receiving your letter, I came to know all about you. As you have come to the shelter of Sri Ramakrishna, he will surely save you. Slowly everything will be all right; you need not worry, my child. Do *japa* and meditate as much as possible; do not give that up. By practice, a taste for repeating the Lord's name will come and you will know peace and bliss. I bless you that through his grace your worries will vanish. Let there be real faith and devotion to his lotus feet.

My body is well. All are well here. Hope your health is all

right now. We shall meet again in the future, do not worry about that. Open your whole heart to the Master; He is *Antaryami* (the Indweller). He will surely hear the earnest prayer of his devotee.

Accept my blessings and good wishes and convey them to the others in the house.

Wishing you well,

Calcutta
July 25, 1927

Received your letter of July 19 in time and the one written previously. I could not answer as I was busy with much troublesome work. Please do not mind the delay . . . Accept my blessings and good wishes always and convey them to C. and all others of the Ashrama. . . . I am managing much as usual.

The rains have begun here again since yesterday. As far as possible I have answered your questions. Hope this will be able to solve at least a little of your doubts.

Wishing you well,

1. How the Lord attracts the *kundalini shakti* and the place from which that power rises up and the exact place in the brain where it meets the *Paramatman*—these things can be understood only when samadhi has become customary. It is not possible to make one who has never experienced samadhi understand that: For this is a thing to be experienced; it cannot be understood by reasoning.

2. What is written in *Sivasamhita* and other books, i.e., the *kundalini* rises up from the four-petalled lotus in the *muladhara*, is correct. The same thing is written in Swamiji's *Raja Yoga* (p.66): "The aim of *pranayama* is to awaken the *kundalini shakti* that is coiled in the *muladhara*." The picture was done in America and the artists of that country did not draw it exactly right.

3. "The *jiva* enters into samadhi when the mind rises to the *ajna chakra* situated in the brow" (*Lila-prasanga* III, p. 70). "It seems I am merged in Him and become one with Him, but actually not yet become [entirely] one. If the mind gets down from this *chakra*, it may, at the most, come down to throat or the heart, it cannot sink below that" (*Lila-prasanga*, p. 73). The desire

to stay with Him day and night indicates the stage the mind has reached.

4. The seat of *jivatman* is in the heart—the lotus of *anahata*. The difference between the *jivatman* and *Paramatman* is this—as Sri Ramakrishna used to say, "*Jiva* is in fetters and Siva is free from fetters." You will find something similar in the Katha Upanishad: "*Atmendriya manoyuktam bhoktyetyahur manishinah.*" When the *Paramatman* feels that He is with the sense organs and the mind, He assumes the feeling of the *jiva* and enjoys the pleasures and sufferings of the world. Becoming unattached to the sense organs and the mind, the Paramatman leaves the feelings of the *jiva* and remains aware of Himself; that is called the stage of *tadakarakarita*.

The visions of the gods and goddesses [that come when the *kundalini is*] in the fourth and fifth *chakras* are also called samadhi.

This is *bhava* samadhi or *savikalpa* samadhi.

If the *kundalini* of the *jiva* rises to *ajna chakra,* the mind does not come down. Remaining for 21 days constantly in samadhi, it merges completely with the *Paramatman* in the *sahasrara*. At this stage, if it is necessary that the body should remain in this world, everything is done through the grace of God and an arrangement is made for breaking his samadhi by feeding him.

Antaratman is the *Atman* with *antahkarana* (the mind-stuff). The seat of this *antahkarana* is the middle of the brow to the navel. The seat of *buddhi* is in the brain, of the mind in the throat, of *ahamkara* in the heart, and of *chitta* in the navel.

5. Intoxication caused by taking *siddhi* and hemp will subside by drinking water that has been used to wash rice. Possibly the intoxication of wine will also subside.

6. If the vision of the cremation ground comes during your meditation and dreams, it is good, not bad.

7. Some *sadhakas* remain sitting after they enter the samadhi that is experienced when the *kundalini* rises to the *ajna chakra*.

Calcutta
25 *Pausch* 1328 B.E.

Happy to receive your letter dated 29/12/21.

... While practicing *nadi-shuddhi* (purification of the blood and nervous system), the number of inhalations and exhalations should be the same. For example, if the time devoted to *puraka* (inhaling) is 16 *japa*, the *rechaka* is to be done to the same count of 16 *japa*.

I am well. Accept my blessings.

Wishing you well,

Calcutta
4 *Magh*, 1329 B.E.

Dear S.

Glad to receive your letter of the 1st *Magh*. The gout in my leg is almost cured; I can even walk a little now. I went for a walk near the Ganga last evening.

Yogin Ma's health is as before...

We have decided to take her to Kasi on the 15th *Magh*. Now whatever the Master and Mother will, that will be done.

I think you are not yet cured. That is why your mind is still weak. Over and above that, worrying about the illness of Yogin Ma makes your mind weaker and makes you think restlessly. Anyway, if it recurs again while sitting for *japa* and meditation, then for a week make *japa* for only 108 times (just to observe the rule) and read the Gita, the *Kathamrita*, the *Stavamala*, etc., for the rest of the time. It seems to me that the mind will again come back to *japa* and meditation if you do this for two or three days. This restless condition of the mind comes now and then to everybody; it is nothing to worry about. After a while, this restlessness will go away and you will be able to make *japa* and meditate with more devotion than before. Those who have been blessed by the Master and Holy Mother need have no fear. Know that the Master and Holy Mother always hold them by the hand.

Golap Ma has been in bed for the last three days because of gout in her leg. All are doing well in the Boarding House. R. had to go away all of a sudden because of a telegram from his sister. His sister had come to Hardwar on a pilgrimage and it will be more convenient for her if R. is with her.

Accept the blessings of Yogin Ma for yourself and convey them to the others. Know you have my blessings always and inform me when you write again whether the restlessness of the mind is gone or not.

Wishing you well,

Calcutta
10 *Sravan,* 1330 B.E.

Accept my blessings. Answer to your letter dated 8 *Ashad* is given below:

1. The general rule is to do two *pranayamas* each time you sit for *japa* and meditation, e.g., in the morning and the evening, etc. In the morning when you first sit down, do one *pranayama,* and then at the end of the *japa* do another, and offer the *japa* (as I have told you previously). In the evening, repeat this. Those who pant for breath while doing the big number of 8-32-16 or feel a pain in the chest after doing it, should only do 4-16-8 in the preliminary stage. *Pranayama* is to be done on an empty stomach, i.e., before taking food. With a full belly you can do *japa* but not *pranayama.*

2. There will be no harm if the *pranayama* is done four hours after taking your meal. Observe this rule of *pranayama* during the day and at night. While doing *pranayama,* imagine the mantra is mixing with the air awakening the *kundalini* in the *muladhara chakra* (below the spinal cord) and then merging into the effulgent *Paramatman* in the head.

3. Meditate on Sri Guru sitting on the twelve-petalled, white lotus above the eyebrows. The *slokas* (stanzas) of meditation on Sri Guru are to be chanted at that time—Sri Bhagavan takes the effulgent form of him from whom initiation is taken and resides as Sri Guru on the twelve-petalled lotus. While sitting for *japa,* meditation, worship, etc., first of all chant His *dhyana mantra,* think of Him, and make *pranams* to Him by chanting, "Om Akhandamandalakaram," etc. . . .*

4. You are to visualize the *Ishta* or Sri Guru face to face, i.e., if you sit eastward think that He is sitting westward.

---

* Om Salutations to the Guru, who has made it possible to realize Him by whom this entire universe of movable and unmovable objects is pervaded.

5. Thousand-petalled lotus is colored in different hues, not of one color. All the lotuses are inside the spinal column. All the *sadhanas* are [accomplished] through yoga. Don't confuse your mind by reading books. Afterwards you will know what should be done.

6. It is best to do *japa* mentally, i.e., neither moving the tongue nor the lips, etc.

7. During *japa* imagine the form and do the *japa* along with that.... Accept my blessings. Tell S. that I shall answer his letter at my earliest convenience. Convey my blessings to him.

Wishing you well,

Calcutta
31 *Sravan*, 1330 B.E.

Happy to receive the news of your returning safely in your letter of August 12. I am sorry to hear that most of you were ailing a little while at Dacca. Now I hope through the grace of the Master all of you are fully well.

I am glad to hear that eight or ten devotees gather together in your house every day and take part in holy reading, discussion, and singing. This is a very good thing. Singing the name and glory of God with other devotees helps to increase devotion and faith. Do not stop; pay no heed to what people with opposite views say. If they see that there is an improvement in your life, they will then discover its benefit. It is not proper to argue or quarrel with anybody on this subject; it is harmful.

Please accept my blessings and convey them to the others. My good wishes to the circle of devotees assembled there.

Wishing you well,

Calcutta
25 *Agrahayan*

Received your letter of *Agrahayan* 21. The guru is to be visualized on the twelve-petalled white lotus. The white lotus is, in a way, part of the thousand-petalled lotus. That is why some hymns of meditation have instructed [that the guru be] visualized "in the thousand-petalled lotus," etc. You may go on as you were doing.

The birthday festival of the Holy Mother will be celebrated on December 30. If I go to Kasi, I shall do so after that. I am well. Accept my blessings. All are well here.

Wishing you well,

Calcutta
31 *Ashad*

Received your letter of July 8. Call on the Holy Mother as you have been doing for so long.... Meditate on the Mother in the way which gives you joy. Do not think that she cannot be called upon without reciting the Sanskrit mantras. Do the worship with feeling. Just as we do when the beloved ones come to our house—give them a seat, wash their feet, put garlands around their necks, offer them a bath, and feed them—also do for the Master and Mother. The essential thing is love; if it is there, everything will be there. When the *japa* and *dhyana* (meditation) are finished, offer *japa* saying, "Lord, do that by which knowledge and real good come," and then pray to him. Self-surrender is the best worship. Even if you do not get flowers, sandal paste, etc., think, "Lord, let the feeling that I give away everything at your feet be constant." Of course, the scriptures say that the guru should be visualized as seated on the white lotus in the head and the *Ishta* on the red lotus in the heart. I do not know whether you will get joy in doing that. Do what gave you joy before.

Know you have my blessings and good wishes always and convey them to your husband, children, and the others. I am well. All are well here. We got the pineapple you sent. I also took from it; it was very good. Let the Lord keep all of you well, that is my prayer.

Wishing you well,

Puri
Sashi Niketan
August 13, 1915

My dear Jayachandra:

I was pleased to receive your letter of some time ago. It was delayed since I left Calcutta in June and was staying at the above address. My plan is to continue my stay here until August 29 and then return to Calcutta.

You are thinking of visiting Belur Math during the Durga *Puja* holidays. That is a good idea. The Math belongs to all. You are welcome to be a guest of the Math whenever you wish to visit it.

What advice am I to give you? Make the pure lives of Sri Ramakrishna and Swamiji your ideal. Always remember their noble virtues and try to follow the path taken by these two great personalities. Apply yourself intensely to your studies for the attainment of knowledge and try to be pure in thought, word, and deed.

Our revered Holy Mother is now living in her village home in Jayrambati. Probably she will come to Calcutta before winter. Accept our love and blessings.

Your affectionately,

P.S. Please convey my love to your father* when you write to him.

Almora
23 August

My dear Naren & Gangis,

Very glad to learn from Pramada Babu's letter today, that you have come to Benares and are about to start for Almora. We are very anxious to see you both and have for this reason loitered here for so long. If we fail to see you this time, we do not know when it will be possible to meet with each other. Pray be good enough to come up here as early as you can; please grant our request. We must wait here till your reply or as late as the 2nd proximo. Upon hearing from you, Badri Sah is willing to make arrangements for your trip from Ry. Stn. up to here. We are all right. God be blessed that you are in good heatlh.

Affectionately yours,
Sarat

Dear Pramada Babu,

Very happy to receive your letter and learn that you are in good health. Many thanks for your loving and good heart. There

---

* Sarat Chandra Chakravati, an ardent disciple of Swami Vivekananda and the author of the book *Talks with Swami Vivekananda*.

is no use sending any passage money now because, by the Lord's mercy, we are well off here. If we should need [money], then we would have to ask you. Please send word quickly [of the date] when Naren and Gangadhar plan to arrive. We must wait here until we hear. We are in good health and hope you are, too. With our best compliments and love to you we are

   Affectionately yours,
   Sarat

Calcutta
May 15, 1925

My dear Beatrice:*

Your kind letter of May 9 has arrived. The question that you have asked is a very subtle one. I do not pretend to know everything and what I give you below are suggestions only. You are free to accept or reject them partially or wholly.

The Puranas, which discuss the various incarnations of God, such as Rama, Krishna, Buddha, Chaitanya, and others, say that these Godmen with their followers form, as it were, different families, each having its own family type or form. So Rama with his followers has a distinct, separate form from Buddha or Jesus with each of their followers. And every individual of one of these families, when perfectly developed, will become one with the Godman who started that family type or form.

From that form, the individual will, in time, attain the Formless One. The Godman of the present age, Sri Ramakrishna, has started a family type that gathers all the former family types into it. What the Master saw in his disciples was their family types or forms attached to their subtle bodies, and so he could immediately recognize from which family type each of them came. He saw that Swami Vivekananda belonged to a rare type of those who had become almost one with the Formless One, and were residing in a place high above the realm of the Gods, in short of all duality. He saw that Swami Brahmananda was the playmate of Sri Krishna, and so on. The disciples of the Master who formerly belonged to different family types have attained an even higher

---

* Mrs. Beatrice Cook, an English disciple.

type or form by their acceptance of the present Godman and from that will reach the Formless One.

I do not know whether I am clear or not, but I believe you will find some kind of sense in it if you think it over seriously. I would like to know what each of you thinks about my suggestions.

Hoping this will find you all in good health and spirits, and with love and blessings to each of you,

I am yours affectionately,

Sasi-Niketan, Puri
August 18, 1925

My dear Beatrice:

All your kind letters have arrived. And, though I have not written for so long, you and your affairs have always been in my thoughts. My long silence has disconcerted you a great deal, as your letters showed, and yet I could not write and tell you what was on my mind. Many things are responsible, some of which you can understand if I tell you, while a great many you cannot understand, even if I tell you.

It is literally true and I am rediscovering it every day that we cannot do anything, however little or simple, unless the divine Being wills it! So I will not try to explain matters. I have given you entirely into the hands of the Master, and I am sure he will lead you safely and surely in his own time to truth and peace everlasting.

With my love and blessings to you always,

Yours affectionately,

Calcutta
November 4, 1925

My dear Beatrice:

Two of your kind letters, those of October 5 and October 10, are waiting for replies.

As regards to Enid's affair, I trust it is a trial which has come to you to make you firm in your vow that the children are the Mother's and not yours. You will learn from it how even the best of us deceive ourselves in our attempts to give up everything to the Lord.

We think that we love without selfish taint or hope of reward, but deep within us there lurks the expectation that it should be returned, and we are at a loss when we find the response to be not exactly up to our inmost wishes. To make our words move always in unison with our thoughts is the highest of all attainments, Ramakrishna said; and Jesus said, "Be ye therefore perfect as your father in Heaven is perfect." Remember always that children have brought their own karma with their birth and will develop according to their own lines. To hold before them the highest ideal by our own way of life is all that we can do to help them.

Now regarding advice: in a general way we all believe in giving advice; but applying the giving of advice to our daily lives is a very complex and puzzling affair. Indiscriminate advice never brings the desired result; in many cases, it brings just the opposite result. So, we try to give advice only when we care about the person and when we think our words will carry some weight. In the case of someone who is stubborn and very near and dear to us and who, due to his lack of experience is in imminent danger of being harmed by an insincere person, we must take the risk of being disbelieved and misunderstood and offer the advice and then leave the matter in the hands of the Lord.

So you see, it is not possible to state a general rule of conduct. We must adapt ourselves to each individual case. The best we can do under such complex circumstances is what our Holy Mother used to do herself—meditate and calm your mind; then, after thinking over the various aspects of the problem, pray to the Lord and do what flashes into your mind.

Yes, the Holy Mother initiated D. without his asking because she knows D. more than he does himself and knew that he "would one day need it and love it."

With my love and blessings to you and the children always.

Yours affectionately,

COMMENTS ON SPIRITUAL EXPERIENCES

(ADAPTED FROM *SRI RAMAKRISHNA, THE GREAT MASTER*)

Samadhi or superconsciousness is not a disease of the brain. Granted it is not generally or usually experienced, but neither is it abnormal in the sense of being a pathological state.

The subtle experiences of the spiritual world can never be objects of knowledge to the ordinary human mind. Such experiences require instruction, training, and constant practice. The extraordinary visions and experiences that come with long and serious discipline purify spiritual seekers and gradually make them fit for realizing God by filling them every day with new vigor and creative ideas. It is through these visions and ecstasies that the next step of spiritual development can be gained.

However the goal of visions and ecstasies, the highest level of samadhi, the *nirvikalpa* state, can be reached only through the cessation of all mental modifications. Thereafter the non-dual plane of consciousness becomes normal. As an example of how ecstasies are a means for going beyond such experiences, Sri Ramakrishna used to say, "When a thorn runs into the body, one has to take it out by means of another and then throw them both away." Forgetting the ultimate Reality, we come into this state of relativity and think that the world is real. Gradually the universe of sights and sounds is attenuated by spiritual visions and experiences that eventually lead us back to the knowledge of non-duality. When that happens we learn the truth of the *rishi*'s utterance: "He verily is Bliss Itself." This is the process. All the doctrines, the experiences, and the visions of spiritual life are valuable only as they help us to go forward to that destination.

Swami Vivekananda often said that these visions and experiences indicate how far the devotee has gone forward toward the goal; he called them milestones on the way to progress. It would be a mistake to think, when there is a little intensity of a particular spiritual mood or a vision of the *Ishta* during meditation, that spiritual realization has reached its culmination. Falling victim to this error, devotees miss the goal, become one-sided and even fanatical and bigoted, filled with hatred and animosity towards one another. Believing visions to be the goal of religion has lead many people to conclude that someone who has not had such experiences is not religious. Spirituality and aimless miracle-mongering seem to them to be the same thing. But this kind of hankering does not make people religious; on the contrary, it weakens them. That which does not lead to steadfastness and strength of character, that which does not enable people to stand on the rock of purity for the sake of truth in defiance of the whole world, that which entangles them in desires instead of setting them free from desire is outside the realm of spirituality. If you have visions and ecstasies without having a corresponding strengthening of character, you are outside the frontier of spirituality; then they are due to a weakened brain and are of no value. If, on the other hand, instead of having visions, you find yourself acquiring strength, know for certain that you are on the right path and that you will yet enjoy spiritual experiences at the proper time.

Finding that some of the devotees of Sri Ramakrishna were experiencing ecstasies, a friend of ours, who had visited the Master for a long time, but had no such experience, felt much perturbed. He went to the Master with tears in his eyes and laid bare his distress. Sri Ramakrishna said, "Don't be foolish, my child. Do you think everything is gained when that is attained? Is it something very big? Know for certain that true faith and renunciation are far greater. Why, Narendra (Swami Vivekananda) does not have these visions, but just see how great his renunciation is, how great his faith is, how great is his vigor and how steadfast is his mind."

Becoming one with the divine Lord comes through the elimination of desire with the help of steadfastness, faith, and single-minded devotion. There are certain pure desires such as the desire to help others that some realized souls cultivate. Even though such desires are pure, under their influence they cannot remain in the non-dual state. They come down just a little from that highest place of consciousness to the realm of "I" and "mine" again. But that "I-ness" of theirs is in constant and unbroken consciousness of an intimate relation with God. They feel I am a servant or a child or a part of Him. That "I" cannot devote itself to lust and gold. Knowing that God is the quintessence of everything, that "I" does not hanker after the enjoyment of worldly objects. It experiences only as much of worldly objects as is necessary for their relationship with God and no more. Those who were in worldly bondage but have attained perfection by means of *sadhana* and are living in the world in some loving relationship with the divine Lord are known as *jivanmuktas* or persons who are liberated during their life.

Transcendental consciousness—samadhi—can be attained through the awakening of the *kundalini,* the coiled reservoir of spiritual energy (*shakti*) lying at the base of the spine. The yogi says that the supreme Self, the divine Lord who is indivisible Existence-Knowledge-Bliss, resides in Its own nature of pure consciousness in the crown of the head. The *kundalini* has a great attraction for It, or to put it another way, the divine Lord continually attracts the *kundalini*. But as the spiritual energy is not awake, it does not feel the attraction. The moment it is awakened, the *kundalini* will feel its attraction and approach the divine Lord. The passage leading the *kundalini* to the Self starts at the lowest center of consciousness, the *meru chakra,* called the *muladhara* or the basic center of consciousness, which is situated at the end of the vertebrae and goes straight through the spinal canal to the seventh center, the *sahasrara chakra,* in the brain. This passage has been spoken of in the scriptures on yoga as the passage of *sushuma*. The western physiologists have labeled this as *canal centralis,* but they have not yet discovered its function.

After its initial separation from the Self, the coiled power came down from the brain by this passage to the lowest center, the *muladhara chakra,* and lies asleep. The *kundalini* will return by this path, crossing one after another of the six centers situated one above the other in the spinal canal. As the awakened spiritual energy moves upward from center to center, the apprentice begins to have spiritual experiences. And when the *kundalini* reaches the seventh center in the brain, the apprentice realizes the ultimate goal—the supreme knowledge of Brahman, the consciousness of non-duality, that oneness of the self with the Self. The Master would say of the non-dual state, the state beyond all states, that it is the last word.

The knowledge that we gain from studying holy books is

good, but there is another knowledge that is better. Hearing the Master speak of the Veda, of the philosophy of Vedanta, and of the science of yoga, some of us have asked him, "Sir, you never went to school or even learned to read and write. How do you know all this?" The question did not annoy the Master; he would smile a little and say, "Ah, it is true I did not study, myself, but I have heard much and I remember everything I have heard. I have heard the Vedas and commentaries on the Darshanas, Vedanta, and the Puranas from good and reliable scholars. After hearing them and learning what they contained, I made a garland of them all (the books) by means of a string, and putting the garland around my neck, I offered it to the lotus feet of the Mother, saying, 'Ah, Mother, here are Thy scriptures.... Please grant me pure devotion; please give me pure love for Thee.'"

Doubt can cover your mind like a dark cloud, making you feel confused, lonely, and forsaken. This conversation between Swami Saradananda and a young man who had come to him in such a dark mood shows us the way out of the darkness.

A Conversation

STUDENT: Sir, when I had my initiation, I had faith in God. But now all seems to be vague and doubt is creeping into my mind. Please tell me what to do.
SWAMI: Frankly, doubt is a sign of disease. It is not the mind's normal condition. What the great sages have said, what Sri Ramakrishna himself taught from his own experience, has been written in books for you to read. If you doubt the truthfulness of their words, what chance is there for my words to bring conviction to your mind?
STUDENT: Who knows, sir, their words, having passed from generation to generation, may have become unknowingly misrepresented by people of diverse temperaments. I want to hear from you what you have personally experienced.
SWAMI: The life and the teachings that I have presented in *Sri*

Ramakrishna, The Great Master, are the record of my experiences. Do you think that I have spun them out of my own imagination?
STUDENT: Not necessarily so. It seems possible to me that the disciples, through enthusiasm and love, may have magnified the facts and may have seen them in an exaggerated manner. Perhaps they were even unconscious of this mental process.
SWAMI: Look, we were not devotees of Sri Ramakrishna from the very beginning. I was a member of the Brahmo Samaj. Disbelief, skepticism, and the spirit of criticism had full possession of my mind. I had no intention of holding aloft the banner of Sri Ramakrishna and proclaiming him to be an incarnation of God. Gradually everything began to change. I was forced to believe in him and his experiences. When I saw that Ramakrishna knew more about me than I knew about myself and that his word when tested was always true, I had to accept him and all he stood for.
STUDENT: Besides the historical record of Sri Ramakrishna's life, does he still exist in a real way?
SWAMI: Certainly, otherwise how could one see him? And talk to him?
STUDENT: Have you personally had any proof of it?
SWAMI: Of course. Do you imagine I am simply wasting my time, living here without accomplishing anything?
STUDENT: If Sri Ramakrishna really existed after his death, why couldn't Swami Vivekananda talk to him whenever he wished?
SWAMI: Undoubtedly Swami Vivekananda spoke to our Master often. Just as I am sitting and speaking to you, Swamiji spoke to Sri Ramakrishna in close intimacy. I know it definitely; however, such a conversation was not possible when Swamiji was on the normal plane. Suppose you live in Sankharitola. If you want to talk to me, you will have to arrange for transportation to come here and interview me. Then alone will you be able to see me and speak to me. Swamiji was not always in the same plane as Sri Ramakrishna. When a person is in the vortex of activities, his mind remains below the transcendental plane where spiritual communion is possible.
STUDENT: Sir, are you all able to see Sri Ramakrishna whenever you want to?

SWAMI: Just now I have told you that we do not live on the same plane on which Sri Ramakrishna lives all the time, and therefore I do not talk to him all the time. From the beginning you have started with a preconceived notion, and so your conclusion is incorrect.

STUDENT: If the disciples have direct communion with the Master why are there differences of opinion among them? Why did Swamiji encounter opposition from one of his brother disciples when he was formulating his plan for establishing the Ramakrishna Mission?

SWAMI: When establishing the Ramakrishna Mission, none of his disciples referred the matter to Sri Ramakrishna: the matter was placed for discussion among them all. It was only natural that there were differences of opinion, but finally Swamiji's idea was accepted by all.

STUDENT: Is there any proof that God is truly real?

SWAMI: Yes there is.

STUDENT: The references to God's reality that I have found in the scriptures, as well as those in the lives of the saints, may be due to imagination resulting from prolonged meditation that may have crystallized into a set pattern of thinking.

SWAMI: Even if this were so, behind every imagination there exists the unfathomable, infinite Reality. Suppose you love a girl and cherish an exalted opinion of her and then you marry. After you have lived together for some time you realize that your ideas about her are changing, and gradually you become disillusioned. No more do you consider her the possessor of many endearing qualities, as you once did. What has happened? The object has remained the same. Only you have viewed her differently as the result of a different state of mind. Similarly, man can have wrong ideas about God, but there must be something real to have stimulated the ideas. Swami Vivekananda used an illustration: Suppose you take a photograph of the sun from where you are, and then travel a great distance upwards to take another photograph of the same sun. There will be a vast difference between the two photos; in one the sun is big, and in the other small. But both are reproductions of the same sun. Similarly, man sees God differently from different planes of consciousness.

STUDENT: Apart from the manifestation of some special powers, is there anything unique in the concept of divine incarnation? Does God really descend on earth as man?

SWAMI: Certainly God comes down and manifests himself as man. We have heard from Sri Ramakrishna that the same power that appeared as Rama and Krishna has manifested in this age as Ramakrishna. In other words, that same godhead assumes different forms and incarnates according to the needs of the time. Sri Ramakrishna has said that he would come again after two hundred years, incarnating in the direction of the Northwest. Indeed, the whole world is nothing but a manifestation of God: yet there is a special manifestation that appears at a particular place at a particular time and abundantly fulfills a specific purpose according to the needs of humanity.

In order to console the young aspirant, Swami Saradananda said in a tone of sweetness and love: Well, when doubt arises, what is to be done? You will perhaps listen to my words with rapt attention as long as you are with me, but by the time you reach home, you may be assailed by doubts once more. Sri Ramakrishna used to say that some people possessed an inborn tendency to doubt everything, and nothing could be done to change that attitude. I know that you do not belong to that category. The grace of God is upon you. This doubting is a state of mind which will not last. After some time you will find that your doubts have gone the way they came. Even if you want to hold onto them, you will not succeed. They are destined to go. Pray to God; call on Him. If you are in doubt, pray to Him in this way; "O God, if you really exist, do such and such a thing for me that I may believe in you." Even such a prayer is helpful. Meditation and prayers, even when they do not bring any material gain, are conducive to immense spiritual good. It is through meditation and prayer that the mind is able to withdraw itself from gross sense objects and lift itself to a higher plane. Is this a small gain?

STUDENT: I want to renounce the world and join the Ramakrishna monastery. If I do, will there be any harm in my being negligent of my duties to my parents who need me?

SWAMI: It is your immediate duty to make provision for the maintenance of your parents.

STUDENT: That has been taken care of, but they need me for personal attendance on them.

SWAMI: Then you should take care of them. There is no guarantee that you will accomplish your purpose simply by renouncing the world. On the contrary, if you stay in the world, you will have to face resistance which will prompt you to turn your mind to God. In an immature state, if one renounces the world and meets with no resistance, one loses the power of attraction for God. How one will reach the goal none can say.

Remember this: None can renounce the world by calculation and plans. When there is an inner urge, no considerations arise in the mind. All this is to be settled within yourself. Will you be able to come to any decision by asking this? Go on working as you are doing now until you feel a strong yearning for God. If your yearning is true, you will find everything in good order and nothing to worry about. Furthermore, behind the renunciation of some, there is a selfish motive—the desire to escape the responsibilities of life. Such renunciation causes more harm than good. Have we renounced the world through our own planning? We had ambitions to be great, to earn more money, and to be influential; along with that we had the desire to help people in distress. But everything was turned in another direction.

What will happen in the future none can foresee. When intense desire comes, nothing can stand in the way. What you wrote in your letter—that you first thought spiritual disciplines easy, but that now you thought differently—is very true. That is the right understanding. One can do one of three things: first, one can believe and then act accordingly; second, one can disbelieve and give up the pursuit completely; third, one can keep an open mind and patiently search for Him. The last one is the true scientific spirit. Keep that spirit alive in your heart and devote yourself to meditation and prayer.

STUDENT: Please bless me that these recurring doubts may pass away.

SWAMI: Yes, my child, I bless you wholeheartedly that you may overcome these negative attitudes and attain purity of heart. Be not troubled; call on Him with sincere longing, and all will be set aright.

STUDENT: From my early boyhood, I have made Sri Ramakrishna the Ideal of my life. I feel sore at heart and ill at ease on account of these haunting doubts.

SWAMI: That is quite natural, but they will pass away. I assure you they will not linger long. Pray to Him with a concentrated mind and always discriminate between what you really are and what you appear to be. The more you practice austerities and meditation, the more you will enjoy the blessings of God. Without practice nothing can be achieved. Always use the power of right understanding, and you will know for yourself where you are, how much you have progressed, and how far you have to go to reach your destination. You have received a sacred name from your guru. Hold onto it with an unwavering mind. May God bless you!

Notes from the Lectures

"Sri Ramakrishna and the Yoga of Devotion" (adapted from *Sri Ramakrishna the Great Master*)

Incarnations of God discover new religious doctrines, new paths to God. They impart the power of spirituality to others by a mere touch. Their lives demonstrate that they were born to show us the path to God realization. They do not live for their own enjoyment or the attainment of their own liberation, but their love of others and their compassion for human misery have urged them to demonstrate with their lives the means of removing sorrow and misery. The author of the *Panchadasi* said, "A man does not like to change, after attaining samadhi, the circumstances or environments in which he was before attaining it." And this is because all circumstances except the reality of Brahman seem hollow to him.

The religious books of all peoples report that even a little devotion correctly practiced molds the devotee to the object of his worship. If our love and devotion to Sri Ramakrishna do not make our daily lives, at least a little, similar to his, then our love and devotion are not worthy of the name. Can every one of us become a Paramahamsa Ramakrishna? Each of us can surely become like one who has been cast in the same mold. All the world's great souls are special molds. The successive generations of their disciples have been preserving those molds, and the process continues to our own day. For most of us, a whole life's effort is not enough to become an exact replica of any one of those prototypes. To fashion one's inner life to such a model requires that all one's physical and mental actions become harmonious with the spirit of the great soul. The mind and body of the disciple then become fully developed instruments for containing, preserving, and imparting to others that great power that astonished the world during the lifetime of the founder of the faith.

In their power and spirituality they are similar, but each of the great souls has manifested that power and spirituality in an unprecedented life and so left new and different molds behind him. Here are a few details of the manner in which Sri Ramakrishna lived from day to day at Dakshineswar.

It was his habit to keep his body, his clothes and bedding, and other things very clean. He loved to keep things in their proper place; he taught others to do so; and he felt annoyed if anyone were untidy. He attended to details. Before departing on a visit, he would inquire whether his towel, his small bag, and other necessities were being taken, and then, when it was time to return, he would remind the disciple who attended him not to forget these articles. He used to be anxious to do a thing at the exact time when he said he would, and, lest he be guilty of falsehood, he would not take something from the hand of anyone else but the person from whom he promised to take it. For the sake of his word, he would put up with any amount of inconvenience for any length of time.

When he saw torn clothing or a torn umbrella or some such thing being used, he would say, "Fortune frowns at the man who uses such things and he loses grace," and then he would instruct the person to buy a new one or sometimes he would buy one for him. Words of pride or egoism never came out of his holy mouth. When he had to speak of his own ideas, he pointed at his body, saying, "The idea of this place..." or "the opinion of this place...."

Sri Ramakrishna had the quality of making his devotees feel that he loved each of them more than he did all the others. Probably that impression came from the deep sympathy he had for each of us; for although sympathy and love are two different things, their external characteristics are not very different.

From his childhood onward he made the fullest use of his eyes and other senses. This self-education stood him in good stead in molding human character. He used to study the conformation of his disciples' features and limbs, as well as their actions, and from this he learned the workings of their minds and the degree of their spiritual development. In our intimate dealings with him, we never found him wrong in such matters. It was an innate characteristic of Sri Ramakrishna to become completely absorbed in whatever he was thinking. This ability to concentrate enabled him to know what was beneath the surface of his disciples and to prescribe what was needed for their improvement.

He took special care that his disciples learn to use their sense and to think before performing any action. We heard him say again and again that it was reason alone that could reveal the merits and demerits of our circumstances and make the mind go forward towards true renunciation. He never enjoyed a person of narrow intellect or one devoid of it. Everyone has heard him say, "You should be a devotee, it is true, but why should you, therefore, be a fool?" Or, "Don't be one-sided: that is not the attitude of this place; the attitude of this place is, 'I'll eat [fish] in different preparations, as soup or with a pungent or sour sauce.'" He called a one-sided intellect dull and drab. "How monotonous," were his words of scolding to a disciple who could not feel delight in any but one particular aspect of the divine Lord. He used these words of scolding in such a way that the disciple had to hide his face for shame. It was undoubtedly under the impulse of this liberal, universal frame of mind that he began to practice the *sadhanas* of all faiths and so was able to discover the grand truth: "As many faiths, so many paths [to God]."

"Bigotry, Religion, and Philosophy in the Light of the Teachings of Sri Ramakrishna and Swami Vivekananda"

Today I shall present you with only a few observations, as there are a number of speakers abler than I to do full justice to the subject. I say they are abler speakers advisedly, for we have a Sanskrit proverb: One should desire victory everywhere but defeat from the son. The speakers of this afternoon are like sons to me and hence I do not hesitate to call them my betters.

Calcutta today is in the midst of bloody communal riots, and the news of them is filtering to us here. The cause of this strife lies mainly in the country's failure to accept the catholic and tolerant ideas of Sri Ramakrishna. If we could have won the country over to his message of harmony, love, and toleration, we would certainly have been spared the pain of witnessing this hatred and jealousy, this fighting and bloodshed.

Sri Ramakrishna dared to test the validity of the Islamic faith. After taking proper initiation from a Muslim holy man, he discovered that the mode of worship described in the Koran, if practiced sincerely and honestly, leads the disciple to the realization of the Truth. If our countrymen could understand and accept his realization of the Truth through the disciplines of the Koran, they could not have committed those sacrilegious acts of breaking into and defiling mosques and images.

You cannot expect these two communities to unite unless there is that purification of heart, unless there is that sincere respect for each other's ideals and beliefs that Ramakrishna's life demonstrated. You cannot achieve unity by social intercourse, by eating together, or other co-mingling. Hindus must believe that Islam as a religion is as true as Hinduism and the Muslims must believe that the Hindu religion with its variety of creeds and customs is as true as Islam. Sri Ramakrishna saw and said long ago that there was a mountain-high barrier separating these two great communities. They come from two distinct streams of civilization and differ widely in their ideas and outlook. Still, there is hope for their union if only we can eliminate the narrowness and bigotry that pass for religion today.

In studying the fundamental ideas about religion that Sri Ramakrishna has left for us, the first that we come across is that God can be seen and talked to, just as we talk to each other. We have to believe this. Secondly, if we are to reach God, we must establish a relationship with Him, be it that of father or of friend or some other relationship that can root deeply in our nature. And we must work at that relationship with single-minded devotion. There are, of course, other more abstract concepts of the

Godhead, but most people need form and symbol and cannot follow the impersonal path to its logical conclusion. Sincerity and wholehearted devotion to God are the determining factors in *sadhana* and in life.

The greatest obstacle in our way to God is the ego. As long as there is the "I," God is far from us. The "I" must be completely merged in the "Thou." We must resign ourselves completely at the feet of the Lord; then only can we realize the Truth. Believe in any form, in any personality, and establish any type of kinship with him, but surrender completely to him, make him the only thought of your life and actions, become wholly absorbed in Him, and then only will you be blessed.

This "Address of Welcome" was delivered by Swami Saradananda on April 1, 1926 at the convention of the Ramakrishna Math and Mission at Belur Math. It was published on page 17 of the book commemorating the convention.

Address of Welcome

To the Delegates of the Ramakrishna Math and Mission Convention

It seems to be the invariable rule that every new movement should pass through the stages of opposition and indifference before its principles are accepted by society and humanity at large. And as human nature is the same everywhere, we find this rule displayed alike in the East and the West. The more radical the ideas of your reform movement, the more vehement will be the opposition. People will say the principles of the movement will ruin the very foundation of everything that is good and useful. But if the movement has real life in it and is based on the essential truths governing human nature, it will survive, grow, and win over the hearts of people despite the opposition. Outside opposition actually helps concentrate the energies of the movement and stimulates the expression of the fundamental truths on which it stands; so we cannot say the process of opposition is all bad, after all.

After a period the opposition wears away and gives place to indifference, when those who first opposed the movement begin to say that after all there is nothing so very new in it: "For have we not in such and such passages of our old histories and scriptures a mention of the principles which it preaches? This is sufficient proof that our forefathers knew these principles and carried them into practice long ago, so we need not think much of it." During this second stage the movement spreads unhindered far and wide and finds secure footing in due time through the recognition of its existence and utility by society.

At the end of the second stage we find the movement accepted by public opinion; the ranks of its members swell rapidly with this social acceptance and recognition.

However the third stage, complete public acceptance, is not to be regarded as the millennium. Security of position brings a relaxation of spirits and energy, and the sudden growth of extensity quickly lessens the intensity and unity of purpose that were found among the early promoters of the movement. In place of outside opposition we find the mushrooming of internal opposition due to the varied opinions of its members and later, in place of the former spirit of sacrifice for truth, a struggle to maintain the secure social position by compromising truth with half truths and clinging more to the appearance than to the spirit of things.

If the leaders of the movement are not watchful or neglect to find remedies to check these evils, you can well imagine the result. First and foremost, the unifying bond of love within the movement slackens from the pressure of selfish motives and the members, losing sight of the welfare and improvement of the movement as a whole, detach themselves into groups with a view to improving and making permanent these separate groups that are unrelated to the whole. This process of disintegration goes on dividing the work to pieces. In the course of time disobedience to superiors, vanity, indolence, and a whole host of other faults crop up within the work to ruin it forever.

The Ramakrishna movement passed through the stages of opposition and indifference a few years before the time when its great leader, the Swami Vivekananda, left us after giving the movement a working shape and organization under the name of the Ramakrishna Mission. Since then, the Mission has been working steadily for the last quarter of a century and has brought itself to the point where it has found recognition and acceptance in the hearts of the people of India and of several countries abroad. From a simple minor organization working mostly in Bengal, it has in this short period quickly spread to all the presidencies and provinces of India and even farther to Burma, Ceylon, and the Federated Malay States and to the west, America and England and some parts of Europe as well.

You, friends, and your brother co-workers, had the good fortune to be willing instruments, starting centers of philanthropic works at Benares, Kankhal, and Brindaban. You depended solely on the Lord and have proved to the public what your prophetic leader, Swami Vivekananda, said in some of his speeches that not money but men—men fired with zeal for a noble cause, men who have character and fixity of purpose—are wanted to make such works permanent and successful. You started teaching at Murshidabad, Madras, Bangalore, and many other places in Southern India and more recently at Nagpur, Bombay, Kuala Lumpur, and Rangoon, which have drawn the attention and the respectful cooperation of the communities. Your frequent relief projects to help the poor and the sufferers of famine, flood, fire, and plague in areas all over India has helped to create the present confidence in the Ramakrishna Mission in the hearts of the people. You have persevered with wonderful patience for twenty years and more, in some cases for a whole lifetime because relieving hands could not be found.

The Master and his chosen leader (Swami Vivekananda) have done wonderful work to help poor India and other more fortunate countries through you. But still greater works remain to be accomplished, and the Master and Swamiji will do it all in time through you—if you hold fast to their purity and singleness of purpose, their sacrifice and self-surrender to all that is good, true, and noble, and continue in that meek and humble spirit with which you have followed them. If we work in any other spirit and think too much of ourselves because we have been chosen and allowed to do their work thus far, we shall find to our great regret that we have been rejected and that others have been chosen to take our places. Remember, when in their vanity the Israelites thought themselves so privileged in being God's children that they heeded not the Master, they were warned by John the Baptist that "God is able of these stones to raise up children. . . ." Remember also the history of some of our once-powerful sects in India.

Therefore, wonderful as it is to think of the growth that our Mission has attained in the past quarter of a century, we should seriously consider whether we have gained this growth at the cost of that intense spirit of sacrifice and love for God that inspired us at the beginning—whether the work that we did in the beginning for the love and glory of God has turned into slavery and bondage through undue attachment on our part to name, fame, power, and position.

The present convention gives us the opportunity to examine our motives. It affords you the rare privilege of meeting many of your senior co-workers and elders in order to profit from their experiences, to initiate and settle future plans with them, and to discuss the welfare of the Mission as a whole, including the need to ward off the evils that threaten to overtake all institutions at this critical stage. Join these discussions with sincerity and openness and with a view of making a thorough and sifting inquiry to find out if we have swerved away from God in our struggle to keep up with the demands of expansion. Hold fast to God, for God contains the stored-up energy—the *kundalini*—behind every movement; judge yourself and others by God's effulgent light. This spirit of rededication will make the convention a success. Remember this is not a new and untried path we are inviting you to travel. The Buddhists walked this way, pushed by the enormous spread of their congregation, and successfully warded off the ruin of their noble work for a long time. The followers of Jesus the Christ and of the prophet Mohammed applied the same technique from time to time in their past history. The approach to the problem is not new; the success of its application depends entirely on the sincerity and unity of purpose of those who use it. So in the words of our leader (Swami

Vivekananda), I call on every one of you to arise, awake, and stop not until the goal has been reached—until by the grace of the Master you have accomplished the noble task that you have imposed upon yourselves. Friends, brethren, children, co-laborers in the vineyard of Sri Ramakrishna, I welcome you with all my heart in the name of our Master, our illustrious leader, the Swami Vivekananda, and our late revered president, the best beloved of the Master, the Swami Brahmananda.

These conversations of Swami Saradananda with various disciples are taken from the book Spiritual Talks (By the First Disciples of Sri Ramakrishna), *published by Advaita Ashrama, Calcutta, 1968.*

Spiritual Talks with Swami Saradananda

DISCIPLE: [A religious teacher] instructs his disciples not to practice *japa* without taking a bath, etc. Are such observances compulsory?

SWAMI: The Master came to make religion easy. People were being crushed under the weight of rules and regulations. To repeat the Lord's name and to worship Him, no special time and place are necessary. In whatever condition one may be, one can take His name. The Master never used to give too much importance to these external observances. As to means, adopt whichever suits you best. If you like God with form, that will lead you to the goal. If you like God without form, well and good; stick to it, and you will progress. If you doubt His very existence, then better put the question to Him thus: "I do not know whether you exist or not, whether you are formless or with form. Make me know your real nature." As to changing clothes, taking a bath, and other external observances, if you can observe them, well and good; if not, go on calling on Him without paying much attention to these details. The Master once sang this song to me and told me, "Assimilate any one of these ideas and you will reach the goal":

> O Lord, Thou art my everything, the sole support of my life, the quintessence of reality. There is none else besides Thee in this world whom I can call as my own.
> Thou art happiness, peace, help, wealth, knowledge, intellect, and strength; Thou art the dwelling house and the pleasure garden; Thou art the friend and relative.
> Thou art this present life, the sole refuge; Thou are the life hereafter and the heaven: Thou art the injunction of the scriptures, the guru full of blessings, and the store of infinite bliss.
> Thou art the way and the goal; Thou art the creator and preserver and the worshipped; Thou art the father that punishest Thy child, the loving mother, and the storehouse of infinite bliss art Thou.

DISCIPLE: What do you think about astrological calculations as to auspicious and inauspicious moments?
SWAMI: The Master used to observe these things. He believed in auspicious and inauspicious times. And because he used to observe these things, we too observe them. But then, these calculations, nowadays, are not absolutely correct. There have been many changes in the position of the constellations and planets, but these astrological calculations have not been corrected accordingly. So I do not observe them so much these days.
DISCIPLE: The Master used to say that *shraddha* food (offered at the last funeral rite) is harmful to *bhakti* (devotion). Why is it so?
SWAMI: The object of food is to build a strong body and a fine intellect. Unless the body and the mind are pure it is not possible to do spiritual practices. It is the food offered to God that builds a pure body and mind. The *shraddha* food is offered to the *manes* and not to God, and as a result, instead of building a pure mind and body, it affects people otherwise. Food builds the body and the mind, and the nature of the food also affects them. In Chaitanya's life we have a case where an ordinary man who happened to touch him in a state of ecstasy was also overpowered by religious emotions. He was told to take *shraddha* food to get

over these emotions, and as a matter of fact this food did put an end to that person's ecstatic moods.

DISCIPLE: Why is the time of an eclipse considered auspicious for the practice of *japa*?

SWAMI: Man becomes thoughtful when such a natural phenomenon takes place. An eclipse brings about a great change in the physical environment. At this time the mind becomes calm and so the time is favorable for the practice of *japa* and meditation.

DISCIPLE: Have any realized God through mere work?

SWAMI: Through selfless work the mind gets purified. And when the mind becomes pure, knowledge, and devotion grow. Knowledge is the very nature of the Self, but being covered with ignorance, it is not manifest. The object of selfless work is to remove this covering. As a matter of fact knowledge dawns as soon as the mind becomes pure. In the Mahabharata you have the story of the chaste lady who attained knowledge through service to her husband and through other household duties. In the Gita also you find, "By work alone Janaka and others attained perfection." Not one but many attained perfection through work, for the text adds "and others."

DISCIPLE: Does work here mean *japa*, meditation, etc.?

SWAMI: No. That meaning is given by the commentators. If it were so then Sri Krishna would have asked Arjuna to ring bells and wave lights before an image of God. Instead, he told him to fight.

DISCIPLE: Did Arjuna fight without any sense of ego, as an instrument in the hands of the Lord?

SWAMI: Certainly. If the ego persists even after the vision of the Universal Form, then of what use is the vision? Arjuna says, "My delusion is destroyed, and I have regained memory through Thy grace."

DISCIPLE: What is the meaning of the word *memory* in that verse?

SWAMI: Arjuna had forgotten the teachings of the scriptures and of the guru; he was overcome by delusion. Fear, love of relatives, and respect of his elders had created this delusion. The Advaitists interpret *memory* as the regaining of the consciousness of his real nature. They too have given a very fine interpretation: When the Vaishnavas progress in their spiritual practice and reach the *advaita* consciousness, they avoid it and try to keep permanently a relationship with the Lord. They consider that to become one with Him is an obstacle in their way and so the moment they get a scent of this consciousness, they become alert to ward it off. In fact, they give the lowest place to *shanta-bhava*, or peaceful devotion, which is the culmination of *advaita sadhana*. They develop the emotional side and direct it towards the Lord—this they think to be the highest goal. From the highest pitch of emotion we have the *madhura-bhava* or the sweet conjugal relationship with the Lord.

DISCIPLE: What is the meaning of the verse, "Relinquishing all *dharmas*, take refuge in Me alone?"

SWAMI: Here *dharma* means ritualistic works, *japa*, etc. Tilak interprets it as the *dharma* spoken of in the Mahabharata, such as service to parents, guests, etc. But this is not correct, for even though through such service some attained knowledge, his interpretation of the Gita is one-sided: he wants to show that the object of the Gita is to establish the superiority of the path of work. The Gita highly praises self-effort (*purushakara*). In this verse the Lord hints that this self-effort has a limit.

DISCIPLE: Which is the best season for spiritual practices?

SWAMI: The rainy season is not suited to them. One gets drowsy when one tries to meditate. We experienced this. In that season the mind becomes more restless. Winter is best suited for meditation. Those who want to meditate must take healthy and substantial food. Ghee, butter, etc., are good.

DISCIPLE: Why is the *kundalini* imagined to be like a snake?

SWAMI: I am not sure of the exact reason; probably because of the impressions of myriads of lives heaped up in coils, or the upward motion of the awakened *kundalini* which is zigzag like that of a serpent. Describing the *kundalini* the Master once said while in ecstasy, "Have you seen the serpent?"

DISCIPLE: What is the nature of the meditation on the formless?

SWAMI: The meditation of the Lord in the *sahasrara*, which you do at the time of *bhuta-shuddhi* in ceremonial worship, is meditation on the Formless. When you do not like any form meditate on the Formless. If meditating on the form of the guru is more appealing at any time, then better meditate on the guru, for the

Lord manifests through the guru.

DISCIPLE: Is mechanical repetition of the mantra of any use?

SWAMI: The Tantras say that through the repetition of the mantra, realization is attained. I should think so.

DISCIPLE: I am trying to follow all your instructions, but somehow I find that I am not quite at home in my spiritual practices. Sometimes they are mechanical without any life in them.

SWAMI: If you follow the same routine every day, it is natural that you should feel so sometimes. But then on those days when you like any particular portion of the *sadhana,* devote yourself to that and let the other parts go. In this way probably you may be neglecting particular practices for three or four days at a stretch. But that does not matter. When you renew these practices you will find delight in them.

Before you meditate think of the Master. If you do that you will see that whatever you do will yield good results. Sometimes think that he is in everything and everywhere and that you are immersed in him even as a pot is immersed in the ocean. Think: That supreme state of the all-pervading Deity is like the sky extending as far as sight can go. He knows everything about you. You cannot hide anything from Him. He knows your inmost thoughts.

Of course one is much benefited by regular practice. If one practices regularly for some time every day, one gains strength and finds pleasure in spiritual practices.

DISCIPLE: I have read much about the Master. Through books I have been able to know much about his life. Yet when I think of his life, I do not find pleasure in it. Why is it so?

SWAMI: To find pleasure in anything both the brain and the heart must unite. Through mere intellectualism one does not get pleasure. Everything becomes lifeless. If what you have read about the Master appeals also to your heart, then alone you will enjoy thinking about his life. He would then seem to be living.

DISCIPLE: Is it due to want of imagination then?

SWAMI: All your doubts will be solved in time.

DISCIPLE: Formerly I was eager to give up service and devote myself wholly to spiritual practices. Now I do not feel such a hankering. I don't want to change my environment, but I find that my mind is more and more attracted to *japa* and meditation and the reading of the scriptures. How is it that I do not have that former longing for solitude?

SWAMI: What of that? The scriptures say that if one can attain knowledge through spiritual practices even when he is engaged in work, then one need not give up work. Have you not heard of *Dharma-vyadha*? He did not think even the work of a butcher to be bad after he had attained knowledge. If the mind is drawn towards Him, then what is the need to change the environment? When nothing is possible without His will, then what is the use of planning? It is better to depend on Him and do as He makes us do. Moreover, if you change your environment, it will be hard to adjust to the new conditions. Therefore let the environment remain as it is. Go on calling on Him. When, through His will, the environment changes, then accept it.

The question of karma yoga was raised by someone.

SWAMI: You have no right to the results of your work; the result depends on various factors among which your effort is only one. The aspirant must try every means to fulfill his duty but should not get disappointed if he is not successful. Even though he did his work well, the work may not be successful for want of the other factors. To do one's best and be at peace without being anxious about the result is called karma yoga.

DISCIPLE: Does "renouncing every undertaking," as the Gita tells us, mean the renunciation of all work or the performance of work without the idea of ego?

SWAMI: Do the work in hand to the best of your abilities. You have to plan or utilize various means for the fulfillment of this work. But then do not take in fresh work. Do to the best of your abilities that work which has fallen to your share. It is not good to take up work aggressively. If you take up work like that, you will find that you cannot perform any task well. As a result you get worried and your mind is upset.

There was a talk on the refraction of light.

SWAMI: When I was traveling by train through Guja-rat I used to see water on either side of the line extending for miles and miles. I wondered from where so much water could come. But afterwards it struck me that it must have been a mirage. After one has realized God, the world seems to be like a mirage. There is nothing in it that can attract one. Just as one who sees water in a mirage knows full well that there is no water there; so also, though the world of names and forms is there, one knows that it is all Maya, an illusion. First, you have to attain knowledge. After attaining knowledge when one returns to this world of diversity, one will see everything as before but will no longer be attached to it. Before knowing it is an illusion, one hopes for water in a mirage, but when one realizes its nature, though one sees the mirage, one no longer expects to find any water. So also, though the world of diversity would still have to be experienced after attaining knowledge, yet one no longer takes it to be real and so has no longer any attachment to it.

Science has reduced our attachment for many things. Take, for instance, the phenomenon of color. In reality no object has any color of its own. The solar light is composed of seven different colors. Different objects absorb different colors of this light and reflect the rest. Those colors that are reflected give the color to that object. We are attracted by the beauty of colored objects, but in reality their beauty depends on the light of the sun. If we remember this, then we can no longer be attracted by them. That which to us is now beautiful may lose its beauty due to a change of conditions. As a matter of fact, objects do lose their beauty.

Take the case of touch. In reality we have but one organ and that is the sense of touch. Sight, hearing, smell, taste—all these depend upon touch or contact. Without contact none of these experiences is possible. The Gita also says, "Enjoyments that are born of contact give birth to misery." Sound according to time and place is experienced as either sweet or harsh. Sound is carried through the air. So here there is also the necessity of touch or contact with the ear.

January 31, 1925
DISCIPLE: Maharaj, the Master has exhorted us to "make the thought tally with speech." What does it mean?
SWAMI: That you must be sincere, that your inner life should correspond to the outer.
DISCIPLE: It is naturally so. Whatever we speak we think in our mind.
SWAMI: But is it not rare? We utter the name of the Lord

superficially, too superficially. We say, "I am Thy servant; Thou art my Master; Thou art my Lord; I have renounced all for Thee; I call Thee, Lord, come unto me." But we harbor all sorts of evil thoughts in the mind. This won't do. As you speak, so you must think. This means, while you take the name of the Lord, think of Him alone. Sri Chaitanya used to say, "That is verily That." That is to say, God's name is verily God Himself. They are inseparable.

DISCIPLE: Well, Maharaj, is mere repetition of God's name enough in the beginning? We cannot concentrate in the beginning.

SWAMI: So it is. But the idea corresponding to the name slowly grows.

DISCIPLE: We have the infinite compassion of the Master and Swamiji upon us. You too have showered blessings on us; yet we do not seem to be making any appreciable progress.

SWAMI: Compassion and blessing undoubtedly are there. But can deep-rooted *samskaras* (past impressions) be erased in a day? They are erased gradually. You have renounced your family and home for the sake of God—this itself is an attainment. You are surely progressing, and you will do so more and more. The Master and Swamiji have infinite compassion on us. Make up your minds now and plunge into *sadhana* (spiritual practice). Then you will see for yourselves whether you progress or not. You must labor hard before you realize the Truth.

DISCIPLE: What are we to do if any other image than that of the *Ishta* (Chosen Deity) appears during meditation?

SWAMI: Think that the *Ishta* has appeared in that form. Thus the form will slowly disappear and the *Ishta* will reappear.

DISCIPLE: Should we do so whatever the form that appears?

SWAMI: No. Do this only when the form of a saint appears.

DISCIPLE: What about an ordinary form?

SWAMI: Drive that resolutely away and try to reinstall the image of the *Ishta* with all your might. How can you meditate if a shoe-maker's shop suddenly comes and distracts your mind?

DISCIPLE: The Master used to say, "After making the knowledge of Oneness your own, you can go wherever you like." What does it mean?

SWAMI: Not "go wherever you like," but "do whatever you like." He meant that after attaining Supreme Knowledge, one cannot commit any evil deed. How can one who has realized God or attained knowledge through discrimination, renunciation, love, devotion, and purity do mischief? Such a man necessarily can do no wrong.

DISCIPLE: Is it possible to attain the knowledge of Oneness through *sakara upasana* (worship of divine forms)?

SWAMI: Why not? In time it leads to the knowledge of Oneness.

DISCIPLE: How, Maharaj? Is it that the immanence of God is realized in all things, or does everything disappear completely?

SWAMI: Both. You will understand it as you progress in your *sadhana*. Practice, and you will feel. What's the use of idle talk? Take to *japa* and meditation for some time at least. Otherwise, it will be like the utterance of some self-deluded monks, "Thou (Brahman) art verily my own nature," while enjoying lavish dishes. Labor hard and you will know everything in time. There is no use in asking abstruse questions. It leads to nothing. Everyone talks but no one does anything. Exertion brings its own reward. Why not practice as per instructions?

DISCIPLE: Maharaj (Swami Brahmananda) has said, "Meditate in the heart." By *heart*, what particular spot is meant?

SWAMI (Placing his hand on the diaphragm): This is the heart. Here one should meditate on the *Ishta*, seated on a red lotus of eight petals. The image of the guru in a white lotus should be meditated upon in the head above the eyebrows.

DISCIPLE: Who is an *ishvarakoti* (divine soul)?

SWAMI: I am not an *ishvarakoti* that I can properly explain it.

DISCIPLE: I wish to know what the scriptures say about it.

SWAMI: *Ishvarakotis* come to the world to fulfill divine missions. They are born with perfect knowledge. Such were sages like Narada, Shukadeva, and others.

DISCIPLE: What is then the difference between a *jivanmukta* (living-free) and an *ishvarakoti*?

SWAMI: An ordinary *jiva* (mortal) has to attain everything through tremendous exertion. When he reaches the *advaita* (non-dual) stage he can no longer return to the ordinary plane of existence. But *ishvarakotis* are born with Incarnations of God for the good of the world with Maya's veil outside but perfect knowledge within. They can come down even from the supreme state. But is it possible for ordinary souls?

DISCIPLE: What is an Incarnation of God? Is he always conscious of his real nature?
SWAMI: Yes, he is always established in perfect knowledge. But according to his sweet will, he occasionally puts on the veil of Maya.
DISCIPLE: What then is the significance of his *sadhana* (spiritual exercises)?
SWAMI: Putting on the veil of Maya by his own choice, he feels desire like ordinary mortals. This explains *sadhana* etc. Do you know what ordinary people are like? They are like salt dolls which go to sound the depths of the sea. They get dissolved in the sea water and never return.
DISCIPLE: Maharaj, is it due to the difference in power or knowledge?
SWAMI: It is due to the difference in power (*shakti*). You know what the Master said about it. Three men were taking a walk. Suddenly they heard music inside a big enclosure near the lawn. Finding no door to go into the enclosure, one of them fetched a ladder and got upon the wall with great difficulty. He saw to his amazement that there was a wonderful performance of dance and music. Overwhelmed with delight, at once he leaped inside without saying anything to his companions. The second man also went up and leaped in like the first. But the third behaved differently. Standing on the wall, he also saw what was going on inside. But he considered, "Should I be so selfish as to enjoy this alone? No. Let me call the others. Let them come and see and enjoy." So he returned and told everyone who would listen what he had seen inside the walls. Incarnations of God are like this. It is due to a difference in the manifestation of *shakti*. A great heart alone can share with others what it acquires after hard struggle. What a renunciation! What patience! All these show the degrees of the manifestation of power.
DISCIPLE: Maharaj, did Totapuri (the Master's teacher) reach the *advaita* state?
SWAMI (After a pause): Why do you ask such a question? Am I Totapuri that I should know everything about him? You can easily find out from books which deal with these things.
DISCIPLE: I ask this because you have just said that it is *ishvarakotis* and Incarnations alone who can return to the normal

plane after reaching the *advaita* consciousness in the *nirvikalpa samadhi* (absolute absorption in Brahman).

SWAMI: Why? What happens with the *jivanmuktas*? They also live after attaining knowledge. It is a matter of realization alone. Mere questions don't help. Be pure. Give up evil thoughts and work hard. Gradually you will come to understand everything. It is impossible to understand these things without intuitive knowledge. Practice hard. Don't take up spiritual practice in the spirit of forced labor.

DISCIPLE: You have placed the heavy work of the (Ramakrishna) Mission upon our shoulders. How can one devote oneself completely to *sadhana* with such heavy work?

SWAMI: Heavy work, indeed! Don't you realize that had there been no such work, you would not have done even what little you are doing now? Give up work for a single day if you can. Take meals from the *satra* (almshouse) and practice hard. Let me see how far you can proceed. You won't be able to do this even for a day. After a few days you will be idling away your time. Swamiji started these works for the service of humanity—service with the fullest knowledge that man is a veritable symbol of the Lord. This is a new path—a simple, easy path. But this does not suit you! Why not leave work and see the result? You will fail to do even what little *sadhana* you are putting in in the midst of work. Now you are performing selfless work, but if you give it up, you will plunge headlong into selfishness. This will be the result.

Don't you see how hard people in the world have to work! Why not enter into the world and see the fun? Many people are at their wit's end simply for serving their parents. Give people a sumptuous meal without any work because they prefer to practices *sadhana!* This won't do. One can certainly gain one's goal in the midst of work. Is there any shade of difference between spiritual practice and the work of the Mission, which is the Master's work? One's longing for spiritual practice loses much of its keenness when work is abandoned. As long as there is an obstruction in the path, there is manifestation of power. So long as one lives in one's home, one's desire to become a monk remains intense. But how long do good intentions prevail after one has become a monk? (Keeping silence for a while) Regular study, special care of parents, marriage, etc., are obstructions, and consequently one struggles harder to overcome them. But when one renounces home, one thinks that the goal has been reached and struggles no more. Take an embankment for instance. Water presses hard to break away as long as there is the embankment. But when it finds a way out, it is spread all over. Nothing is left of that force. Being scattered all over, the concentrated force is lost.

DISCIPLE: It may also stop without forcing a way out and thus lose all its strength.

SWAMI: Yes, sometimes it is actually so. But that is rare. Power seeks channels for its manifestation and gathers force from obstructions. The mantra that you have received—why not repeat it regularly? But this, none of you will do. Follow your guru's instructions. How many of you do it? At most one sits for half an hour—and that in not too calm a mood—and tells the beads as if it is a drudgery and then gets up. This won't help. Who has been following the rules after receiving the mantra? One nowadays takes a fancy for *sannyasa* (monasticism). This seems to be your usual way. *Sannyasa* means an inward unfoldment. Mere formality cannot go far. Is there anything in formality? One must make oneself fit for *sannyasa*. This requires an inward growth. How many people work in a true spirit? Working like a day laborer—what can it pay? The spirit that we are serving—Narayana, God in human forms, and the *Ishta* in all men—is what counts in the long run.

DISCIPLE: Is it possible to visualize the *Ishta* and external objects at the same time?

SWAMI: The idea is that the *Ishta* is visible in everything, as the Master himself saw the Divine Mother in everything. (After a pause) Strive, strive, exert yourself.

DISCIPLE: Maharaj, we do not see God. How can we love Him without seeing Him? How can we love a Being who is unseen and whose very existence is doubtful?

SWAMI: Act according to the instructions of the guru. If you can strictly follow what the guru has prescribed for the realization of God, everything will be smooth at last. Meditation comes afterwards. If one fails to meditate, one should go on repeating the mantra very earnestly. Do you follow the guru's instructions? Who practices even half of what the guru has instructed? If you practice, surely you will get your reward. Do you know *puras-*

charana of the mantra? A mantra becomes "conscious" (kinetic) when you repeat it a *lakh* (100,000) times a day. The utterance of the mantra in a proper spirit even one time purifies the mind. Instantly the mind becomes delighted and blissful.

DISCIPLE: Will it do to repeat it a *lakh* of times a day?

SWAMI: That will certainly be very good. Repeat it a *lakh* of times or even ten thousand times according to your capacity. Even five thousand times is good if the mantra is a big one, or even two thousand times if the mantra is very long.

DISCIPLE: Maharaj, it will take five to six hours to repeat the Gayatri two thousand times.

SWAMI: All right, if the mantra is too big, why not repeat it at least a thousand times? One should rise at dawn every day and practice. If the mantra is comparatively small, at first repeat it two thousand times, then slowly increase the number. This will do. No one practices; everyone whiles away his time. Strenuous practice is wanted before you can succeed. Labor hard and success is sure. Everyone finds time for eating and sleeping, but not for spiritual practice.

February 1925

SWAMI: What do you read nowadays?

DISCIPLE: *Adhyatma Ramayana.*

SWAMI: Good. The Master liked it much. Many portions of it he got by heart. He had a wonderful memory. He was a *shrutidhara* of the first order—he could remember anything he heard but once. Swamiji (Swami Vivekananda) was one of the second order, he had to read or hear anything twice and only then he could remember it.

DISCIPLE: Maharaj, how does one get this wonderful power? Is it that their minds are fine or subtle, or is there any other reason?

SWAMI: Certainly. These people have great control over the mind. Whatever they concentrate on gets stuck in their minds at once. It requires great powers of concentration. Whatever they say or hear they remember for years.

(After a short pause): *Shraddha,* or unswerving faith, is one of the "six treasures" (calmness of mind, control over the senses, etc.). What really counts in the spiritual domain is this faith—

faith in the words of one's guru, in the Lord, in the scriptures. The guru has asked me to do such and such a thing; if I follow his instructions, I am sure to attain success; it can never be otherwise. Such burning faith in the words of the guru is what is really required.

What's the difference between a *shrutidhara* and an ordinary man? A *shrutidhara* can focus all the powers of his mind to a point, whereas the mental forces of an ordinary man are scattered and he has not the power to focus them on one thing. The mind of worldly people is divided among many things. If they get married half the mind goes to the wife, and the greater portion of what remains goes to the children, money, property, etc. The little that is still left is scattered over things of enjoyment. It is almost impossible to concentrate such a mind. The Master would compare the mind to a packet of mustard seeds. "If the packet is once untied the seeds get scattered in all directions. How difficult it is to collect them again! Some are perhaps lost forever." But absolute faith makes the impossible possible.

(After a pause): Reality must not be lost sight of. One must have a tight hold over it—the Truth, the only abiding thing in this fleeting world. The Master once told Hari Maharaj (Swami Turiyananda), "You are studying Vedanta. What's the essence of it? Brahman alone is true and the *jagat* (the world) is false. Isn't it? Or anything else? What you require is the essence; throw away everything else." The Master first heard what the great saints of different sects and faiths had to teach, then one day he collected a good number of scriptures, made a garland of them and, having put it on, danced for awhile, and then tore the books to pieces. You get a letter requesting you to send certain things to the writer; when you send them on, you have no need of the letter. The Truth is what we require—the essence of this universe.

October 1926
DISCIPLE: Maharaj, at the time of meditation, I can fix my mind neither on the *Ishta* nor on the image of the guru.
SWAMI: It will be of no avail to say that you cannot. You must practice regularly. Incessant effort is required. There is no other

way out. Every day at fixed hours, in the morning and evening, you are to practice diligently. Keep a portrait of your *Ishta* before you and try to meditate.

DISCIPLE: What if I fail to observe strict punctuality? If I cannot sit to meditate at the proper hour?

SWAMI: There is no harm if you cannot be punctual for a day or two. But you should remember Him and think of Him while engaged in work. Do it.

DISCIPLE: Can the desired object be attained by mere work if *japa* and meditation are given up?

SWAMI: It can be attained provided one works in the proper spirit. But ordinarily it is not possible. Spiritual practices are essential.

DISCIPLE: How many times shall I repeat the holy name?

SWAMI: As many times as you can.

DISCIPLE: Frequently evil thoughts arise in my mind. How can I be saved from them?

SWAMI: One should drive them away resolutely. You have read in the Gita, "The Self is attained by continual practice and renunciation." There is no other way. Surrender yourself to the Lord. Make Him your own and evil thoughts will pass away. It is absolutely necessary to make Him your own.

DISCIPLE: Frequently, even at the time of meditation, *kama* (lust) makes its appearance vigorously.

SWAMI: Never mind. It comes to all. Surrender yourself to the Lord and drive it away. But carefully abstain from such food as irritates the stomach and is not easily digested.

DISCIPLE: What is the meaning of our mantra?

SWAMI: May God who is the creator, sustainer, and destroyer of creation, remove my sorrows. This is the significance of all mantras. Have faith in Him; otherwise even thousands of explanations will be of no use. Pray to Him and love Him.

DISCIPLE: Do *pranayama*, *asana*, etc., help to remove the tendencies of the mind?

SWAMI: No. One may derive some benefit from them. The more you will love God, the more will the mind come under your control.

DISCIPLE: Maharaj, I like to meditate on the guru. The *Ishta* does not come to my mind. So I meditate on the guru. Will it do?

SWAMI: No. Why should you make things so easy? After meditation on the guru, meditate on the *Ishta* as well. But if you feel a special yearning for the guru, you may devote a greater length of time to him. If you cannot meditate on the *Ishta* just think that He is. That also will give you peace.

DISCIPLE: I have heard that the two are essentially one. Why then will it not be sufficient to meditate on one?

SWAMI: No. When you will attain that state, when you will realize the oneness of the two, then alone you can think in that way. Why should you make things too easy?

DISCIPLE: Is *japa* to be practiced with meditation or after meditation?

SWAMI: It is to be practiced with meditation. As you progress you will understand how with the intensity of meditation *japa* stops automatically.

The Literary Beauties of the Vedas

The domain of poetry is vast and wide. In its widest sense it includes everything in this world, every expression in the sentient and insentient universe. The minutest atoms obeying the law of chemical affinity, the huge solar systems obeying the law of gravitation, the all-embracing minds of human beings obeying the laws of love—the highest manifestation of the same force which expresses itself in the laws of chemical affinity and gravitation—all are expressing or trying to express what is within. And this manifestation of nature as the universe is poetry.

What is nature? What is this universe? The breathing out of the Infinite Being; the expression of that ocean of absolute Love, as the Vedas say; the expression (or word) of God as the Bible says: "In the beginning was the word, and the word was with God, and the word was God, and the word was made flesh."

Do you want to find the root of poetry? You will find it in the absolute love, which is the essence of the Deity because the expression of that unbounded love is poetry. You cannot separate the word from God, the expression or manifestation from the Deity, the poetry from that infinite Love.

The *rishis* (seers) of the Vedas told the truth and showed their just appreciation of poetry when they addressed God as the first and foremost poet—the oldest of all poets, who never grows old. He is the poet whose writing is this wonderful universe, the expression of whose unbounded love is the limited love and beauty of this world, in whose poem the rhythm is kept by the sun, the moon, and the stars, whose music is the music of the spheres. The condensation of the nebulous matter into this formulated world, of mountains touching the skies, and seas of unfathomable beds, the development of a tiny seed into a blade of grass or a stately tree, of a child into a man or woman, of the gross attraction of the flesh into sweet love for love's sake—these are not only full of poetry but are poetry in the widest sense. Blessed are they who can see poetry in everything and everywhere for they alone have eternal peace and beatitude. They alone attain prophetic vision, seeing the ever-beautiful present in the heart of everything, the unbounded Love behind every mask and form. Thus every real poet is a prophet, and every real prophet a poet.

In a limited sense poetry "seeks to analyze that essential faculty of human nature, the sense of the beautiful." It is the expression of human emotions. Every sentiment, every idea that touches the human heart and sends a thrill into it through devotion or love, through awe and reverence or fear, through heart-rending separation or the great joy of desire fulfilled after struggle and difficulty—the expression of every one of these emotions in human language is what is known to us as poetry. A genuine revelation of the human heart appeals to people of all ages, however much they may be separated by time or space, racial, national, or a thousand other prejudices. That is why the Vedas appeal to us as genuine poetry, although written thousands of years ago in a tongue which is now almost forgotten. That is why Kalidas's *Sakuntala* or Shakespeare's *Hamlet* will be appreciated as long as language will last. Although widely separated, we are human beings, and the same actions still give rise to the same emotions in all of us, even when we express our feelings differently. Expressions may vary but the essence will always remain the same. The same terms of endearment that the lover whispered into the ears of the beloved on the banks of the

Ganges or that Jumna whispered during the time of Kalidasa hundreds of years ago were used by the lover on the side of the Thames when Shakespeare wrote, and the same things are repeated in our own time. The same fullness of reverence and of awe and of the love that made the Vedic seer thirst after God and helped him to rise to the unclouded vision of the superconscious we also find in the lives of the seers of other nations and other scriptures. In our hopes and joys, our fears and sorrows, our thirsts and fulfillments, we feel and think and act alike. We are one with one another, one with the universe. Therefore, shake off all prejudices; let us enjoy the genuine expression of the human heart, wherever we may find it, in whatever nation or clime; let us seek the essence of everything with reverence; let us see and feel the presence of the beautiful; let us listen for a few moments to that deep and sonorous voice of old by the side of the Ganges, whose songs are still reverberating along the snow-covered peaks of the Himalayas and the shady forests of the plains of India.

The poetry of the Vedas is wholly religious. If the Aryans had any other kind of poetry, it is lost entirely, never to be found again. Never was such an amount of religious poetry composed anywhere in the history of the world. The Vedas themselves provide ample internal evidence that the Aryans of India had evolved a high order of civilization. They were a band of strong, sturdy people, full of faith in themselves and faith in God. The hard winters of the Asiatic plains, where they must have spent hundreds of years in migrations and settlement; the mighty rivers rushing toward the sea, which they must have encountered in their gradual passage to India; the strong whirlwinds in the northern deserts and the mountain passes, and the grand Himalayas rising tier above tier, as if to the very gates of heaven—these overwhelming and sublime spectacles must have contributed to the deep emotions we find in the hymns of the Vedas. With each fresh advance into the plains, new experiences came to those deep minds and were embodied in the Vedas and the Upanishads.

Apart from their religious and philosophical importance, the hymns of the Vedas and the Upanishads have a literary value of their own, unsurpassed by any literature of the kind. They are full of life and vigor, purity and simplicity. In later times, some hundreds of years before the birth of Buddha, the Vedas were classified into four divisions, the Rik, the Sama, the Yajur, and the Atharva. Each of these divisions in its turn was divided into three subdivisions—the Samhitas, the Brahmanas, and the Upanishads. The Samhitas are the collection of hymns. The Samhita of the Rik-Veda alone contains 1,017 hymns, consisting of 10,580 verses. The Brahmanas are prose directions for reciting the hymns and their proper order in the rituals to obtain the full spiritual effect. The Upanishads, the books which express the philosophy of the Vedas, are the last of these subdivisions. They form the foundation on which rests the grandest of all religious philosophies—the Vedanta Sutras and the commentaries on them by the great philosopher, sage, and religious reformer, Shankaracharya.

Sincerity, vigor, and the diligent search after truth characterize the Samhita poetry. The poetry of the Upanishads, by contrast, is full of power and yet filled with peace; concise yet strongly appealing to the interest and emotions. The former is like the language of some inexperienced youth, powerful in its rashness and exuberance of life, while the later is like that of the fully developed man, controlled and chaste and conscious of his own power. In the Upanishads there is the inferior devotion through fear; in the Vedanta Sutras and the commentaries there is that highest devotion that knows no fear, that loves its beloved for love's sake, seeking no other reward, finding in love its own fruition. In the former, God is worshipped because he will reward or punish according to our acts; in the latter the worshipper has found Him within himself as "the Soul of his soul, as the light of his eye," as the beauty in everything that is beautiful. "He vibrates and He does not vibrate; He is far and He is near; He is within all and He is beyond all." "Through every hand He works; through every foot He moves; through every eye He sees; through every ear He hears; through every mouth He eats: He pervades everything."

The Upanishads were called the forest books because they were studied in the forest. In ancient India the life of a man was divided into four stages—the student life, the family life, the forest life, and the monastic life. The sacrifices and rituals of the

Vedas relate to the first two stages when a person was struggling for name and fame and wealth, feeling these are the be-all and end-all of existence. Having fulfilled his duties toward his family and his country, he became more calm and controlled, ready to give his place in the world to others; the bitter and sweet experiences of life had left him wiser and made him thirst for something higher. Then, in Vedic India, he would retire to the forests on the slopes of the Himalayas or by the side of the Ganges to meditate upon the mysteries of life and death. In those days the forests were kept cleared of wild animals by the kings and princes to give the sages the opportunity of simple living and high thinking. There, surrounded by the singing of birds and the murmur of running water, in the calm of night and dawn, he would come face to face with nature and feel himself part and parcel of it.

They dived within themselves until they reached the very root of mind and consciousness through meditation and discovered the answer to the vexing problems of life. They realized their oneness with the Infinite Being and found material and efficient causes of this universe: "From Love Absolute has all this universe come out, in Love Infinite does it live after it is born, towards Love Unlimited it flows, and into It it ultimately enters." Can we wonder why the Upanishads are full of living poetry? This highly poetic mode of living was manifested in the beautiful language of the Aranyakas (the forest books). Yet these books are dim expressions of what they felt, for can language ever equal what is thought and felt? Every expression is a degeneration; the spirit can only be revealed in the letter, and "the letter killeth." Who can know the feelings behind such language as this:

> Thou Sun! Thou hast covered the face of truth by thy golden disc; do thou uncover it to the vision of one who thirsts after true religion. Progenitor and controller of all, thou Sun, withdraw thy rays awhile that I may look at thy blissful form, the true cause of thy power. That form of thine is one with the Infinite Being, and I too am one with Him.

The theme of the poetry of the Upanishads is the expression of the inexpressible, the knowledge of the unknowable, the capturing within the bounds of speech and thought that which lies beyond, the clothing of the Infinite is our poor finite human language. No wonder the song of the *rishis* appears in many places to be paradoxical and incomprehensible. Yet the language used, the imageries employed, bring awareness of the Infinite. Nature seems to stop and lift up her veil as you sit listening to the wondrous song; and the Infinite appears to you in such a real and tangible form that you seem to feel that you can touch It, grasp It, realize It, and make It your own. The song rises higher and higher in cadence, everything seems to melt before your gaze; the earth disappears, the sun seems to grow dim before the ocean of light. You appear to grow larger and larger until you cover the universe. Your little personality vanishes entirely and you are one with the ocean of unbounded Love.

A deep calm and repose settle over you like the spirit moving on the face of the waters, and you feel that nothing can disturb you in this world of the senses; nothing can destroy you; your existence lies beyond the changes of mind and body, beyond death and the grave. You experience the inner meaning of the poet's words:

> It, the knower, neither is born nor does It die, nor was It born in some past time. It is birthless, eternal, ever-existent; old and yet ever new; It is not killed with the killing of the body.
> If the slayer thinks he can slay, or the slain that he can be slain, both of them know not the truth; It neither slays nor is slain.
> It is finer than the finest (atom), greater than the greatest orb; seated deep within the nature of every creature, seeing the greatness and the glory of the Self, through Its grace the self-controlled man goes beyond all sorrow.
> He sits still and yet moves far away. He is at perfect rest, and yet goes everywhere. Who can know that effulgent Being, Who is greater than the greatest, except myself?
> Void of form, yet existing in all that has form; changeless, yet remaining in all that is changeable; knowing that Self, the Lord, the great One, the enlightened man never grieves again.
> That Self cannot be gained by much learning, nor by a keen

understanding, nor by the reading of many scriptures. He whom the Self chooses, by him the Self can be gained. To him the Self reveals His own essence.

The theme of the Upanishads is the Absolute, the Infinite, and only a poet who was also a seer could reveal this glimpse of the Absolute:

> There (where the Self is) the eye cannot reach, nor the speech, nor the mind. We cannot say we know That, neither do we know how to teach That to others. That is beyond what is known and what is unknown. Thus we have heard of It from them of old.
> That which cannot be disclosed by speech, but which has given rise to speech, that is the Self, and not this which thou hast been worshipping; know that. That which cannot be measured by the mind, but That by which the mind thinks, that is the Self; know that.
> Those amongst us who think they know the Self perfectly, they know It not; those who think they cannot know It, they know It.

The one peculiarity of the Upanishads is that they rarely try to express the Infinite in terms of matter, in terms of bones and muscles. Almost all other poets, wherever they have attempted to bring before the reader's mind the vastness of the Infinite, have used material pictures and imagery. The sages of the Upanishads have done just the opposite. Their attempt to convey Infinity has been from another direction altogether. They have done it by denying to it everything that is material. The Vedic singers alone have made the unique attempt of negating every positive idea from the concept of Infinity. That which we see, feel, hear, that which comes under the senses is limited; deny it, go beyond it to find the Unlimited. That which we think, imagine, conceive, that which comes within the domain of our mind is limited by the mind; cast if off, go beyond to find the Infinite. That which comes within the realm of time and space, that is limited by them, stop not there to find the Infinite, but go beyond—this is the way of *neti, neti* (not this, not this) of not positing anything of the Infinite:

> That whence speech falls back, baffling the mind unable to attain, is that ocean of unbounded Bliss. Attaining that, the enlightened man goes beyond all fear.
> Neither the sun appears bright there, nor the moon, nor the stars; the flash of lightning is as darkness, not to speak of the brightness of fire. That shining, all else shines; all else is bright by Its brightness.

The similes are so brilliant and striking that they never fail to carry the author's idea to the reader's mind. Notice the use of the great Indian fig tree, the *Ficus Religiosa* to suggest the oneness of this manifested universe with God, to show that it is established in Him and is part and parcel of Him:

> This is the eternal fig tree (that ever changes its form). Its root is fixed high up (in the unmanifested, the Absolute) and its branches are down here below. It is pure; it is the Deity; it alone is the Immortal. All worlds are contained in it; none goes beyond it. It is that Self, the Deity.

This simile was elaborated later in the fifteenth chapter of the Bhagavad-Gita and may possibly be one of the causes of the reverence paid by the ignorant to this species of fig tree. In speaking of the beginning of creation as the beginning of a cycle, the expression used is "In the beginning when all vibration was hushed . . ." In describing the Deity as manifesting Himself in different forms in the universe, the poet said:

> As the one fire, entering the universe, manifests itself in this form and that form and becomes like unto every form (of whatever it burns), thus the one Self within all things manifests Itself in this form and that form, and appears like unto every form and yet exists outside of all forms.
> As the sun, the eye of the whole world, is not touched by the imperfections of the eyes, being outside of them, so the Self within all remains untouched by the evils and imperfections of the world, being outside of it.

The following passage shows the ultimate union of the individual soul with the Deity: As the rivers flowing into the ocean become one with it, leaving all separate names and forms behind, thus the enlightened, liberated from all name and form, approaches the supreme, effulgent Being."

This simile describes the relationship between the human soul and the Deity: "As from a blazing fire come out thousands of sparks of the same nature as the fire itself, thus, O Beloved! come out the different existences from the eternal and unchangeable Being, and enter into Him again." Here a simile is used to show the difference between the controlled and uncontrolled mind: "Know this body to be the chariot, in which intelligence is the driver, the mind the reins, the sense organs the horses, and the soul the lord of the chariot. The horses are running towards the objects of the senses. The mind and organs of the uncontrolled man are like wild, unbroken horses in the hand of an inexpert driver, while those of the controlled man are like the trained horses of a skilled driver." The famous simile from the Mundaka Upanishad describes the progress of the human soul towards the Divine and the ultimate union of the two, putting the whole philosophy of man in religion in one single picture and a few concise words: "Two birds of beautiful plumage, inseparable companions of each other, are residing in the same tree (of life); the one is busy tasting the fruits thereof, while the other, resplendent in its own glory, cares for none. In the same tree the Infinite Being sits, immersed in His own glory, while the human soul sits, lamenting its imperfections. As soon as the lower bird perceives the full glory of the upper one, it approaches, it goes beyond all misery, it finally becomes one with Him."

The stories of the Upanishads are equally simple and strong in character. Persons and events are described to illustrate the main theme, the religious discourse. Often a character is identified by name and described as the son of another, but nothing more is given of his antecedents or of his father's. Some events are related about this unknown person; a fragment of his life is given along with some few words full of feeling and deep introspection from his mouth. Our curiosity is roused; sympathy and love make us go forward and embrace him as a dear friend, when suddenly the vision vanishes, and we awake with a start with those ennobling words resounding in our ears. Nothing more can be known of the unknown. His footprints remain, but he himself has winged his course like an eagle to the bosom of the Infinite forever.

The Upanishads also give us glimpses of the thought of the people of that time such as this story from the Talabakara Upanishad: Once upon a time the bright ones, Indra and the other gods, became very proud of their victory over the demons. They forgot that there was any power higher than themselves. They imagined themselves to be the lords of the universe, the creators, when suddenly a bright light appeared before their eyes. Dazzled by the radiance, they became unable to see the form of the effulgent Being before them. They held a hurried counsel and sent one of themselves, the fire god, to learn what it was that had dazzled the region with light. The fire god approached and stood before the cone of concentrated light and heard a voice from within the brightness inquire who he was. The fire god answered, "I am Agni, the fire god; I can burn this universe if I like." A few bits of straw were laid before him, and he was told to burn them. He tried his best but failed, and he returned to his friends shamefaced, saying he knew not who the effulgent Being was. The god of the wind was sent next. The voice asked him to blow away those bits of straw. He tried with all his might with an equal lack of success and came back vanquished. Then the greatest of them all, Indra, went into the presence of this Being, but the effulgent One vanished before his eyes, and in his place a beautiful female figure was seen, who taught him that it is through the power of that effulgent Being alone that the gods had conquered. To Him alone belongs all glory. He is the storehouse of all power, the ocean of all light and love.

Swami Saradananda and Girish Chandra Ghosh

Often when Swami Saradananda visited Girish Chandra Ghosh, he urged the dramatist to write about Sri Ramakrishna. His brother disciples, too, frequently told him, "Girish Babu, why don't you write about our Master? Your reminiscences would be precious, and they would surely be published in the Udbodhan. Whatever you wrote about the Master would be a source of inspiration to the world." Girish Babu always listened respectfully to their urging and always he replied, "If Sri Ramakrishna wills it, it will be done. Without him I am nothing."

Eventually he did write a series of articles about Sri Ramakrishna, the first appearing in the Udbodhan under the title, "The Love of a Paramahamsa Deva for his Disciples." He wrote these articles in strong, simple Bengali prose that sang with poetic charm. I have translated and collected them under the title Memories of Sri Ramakrishna.

While working on these translations, I was struck with the similarity of the paths to God taken by Girish Ghosh and St. Augustine. As a young man St. Augustine, too, led a fast life, breaking free of restraint, flinging discipline to the winds. Then, as he recorded in his autobiography, The Confessions of St. Augustine, from across a wall one day, he heard a child's voice saying, "Take up and read." Soon after, he came across a copy of the New Testament lying on a bench in a friend's house, and opening it at random he read, "Not in rioting and drunkenness, not in chambering and wantonness, not in strife and envying, but put ye on the Lord Jesus Christ, and make not provision for the flesh to fulfill the lusts thereof."* These words sank deep into his consciousness. He joined a monastary and through the practice of study, continence, and prayer he became a new man, a saint, and the most scholarly theologian Christianity has produced.

Mysterious are the ways of the Lord. He does transform the lives of those who come to him. I believe God hears the voice of a contrite heart and replies, "Do as much as you can, but when you can do no more, don't worry. Give me the power of attorney. I will do the rest." That is what happened to Girish Chandra Ghosh and, essentially, that is what happened to St. Augustine. In the language of the Bhagavad Gita:

> Though a man be soiled
> With the sins of a lifetime,
> Let him but love me,
> Rightly resolved,
> In utter devotion:
> I see no sinner,
> That man is holy.
> Holiness soon

---

* Romans 13:13–14

> *Shall refashion his nature*
> *To peace eternal;*
> *O son of Kunti,*
> *Of this be certain:*
> *The man that loves me*
> *He shall not perish.*
> IX: 30-31

Memories of Sri Ramakrishna

When the responsibility of writing an article on Sri Ramakrishna fell on me, I thought it would be a very simple thing. But actually, I find the writing extremely difficult. I thought it would be easy, for I have enjoyed his unfathomable love. I have also heard from each and every disciple of his how Sri Ramakrishna showered his infinite love on him. Many a time with enraptured minds, we have discussed that great love among ourselves. Whenever a disciple would recount his personal experiences, a sympathetic chord in my heart would be touched and his experience would become vivid and living in my mind's eye.

A single word of the disciple, a single incident described, would make me feel that I, too, had heard such words of affection. I, too, had seen many such acts of compassion. With a single word the disciple would relive the experience and the listener would feel a participant. But I wonder if my readers will be able to share with equal vividness my own experiences. Shall I be able to convey them in words? Let me ask a question: "Can you describe the warmth of affection which you have received from your own mother?" For myself, I could not. I could only exclaim: "Ah, mother's love, mother's love!" In every act of my mother, in her every glance and movement, what I have felt is beyond my words to describe. Besides, could anyone really understand a mother's love without becoming a mother oneself? Even were such an understanding possible, an understanding of Sri Ramakrishna's love lies far beyond that. A mother's love can be said to fall within *maya*. Usually love prompted by *maya* desires only the worldly happiness of the son, seeks only his worldly prosperity and nothing more. Very often it is seen that if the son, for the sake of spiritual enlightenment, pays no attention to worldly duties, he becomes a source of annoyance to the parents. In spite of his possessing all the good qualities, if the son prefers monastic life to marriage, he becomes an object of displeasure to his parents. They advise him that there is time for everything... that he should attend to spiritual life after discharging his duties to the world in a proper manner. If the boy does not listen to their advice, though they may not say in so many words that their son has gone astray, they will not refrain from telling their friends and relations with a sigh of regret that he is useless and lacking in purpose. There is selfishness in the love of parents. It is seen that the father is partial to an accomplished son. As long as the son is a mere boy and helpless, the parents are unselfish. But most parents expect that they will be looked after and provided for by their sons in their old age. A father's love or a mother's love is very high indeed, but it cannot be said that it is absolutely free from selfishness.

If I stretch my imagination, I can have a glimpse of my parent's love. But the love of Sri Ramakrishna—that immaculately pure and absolutely unselfish love—how can I comprehend it, how shall I portray it in words? Without attaining the state of consciousness, which is free from the touch of selfishness, free from the delusion of *maya*, how shall I understand the actions of a person who has broken the bonds of *maya* and is without faults? If I had attained to that state in which Sri Ramakrishna lived, the state of being totally free from *maya*, and if I had had a disciple, I could then have gained the power of understanding in a small measure Sri Ramakrishna's love. But I don't know whether I would have been able to express it. I may or may not know the story of my own life, but the story of another man's life is a completely sealed book to me. Therefore in this article I shall tell only my own tale, what I felt about the love of Sri Ramakrishna in relation to me. Beyond that I am helpless. I must speak of myself. My listeners, out of compassion for my pitiable condition, must kindly forgive me.

Those who went to Sri Ramakrishna were all gentle, good-natured, and virtuous. Boys like Narendra and the others, who are considered as Sri Ramakrishna's own, visited the Master at an early age. Being drawn by his love, they left their homes and later embraced the life of monasticism in order to carry out his mission. To describe his love for them will hardly give a correct picture of his love. His affection for these boys, who were pure and spotless and who had taken shelter in him after renouncing everything for his sake, was quite natural. But I too was the recipient of his love. This seems to me something extraordinary. Sri Ramakrishna loved me unstintedly. This was a proof of the fact that he was an ocean of unconditional mercy and boundless compassion. One of the names of God is "Savior of the fallen." I, as no one else, can bear witness that he deserved that name. Some of those who have been with the Master may be fickle-minded, but in comparison with my fickle and restless nature they are all saints. They may have a few weaknesses, their feet may have slipped a few times, but in comparison with my Himalayan faults, those shortcomings are nothing. From my early boyhood I was molded in a different way. I never learned to walk a straight path. I always preferred a crooked way. In spite of my faults, I was the object of his deepest affection. The manifestation of his love was revealed nowhere so clearly as in my case. The readers will get a glimpse of it from the story I shall tell below.

Sri Ramakrishna gave me refuge at a time when I was torn by conflict and brutal agony of the heart. My early training, my lack of a guardian from childhood, my wayward youthful tendencies—all these conspired to lead me away from the path of spirituality. Atheism was the fashion of the day. Belief in the existence of God was considered foolish and a sign of weakness. In my circle of friends if one could prove the non-existence of God, one received the most extravagant praise and honor. I used to make fun of those who believed in God. After reading a few pages about science, I jumped to the conclusion that religion was pure imagination and myth. Priests had concocted it to frighten people into morality and abstention from evildoing. Wisdom lay in accomplishing one's ends by any means, fair or foul. An unworthy act became ignoble when it was discovered and not before that. It was daylight that made sin. To fulfill one's purpose secretly was a proof of talent. To satisfy one's desire through cleverness was a mark of intelligence. But in a world ruled by providence such intelligence does not last. Evil days are bound to come. When they come, they teach hard truths. I learned from them one big lesson—that there is no way to hide a wicked deed. The saying "Murder will out" is too true, as I learned. But my deeds had already begun to bear fruit. A terrible future was painted in vivid colors on the canvas of my mind. It was not the end but only the beginning of the painful consequences that darkened my destiny. Punishment had begun, but the way to its escape had not yet been found. Friendless, and surrounded on all sides by enemies who took advantage of my misdeeds to ruin me, I felt adrift on a sea of despair.

I thought, "Does God exist? Does he listen to the prayers of man? Does he show him the way from darkness to light?" My mind said, "Yes." Immediately I closed my eyes and prayed, "Oh God, if thou art, carry me across my difficulties. Give me refuge; I have none." I remembered the words of the Gita: "Those who call on me only in the days of affliction, to them, too, I bring succor and refuge." These words sank deep in my consciousness and gave me solace in sorrow. I found the words of the Gita to be true. As the sun removes the darkness of the night, so the sun of hope arose and dispelled the gloom that had gathered in my mind. In my sea of trouble I found the harbor of repose, but I had nurtured doubt all these years. I had argued long, saying, "There is no God." Where would the impressions of these thoughts go? It is said that doubt dies hard. Again I fell victim to doubt, but I lacked the courage to say boldly, "God does not exist."

Desire for inquiry came. Looking into the current of events, sometimes faith, sometimes doubt, emerged. All with whom I discussed my problem said unanimously that, without instruction from a guru, doubt would not go and nothing could be achieved in spiritual life. Nevertheless my intellect refused to accept a human being as a guru, for one has to salute the guru with the words, "The guru is Brahma, the guru is Vishnu, the guru is the Lord Maheshwara, the god of gods, etc." How could I say this to a man like me? It would be hypocrisy. But the tyranny of doubt was intolerable. Terrible conflicts pierced my heart through and through, a condition better imagined than described. Suppose a blindfolded man, all of a sudden, is forcibly dragged into a dark, solitary room and kept confined there with no food and drink. What will be the state of his mind? If you can picture his mental condition, you will be able to understand something of my own. There were moments when I was breathless with emotion. Despair bit through me like a saw. At other times the memories of the past revived and the darkness of my heart knew no bounds. Just at such a time, I saw Sri Ramakrishna passing by our lane to the house of Balaram, the great devotee, and I felt irresistibly drawn to him. However, I shall describe this meeting later.

Sometime previously I had read in the *Indian Mirror* that there was a *paramahamsa*, who was living in Dakshineswar. Keshab Chandra Sen visited him frequently, accompanied by his disciples. With my little understanding, I believed that the Brahmos, who had many strange ideas, had created a fake *paramahamsa*. He could not be the real thing. A few days passed, and I heard that the *paramahamsa* would be coming to the house of Dinanath Basu, an attorney of the Calcutta High Court, in our neighborhood. To satisfy my curiosity and to ascertain what kind of a *paramahamsa* he was, I went to see him. I returned with irreverence instead of reverence. When I arrived at Dinanath Basu's I saw that the *paramahamsa* had come and that he was giving instructions to Keshab Sen and others, who were listening with rapt attention. It was dusk. Lights were lit and they were placed in front of Sri Ramakrishna, but he began to make repeated inquiries, asking, "Is it evening? Is it evening?" I thought to myself, What pretention! It is dusk. Lights are burning in front of him. Yet he cannot tell whether it is evening or not. Thinking I had seen enough of him, I came away.

A few years later Sri Ramakrishna was to come to the residence of Balaram Babu at Ramkanta Bose's Street. High-souled Balaram had invited many in our neighborhood to come and visit the Master. I too had an invitation; so I went. After arriving there, I found Sri Ramakrishna had already come and Bidhu, a dancing girl, was seated by his side in order to sing a few devotional songs for him. In the drawing room quite a large gathering had assembled. Suddenly my eyes were opened to a new understanding of the conduct of Sri Ramakrishna. I used to think that those who style themselves as *paramahamsas* or yogis would not speak with anybody; they would not salute anybody. If strongly urged, they would allow others to serve them. But the behavior of this *paramahamsa* was quite different. With the utmost humility he was showing respect to everybody by bowing his head on the ground. An old friend of mine pointed to him and said sarcastically, "Bidhu has had a previous intimacy with him. That's why he is laughing and joking with her." I did not like his insinuations. Just at this time Sishir Kumar Ghosh, the well-known editor of *Amrita Bazar Patrika,* arrived. He seemed to have very little respect for Sri Ramakrishna. He said, "Let us go; enough of him!" I wanted to stay and see a little more, but he insisted and made me come with him. This was my second visit.

Some days went by. My play, *The Life of Chaitanya,* was being enacted in the Star Theater. I was strolling in the outer compound of the theater when Mahendra Nath Mukhopathyaya, one of the devotees of Sri Ramakrishna, came and said to me, "*Paramahamsadeva* has come to see the play. If you allow him a free pass, well and good. Otherwise we will buy a ticket for him." I replied, "He will not have to purchase his ticket. But the others will have to." Saying this, I proceeded to greet him. I found him stepping down from the carriage and entering the compound of the theater. I wanted to salute him, but before I could do so, he saluted me. I returned his salute. He saluted me again. I bowed my head, and he did the same to me. I thought this might continue forever. So I greeted him mentally and led him upstairs and offered him a seat in the box. After arranging for an attendant to fan him, I returned home, feeling indisposed. This was my third visit.

Before I narrate my fourth visit I must tell you the condition of religion that prevailed in the country at that time. During my school days those who were called Young Bengal were the first products of Western education in Bengal. The majority of them were materialists. A small minority had been converted to Christianity; some of them accepted the creed of Brahmo Samaj; few of them had any respect for Hinduism; orthodox Hindus were bitterly torn by sectarianism. Rivalry between Shaktas and Vaishnavas was strong. Vaishnavism was divided into many sects, each contending for supremacy over the other. Moreover there were other faiths prevalent at the time; each condemned the followers of the other faiths to the darkness of hell. Added to this, many Brahmin priests were degenerate, ignorant of their own scriptures, and not even familiar with the formalities of religion.

The youths of the day, having studied a few pages of English, became iconoclasts. The materialists were considered the most enlightened people on earth because of their erudition and scholarship; the sign of scholarship was not to believe in God. But now and then among ourselves we would speculate about the existence of God, and occassionally I attended the services of the Brahmo Samaj. I doubted God's very existence. If he existed, which religion should I follow? I argued much, deliberated much, but found no solution. Thus I passed fourteen long years in a fog of gloom.

Then came evil days that allowed me no rest. There was darkness within, there was darkness without—darkness everywhere. I thought, Is there any escape? I have seen people taking refuge in Taraknath when they suffer from some incurable disease. My condition too was very serious. To get release from my trouble seemed almost impossible. Would it do me good to pray to Taraknath Shiva, the protector of his devotees? Let me test it! I made an honest attempt to resign myself to the will of the Lord. My attempt was successful. I began to believe that God was not unreal.

I was saved from the danger of doubt, but was this the way to ultimate salvation? I was uncertain which way to take. I had seen the glory of Taraknath. Why not call on him again? Gradually faith in God began to grow in me, but they said that no liberation is possible without a guru. Furthermore, I was told that one must look upon the guru as God. The very idea was revolting to me, for nothing seemed more blasphemous than to think of man as God. I must trudge on alone without a human guru. I would pray to Taraknath. Let him be my guru. I had heard of some people to whom the Lord had appeared as guru in a vision and who thus received their spiritual instruction without a human intermediary. If he would shower such grace on me, I would be saved. Otherwise I was helpless. But I had not seen Taraknath.

What should I do then? Let me chant his name in the morning, and then see what happens.

I became acquainted with a painter who was a Vaishnava. I don't know if it was true or not, but he told me, "I offer food to the deity every day and I am convinced by certain signs that he accepts it. Unless one is initiated by a guru, the deity will not accept the offering." My mind became restless. I took leave of him, went to my room, closed all the doors, and began to weep.

Three days later I was sitting on the porch of a friend's house when I saw Sri Ramakrishna slowly approaching, accompanied by Narayana and a couple of other devotees. No sooner had I turned my eyes toward him than he saluted me. I returned his salute. Then he went on. For no accountable reason my heart felt drawn towards him by an invisible string. As soon as he had gone a short distance, I felt an urge to follow him. I could not keep calm, for the attraction I felt was not of this earth; it was something for which no former experience had ever prepared me; it was something unique, which no words could describe. Just at that moment a person whose name I do not recall brought me a message from him and said, "Sri Ramakrishna is calling you." I went.

Sri Ramakrishna went on to Balaram's, and there I followed him. Balaram was lying on a couch, seemingly ill. The moment he saw Sri Ramakrishna he got up quickly and with great reverence prostrated himself before him. After an exchange of a few words with Balaram, Sri Ramakrishna suddenly exclaimed, "I am all right, I am all right." So saying, he went into a state of consciousness that seemed very strange to me. Then he remarked, "No, no, this is not pretense, this is not pretense." He remained in this state for a while and then resumed his normal state. I asked him, "What is a guru?" He answered, "Do you know what the guru is? He is like a match-maker. A match-maker arranges for the union of the bride with the bridegroom. Likewise a guru prepares for the meeting of the individual and his beloved, the divine spirit." Actually, he did not use the word match-maker, but a slang expression, more forceful. Then he said, "You need not worry. Your guru has already been chosen." I asked, "What is the mantram?" He replied, "The name of God." And as an example he told the following story.

"Ramanuja used to bathe in the Ganges early every morning. A weaver by the name of Kavir was lying on one of the steps leading into the water. Ramanuja's feet accidentally touched the body of Kavir. Being conscious of the divine presence in all beings, Ramanuja exclaimed the word *Rama*. On hearing this name from the lips of a holy man, Kavir took it to be his mantra, and by chanting it, eventually realized God."

The talk drifted to the theater, and Sri Ramakrishna said, "I liked your play very much. The sun of knowledge has begun to shine upon you. All the blemishes of your heart will be washed away. Very soon devotion will arise to sweeten your life with profuse joy and peace." I told him that I had none of those qualities and that I had written the play only with the idea of making some money. He kept quiet. Then he said, "Could you take me to your theater and show me another play of yours?" I replied, "Very well, any day you like." He said, "You must charge me something." I said, "All right, you may pay eight annas." Sri Ramakrishna said, "That will allow me a seat in the balcony, which is a very noisy place." I answered, "Oh, no, you will not go there. You will sit in the same place where you sat last time." He said, "Then you must take one rupee." I said, "All right, as you please." Our talk ended.

Soon after this, Haripada and I saluted Sri Ramakrishna and left Balaram's house. "What do you think of him?" Haripada asked me. I replied, "A great devotee." My heart was filled with unspeakable joy, for it seemed as though my search for a guru had ended. Had not Sri Ramakrishna said that my guru had already been chosen?

Looking back at my former objections to a guru, I understood the pride and vanity which had lain behind my rationalizations. I had thought, "After all, the guru is a man. The disciple is also a man. Why should one man stand before another with folded palms and follow him like a slave?" But time after time in the presence of Sri Ramakrishna my pride crumbled into dust. Meeting me at the theater, it had been he who first saluted me. How could my pride remain in the presence of such a humble man? The memory of his humility created an indelible impression on my mind.

A few days after my visit with him to Balaram's I was sitting in the dressing room of the theater when a devotee came to me in a hurry and said with some concern, "Sri Ramakrishna is here in his carriage." I replied, "Very well. Take him to the box and offer him a seat." But the devotee answered, "Won't you come to greet him personally and take him there yourself?" Nevertheless, I went. I found him alighting from the carriage. Seeing his serene and radiant face, my stony heart melted. I rebuked myself in shame, and that shame still haunts my memory. To think that I had refused to greet this sweet and gentle soul! Then I conducted him upstairs. There I saluted him, touching his feet. Even now I do not understand the reason, but at that moment a radical change came over me and I was a different man. I offered him a rose, which he accepted. But he returned it again, saying, "Only a god or a dandy is entitled to flowers. What shall I do with it?"

Sri Ramakrishna came into a special room on the second floor of the Star Theater, which was intended for the visitors of the dress circle to sit in during the concert. A good number of devotees joined him. He started conversation with me, speaking of several things. I felt a spiritual current passing through my body from foot to head and head to foot. All of a sudden, Sri Ramakrishna lost consciousness and went into ecstasy. In that mood he was playing with a young devotee. Many years ago I had heard some slandering remarks against him, made by a very wicked man. Suddenly, I remembered his words, and at that moment, Sri Ramakrishna's ecstasy was broken and his mood changed. Pointing towards me, he said, "There is some crookedness in your heart." I thought "Yes, indeed. Plenty of it—of various kinds." But I was at a loss to understand which kind he was particularly referring to. I asked, "How shall I get rid of it?" Sri Ramakrishna replied, "Have faith!"

Time rolled on. I went to the theater at three o'clock in the afternoon. I saw on my desk a slip of paper with a note that Sri Ramakrishna would be going to Ramachandra Dutta's house at Madhu Ray's Lane, Calcutta. After reading that note, I felt in my heart the same kind of strong urge to go to meet him as I had felt on that day when I saw the Master coming while I was sitting on the porch of a friend's house at the crossing of the roads in our neighborhood. I was eager to go. But again I considered,

"Should I go to a stranger's house without an invitation?" But the pull of the invisible string was strong. I had to go. I went as far as Anath Babu's market, and stopped; then I thought again, "No, I must not go." But I was helplessly drawn. I would go a few steps and then stop. I hesitated even after coming very near to the house of Ramachandra. It was evening when at last I reached the gate. Ramachandra was sitting there, and he ushered me in. Sri Ramakrishna was dancing in ecstasy in the courtyard. Someone was singing accompanied by a drum. The devotees were dancing in a circle around Sri Ramakrishna. The words of the song were: "Nadia is shaken by the surging waves of divine love emanating from the heart of Gauranga." The courtyard seemed a sea of bliss. Tears filled my eyes. Sri Ramakrishna suddenly became still. He was absorbed in samadhi. The devotees began to take the dust of his feet. I wanted to do the same, but I could not, as I was shy. I was thinking what others might say if I went to Sri Ramakrishna and took the dust of his feet. No sooner had this thought crossed my mind than Sri Ramakrishna, coming down from samadhi, began dancing again. While dancing he came before me and stood still, once more absorbed in samadhi. Now there was no longer any hesitation on my part; I took the dust of his feet.

After the music stopped, Sri Ramakrishna sat down in the drawing room. I followed him. Then he began to talk to me. I asked him, "Will the crookedness go out of my heart?" He said, "Yes, it will go." Again I asked him the same question, and he gave the same reply. I repeated it once more, and he said the same thing. But Manomohan Mitra, an ardent devotee of his, said to me rudely, "Enough. He has already answered you. Why do you bother him again?" I turned towards him to answer sharply, for no one who criticized me ever escaped the lash of my tongue. But I controlled myself, thinking, "Manomohan must be right. He who does not believe when told once will not believe even if he is told a hundred times." I bowed down before Sri Ramakrishna and returned to my theater.

One night, in a gay and drunken mood, I was visiting a house of prostitution with two of my friends. But suddenly I felt an urge to visit Sri Ramakrishna. My friends and I hired a carriage and drove out to Dakshineswar. It was late at night, and everyone was asleep. The three of us entered Sri Ramakrishna's room, tipsy and reeling. Sri Ramakrishna grasped both my hands, and began to sing and dance in ecstasy. The thought flashed through my mind—Here is a man whose love embraced all, even a wicked man like me, whose own family would condemn me in this state. Surely this holy man, respected by the righteous, is also the saviour of the fallen."

After these meetings with Sri Ramakrishna I began to wonder: "Who is this man who speaks to me with such intimacy and makes me feel that he is my very own? No longer do I fear my sins, for I feel sure he would not condemn me. Though he seems to know me through and through, a confession might do me great good. I must take shelter at his feet, for he alone can bring me peace."

I went to Dakshineswar. I found Sri Ramakrishna seated on the southern porch of his room. He was talking with a young devotee named Bhavanath. I prostrated myself before Sri Ramakrishna and mentally recited the verse "The guru is Brahma, the guru is Vishnu, the guru is the Lord Maheshwara, the god of gods." He said, "I was just talking about you. And if you don't believe me, ask Bhavanath!"

After a while he started to give me some spiritual advice. I stopped him, saying, "I won't listen to any advice. I have written cartloads of it myself. It doesn't help. Do something that will transform my life." Hearing these words, Sri Ramakrishna was highly pleased. Ramlal, his nephew, was present. Sri Ramakrishna asked him to recite a particular hymn, "Go into solitude and shut yourself in a cave. Peace is not there. Peace is where faith is, for faith is the root of all." I saw a smile playing on the lips of Sri Ramakrishna, and I felt at that moment that I was freed from all impurities. And at that moment, my arrogant head had bowed low at his feet. In him I found my sanctuary and all my fear was gone. I prostrated myself before him and was about to return home. He followed me as far as the northern porch. There I asked him, "Now that I have received your grace, am I to continue the same kind of work that I have been doing?" Sri Ramakrishna replied, "Yes, why not?" From his words I understood that my connection with the theater would not hurt my spiritual life.

My heart was filled with joy. I felt as if I were born anew. I was a totally changed man. There was no more doubt or conflict in my mind. "God is real. God is my sanctuary; I have found my refuge in this godman. Now I can easily realize God." Thoughts like these cast their spell on me night and day. In waking or in dreaming, the same mood persisted: "Fearless am I! I have found my very own. The world can no longer bind me, for even the greatest fear, the fear of death, is gone."

Meanwhile, I would hear from various devotees that the Master had spoken affectionately of me. If anybody would criticize me, Sri Ramakrishna would say, "It is not true. You do not know. He has tremendous faith."

Sri Ramakrishna would come to the theater now and then to visit me, bringing some sweets for me from Dakshineswar. He would first taste them and then give them to me. Immediately my mood would change, and I would feel like a little child, fed by a loving parent.

One day when I arrived at Dakshineswar, Sri Ramakrishna was just finishing his noonday meal. He offered me his dessert, but as I was about to eat it, he said, "Wait, let me feed you myself." Then he put the pudding into my mouth with his own fingers, and I ate as hungrily and unselfconsciously as a small baby. I forgot that I was an adult. I felt I was a child of the Mother and the Mother was feeding me. But now when I remember how these lips of mine had touched many impure lips, and how Sri Ramakrishna fed me, touching them with his holy hand, I am overwhelmed with emotion and say to myself, "Did this actually happen? Or was it only a dream?" I heard from a devotee that Sri Ramakrishna saw me as a little baby in a divine vision. And whenever I was with him, I would actually feel like a child.

Although I had come to regard Sri Ramakrishna as my very own, the scars of past impressions were not so easily healed. One day, under the influence of liquor, I began to abuse him in the most unutterable language. The devotees of the Master grew furious, and they were about to punish me, but he restrained them. Abuse continued to flow from my lips in a torrent. Sri Ramakrishna kept quiet and then silently returned to Dakshineswar. There was no remorse in my heart. As a spoiled child might carelessly berate his father, so did I abuse Sri Ramakrishna without any fear of punishment. Soon my behavior became common gossip, and I began to realize my mistake. But at the same time, I had so much faith in his love that I did not fear for a moment that Sri Ramakrishna could ever desert me.

Many of the devotees wondered why the Master put up with all my wickedness, and suggested that he sever all connection with me. Ramachandra Dutta alone pleaded in my behalf, saying to him, "Sir, he has worshipped you with abuse, according to his nature. The serpent Kaliya asked Lord Krishna, 'Since you have given me poison, how can I offer you nectar?'" Sri Ramakrishna said, "Just listen to what Rama says," But as the others still continued to condemn me, the Master said abruptly, "Get me a carriage. I must go to visit Girish!" My affectionate spiritual father then came to my house and blessed me by His presence.

As the days passed on I began to feel more and more remorse for my conduct toward this gentle holy man who was the very soul of love. Thinking of the other devotees who worshipped him with adoration, I was full of self-reproach. It was in this state of depression that Sri Ramakrishna found me a few days later, and in an ecstatic mood he said, "Girish Ghosh, don't worry. People will be amazed at your transformation."

From my early childhood it had been my nature to do the very thing that I was forbidden to do. But Sri Ramakrishna was a unique teacher. Never for one moment did he restrict me, and that in itself worked like a miracle in my life. Whenever any lustful thought would arise in my mind, it would quickly fade. My head would bow low before Brahman and Shakti, and Sri Ramakrishna would appear in my mental vision. Behind the degenerate words and actions of worldly people, I felt the eternal play of God. Again, it was my habit to tell occasional lies. Though Sri Ramakrishna was very strict with regard to truthfulness and would not allow anyone to tell an untruth even in fun, when I approached him to confess my guilt, he replied, "You need not worry. Like myself, you are above truth and falsehood." Yet afterwards, when a thought of telling a lie arose in my mind, the mental image of Ramakrishna would again appear before me, and no untruth could escape my lips.

Sri Ramakrishna has taken full possession of my heart and bound it with his love. But such a love cannot be measured by any earthly standard. If I have acquired any virtues, it is not through my own efforts, but solely due to his grace. He literally accepted my sins and left my soul free. If any of his devotees would speak of sin and sinfulness, he would rebuke him saying, "Stop that. Why talk of sin? He who repeatedly says, 'I am a worm, I am a worm' becomes a worm. He who thinks, 'I am free, I am free,' becomes free. Always have that positive attitude that you are free and no sin will cling to you."

The significance of the word *guru* has dawned on me gradually. It was a slow process. But its effect was deeply penetrating. Now I have realized that the guru is everything. He is my all in all. Through him my life has been blessed. To this redeemer of my soul I have paid little homage. In a drunken state I have abused him. When given the opportunity to serve him, I have ignored it. But I have no regrets. In my attempts to escape all discipline I found myself disciplined without knowing it. Such is my guru's grace—an infinite ocean of mercy, not conferred because of merit, nor withheld because of sin, but lavished on saint and sinner alike. With a love transcending reason, he has given me sanctuary, and I have no fear. Hail Sri Ramakrishna!

Other Reminiscences of Swami Saradananda

Swami Nikhilananda's Reminiscence

I believe it was in 1916 that I had the good fortune of first meeting Swami Saradanandji Maharaj either at the Belur Math or the Udbodhan. For several years I had cherished a deep yearning to meet a direct disciple of Sri Ramakrishna. As I lived in East Bengal this longing was not fulfilled. But, in the winter of 1915 when Sri Maharaj Swami Brahmanandaji visited Dacca, where I was a student, in company of Swamis Premanandaji, Sankaranandaji, Ambikananadaji, Madhavanandaji, Mohin Babu (brother of Swamiji) and several other members of the Ramakrishna Order, this dream was fulfilled. I earnestly requested Baburam Maharaj's permission to visit the Belur Math during the vacation of 1916. He graciously gave his consent. I was given the privilege of spending some time at the Math. During that period I must have met Swami Saradanandaji, but I do not recall any particular conversation with him.

In 1916 I was arrested for my association with the Bengal Revolutionary movement and put in a concentration camp for about two years. I was released in 1918, just before the first World War was over. I came to Calcutta and went to the Udbodhan to pay my respects to Holy Mother. She had not been keeping well and no visitors were allowed. Either Swami Arupananda or Swami Anubhavananda spoke to Swami Saradanandaji about my eager desire to take the dust of Holy Mother's feet and the Swami graciously gave his permission, asking me to spend only a few minutes with her. One of the Mother's disciples, Surendra Kar of Vishnupur, who had been my fellow detainee at Kagdwip had committed suicide, unable to bear the restrictions of the concentration camp. When I told Holy Mother this sad incident she said in an anguished voice: "O Lord, how long will you put up with the iniquities of the present Government?" At that time I was on the staff of the Smrita Bazar Patrika and lived at Baghbazar. Generally on Tuesdays and Saturdays I visited the Udbodhan to pay my respects to Holy Mother and to Swami Saradanandaji. I do not remember any special conversation with the Swami during those visits. During that period I would visit Sri Maharaj as often as I could at the house of Balaram Bose.

In the summer of 1921 I went to Mayavati with Swamis Suddhananda, Madhavananda and Vireswarananda as a guest of the Ashrama. Swami Yatiswarananda joined us later, and became the editor of the *Prabuddha Bharata*. After several weeks, Swami Madhavanandaji one day asked me to write an English life of Sri Ramakrishna as there was no complete life of the Master available at that time. There were many non-Bengali speaking devotees of the Master not only in India but also abroad. All my pleas about my inability for such a task were brushed aside. I then drafted the manuscript, which was thoroughly revised by Swami Madhavanandaji. Most of the material of the manuscript was taken from Swami Saradanandaji's classic work, the *Ramakrishna Lila Prasanga*, which did not contain, however, the Master's life at Cossipore Garden. I collected that material from several Bengali books. The manuscript was completed in 1923, I believe. I came down to Calcutta in order to read the last chapter to Swami Saradanandaji for any necessary correction. Two things I recall in this connection. In one place I had mentioned that the Master referred to Swami Saradanandaji as the embodiment of Ganesha. I think this was due to my pure imagination because of the fact of the Swami's having written his classic *Lila Prasanga*, a true landmark in the Bengali literature. The Swami corrected me. He said that Sri Ramakrishna had asked him to regard himself as Sri Ramakrishna's sakti. The other incident was about the dying moments of the Master. I wrote that the disciples present in the room had plunged into a sea of sorrow. The Master's body was a mere skeleton covered with skin. Sannyal Mahasaya (Vaikuntha Nath Sannyal) said that when the Master breathed his last the whole room was filled with a celestial light. The Swami, who was also a matter-of-fact man and disliked any unnecessary emotion, said that they did not see any light as all of them were grief-stricken. I remember another incident which he told me. On the Kalpataru day, many of the disciples who were in the Cossipore Garden were in ecstasy as the Master bestowed upon them His blessings. I asked Swami Saradanandaji what he was doing at that time and whether he had witnessed the great event. He said, in a matter of fact way that he was tidying the Master's room and saw the incident through the window but he did not feel like going there because such an experience was not at all new to him.

When the life of Sri Ramakrishna was published, Swami Madhavanandaji asked me to personally present the first copy to Swami Saradanandaji. We both went to the Udbodhan. It happened to be the Swami's birthday. He was pleased to see the book and said that he himself had desired to write an English biography of the Master, who evidently had wanted the book to be written by someone else.

At Mayavati I often listened to the senior Swamis telling of the rare blessings which some of them felt when serving a direct disciple of the Master. Inwardly I felt sad that I had not been fortunate enough to be chosen to live with any of the Master's disciples. I often prayed that I might be able to live with at least one of them. At long last my desire was fulfilled. Swami Madhavanandaji sent me on a tour to Rajputana, Gujerat, Kathiwar and the United Provinces, to give lectures and also to collect funds and subscribers for the Hindi magazine *Samanvaya* which he had recently started. After spending about eleven months on this tour during which I had met a number of Maharajas and other dignitaries, I returned to the Calcutta branch of the Advaita Ashrama which was then located at Sankar Ghose Lane. It was about four o'clock on the afternoon. Swami Madhavanandaji asked me to go at once to the Udbodhan to pay my respects to Swami Saradanandaji who would be leaving for Benares the next evening. Swami Saradanandaji had visited Kathiwar and Gujerat many years before and asked me about my experiences. Suddenly he told me he would go to Benares the next day and would I like to accompany him? I could hardly believe my ears because this was the dream I had so long cherished. But I told him that I should ask permission of Swami Madhavanandaji as I was then a worker of the Advaita Ashram.

He told me not to bother about it and asked Swami Sambidhananda who was to be the leader of Swamiji's attendants, to purchase a ticket to Benares for me. I returned to the Advaita Ashram and reported the matter to Swami Madhavanandaji. He was very annoyed as he had planned to start an ashram at Rajkot with me as its leader. He hurried to the Udbodhan to cancel the plan. Swami Saradanandaji said to him that I could go to Rajkot in January, after Swamiji's birthday.

I accompanied Swami Saradanandaji to Benares with several other attendants. This was perhaps the happiest period of my life. My principal duties were to clean his room and wash his dishes and clothes. We all lived on the second floor of Kiran Babu's house in Benares. The attendants occupied the first room, Swami Saradanandaji and Sannyal Mahasay the middle room and the ladies who accompanied us, the last room. I recall several events that happened during that period. One day one of the ladies who served the dinner gave me two or three luchis and I told her that I could not eat any more. The Swami said: "Look at his stamina. He cannot digest more than three luchis." Then he told us that during the days of their austerities at Rishikesh he used to get seventeen or eighteen heavy chapatis by begging. "How can you meditate if you eat so lightly?" he asked.

One day he asked me to give him a massage. As my hands perspire Swami Aseshananda was asked to stroke his body. It saddened me to be deprived of such a great privilege. One day I was asked to prepare his tobacco. At that time I did not smoke so I did not prepare his tobacco properly. He said to me, "if you want to prepare tobacco properly for me you yourself should learn to smoke." So I stealthily started smoking. After supper the Swami generally enjoyed a few puffs only but I always put a large quantity of tobacco in the clay pot. He scolded me for wasting the tobacco but the next day I put the same quantity in the pot and again he reprimanded me. I asked him to smoke as much as he wanted. He understood then that we were eager for his prasad. After that he would ask me to take the hubble-bubble after he had finished smoking.

One day I said to Swami Saradanandaji that sometimes I felt like going to Rishikesh to lead a contemplative life. He discouraged me with the remark that he himself had lived that kind of life for several years and then became the Secretary of the Ramakrishna Mission after his return from America. Ever since he had been very active in the arduous work of the Mission but he said that he did not feel that his new activities had any less spiritual value than his austerities in the Himalayas. I began to argue and said: "But you had gone to the Himalayas to lead a contemplative life." Immediately he answered: "If you felt the yearning which I felt before I went to the Himalayas you would not have asked my permission. You would have gone without asking me."

Several years later I asked him what should be my main spiritual discipline, should I carry on Swamiji's work or lead a meditative life. I reminded him that Sri Ramakrishna had often told his principle disciples the particular kind of spiritual discipline they should practice. Looking at me for a few minutes he said, "I don't think you should try to practice exclusive meditation. Try to combine work with contemplation."

It was a cold afternoon. There was a drizzle. The Swami had gone to visit the temple of Viswanath. I was alone in the house. One Swami from the Advaita Ashram came to our place and said to me: "Have a bucket of hot water in the bath-room, Swami is slightly rheumatic. It will refresh him to wash his hands and feet with warm water. The attendants of Sri Maharaj always kept hot water for him on cold days for washing his hands and feet." I kept a bucket of hot water in the bath-room. After his return he used the water and and I am sure enjoyed it. Then he asked me who put the water there. I answered I had done so. He asked me the reason for it. I said because it was a cold evening and added foolishly that the attendants of Sri Maharaj always did the same for him during cold days. He became very angry and said: "I see you want to put me on the same level with Sri Maharaj." I felt piqued and went to my room and shut the door. I sat with my back to the door feigning meditation. In a few moments the Swami gently opened the door and asked me in a sweet voice if I would prepare for him a cup of coffee. My anger melted away. Then he gave me a betel leaf to chew. I noticed similar incidents at other times and felt that perhaps that was one of the ways the disciples of the Master gave their blessings to the devotees.

Swami Vivekananda's birthday arrived and a public meeting

was arranged at the Advaita Ashrama, which would be addressed by different speakers in English, Hindi, and Bengali. Swami Saradanandaji would preside. I did not go to the meeting as I was busy with some household duties at Kiran Babu's house. I was boiling milk when one Swami came there quickly and said that the English speaker could not come to the meeting on account of some unavoidable reason and Swami Saradanandaji wanted me to give the English speech as there were some English people among the audience who did not know Hindi or Bengali. I was completely unprepared for the occasion but because of the Swami's order I came to the meeting and told him about my extreme nervousness about speaking in English, but he insisted. I began my talk mentioning the three evil legacies of the British rule in India which Swami Vivekananda wanted to remove. These were "the Bible, the Bottle, and the Battalion." By way of explaining these rather strong legacies I said the Bible stood for the Christian religion, the Bottle for Western materialism and the Battalion for the British military power. I was told that my remarks made quite a sensation not only among the audience but in the whole town. Naturally the few English missionaries present there were furious. They particularly resented my coupling together the Bible and the Bottle. They wrote a strong letter to the head of the local Ramakrishna Sevasram. At the request of Swami Saradanandaji who had read the letter I wrote to the missionary gentleman about the high veneration in which we held Jesus Christ and that I wanted personally to discuss the matter with him, but he was not pacified. However he said he would be glad to see me but any conversation on the subject must be preceded by an apology from me to Christ, whom I had insulted by associating the Bible with the Bottle. Several letters passed between us and then Swami Saradanandaji said to me they were very bigoted Christians and asked me to forget the whole matter.

During the presidential speech I saw Swami Saradanandaji pausing at least three times in the course of his talk for a few brief moments. Later when I asked him the reason for it he said that while he was talking he vividly saw the Master standing there and was overcome.

Here I recall an incident which shows Swami Saradanandaji's wonderful patience. He used to spend a long time in the morning in meditation in Puri and at the Udbodhan. Then he appeared like a statue. One morning Swami Subhananda, the head of the local Sevasram, came to our house when Swami was meditating and said that the Secretary of the Sevasram was very eager to see the Swami. I told him I could not possibly disturb his meditation but he said that the matter was very urgent; furthermore, the Secretary being unwell he could not come to Kiran Babu's house and that the Swami had to go to the Sevasram, which was about ten minutes away. I did not know what to do. I stood at the door of the Swami's room. Sannyal Mahasaya was also meditating, after a fashion, sitting on his bed, right in front of the door. The Swami was seated on his bed on the left side of the room near the wall. One could not see him from the door without craning the neck. As I stood there Sannyal Mahasaya opened his eyes and asked me by a sign what I wanted. I pointed to the Swami. He sternly asked me to go away. But Swami Suddhananda was insistent that the Swami must see the Secretary. After two or three attempts I stood at the door of the Swami's room and said that I must speak to him. The Swami opened his eyes and asked me what the matter was. I told him about the Secretary's wish. He said, "Ah, they won't allow me to meditate peacefully." He asked me to bring in the Secretary. I said that he was unwell and that the Swami would have to go to the Sevasrama. Even now as I recall the incident I feel my heart palpitate at my temerity to disturb the Swami's meditation.

I am active by nature. One day Swami Saradanandaji said to me, "it is good to be active but it depends on several factors. Your health must be good and you must be able to get along with fellow-workers. But suppose you have injured one of your limbs, then it would be difficult for you to work. Therefore I request you to cultivate the habit of reading. Even that is not enough. Suppose you become blind. Therefore it is good that you also practice meditation so that if you cannot read or work at least you can meditate."

At Kiran Babu's house the *Lila Prasanga* was read aloud in the presence of Swami Saradanandaji who now and then answered questions. It was really an unforgetable experience. Generally in the evenings the Swamis and the Brahmacharis of the Sevasram and Advaita Ashrama would come to Kiran Babu's house to pay their respects to Swami Saradanandaji. Most of the time they sat quietly. One day the Swami said: "Why don't you ask some questions?" Still they sat quiet. Then he said to someone: "Ask Nikhilananda to come. He may ask some questions." I remember one day I said: "We have the blessings of the Master otherwise we could not embrace the monastic life. We have your blessings also, but as for myself, I don't have any spiritual experience." The Swami said in reply: "You will feel the effect of the Master's blessings at the hour of death, if not earlier. But if you seek the result now, you must work hard."

There happened in Benares an incident, which together with another incident which took place later, was very significant for me. One afternoon the ladies in the Swami's party went to visit the Temples. They were late in returning. Soon a drizzle started. They had left their clothes on the roof to dry. Swami Sambidananda, our leader, asked me to bring the clothes to the ladies' room. I did not feel inclined to do this, but he said he had lived a long time at the Udbodhan with the Swami and was familiar with the Swami's way of thinking. He would be angry if the clothes got wet. Swami Sambidananda had some pain in one of his legs, otherwise he said he himself would have done it. Reluctantly I went to the roof, gathered up the clothes and put them in the ladies' room. Swami Saradanandaji was seated on the porch and saw the whole thing. He asked me angrily why I had brought down the clothes. I gave as an excuse the drizzle but he wanted to know who had asked me to do so. I kept quiet as I could not denounce my brother monk. I also felt hurt because I thought the scolding was unwarranted. I entered my room, as I had done before, closed the door and feigned meditation. The Swami again opened the door and sweetly asked me to prepare a cup of coffee for him. I learned my lesson, that I should not poke my nose into something which was none of my business. But I shall presently narrate another incident which proves how difficult it is to understand the way of thinking of enlightened souls.

In Benares Swami Saradanandaji did not keep good health. We returned to the Udbodhan. There he was laid up with fever. Dr. Durgapada Ghosh treated him. I had to report to him about the Swami's condition. One day at about 11:00 a.m. Dr. Ghosh came to the Udbodhan and prescribed two medicines which were to be administered depending upon whether the temperature went up or down. The doctor returned home. I took the Swami's temperature which was then very high. I did not know what to do and hurried to Dr. Ghosh's house. Sannyal Mahasaya saw me passing by his house and asked me about Swami's condition. I told him the Swami was running a high temperature. When I reached Dr. Ghosh's house I saw he was resting after his evening meal. I reported Swami's condition and asked him what to do. He wanted me to rest awhile with him and then we would both go to the Udbodhan. I begged him not to disturb his rest but just to suggest the medicine. But he was eager to come. Presently we arrived at the Udbodhan. One of the Swamis asked me not to go to Swami Saradanandaji's room because he was furious with me on account of my having disturbed Dr. Ghosh's much needed rest. Sannyal Mahasaya had already told the Swami about my having gone to Dr. Ghosh's house. But I went with Dr. Ghosh to the Swami's room. No sooner did he see me then he flew into a rage. He sternly rebuked me for this uncalled for anxiety about his temperature and said he would never allow me to come near him again if I ever again acted in such a stupid manner. I was often scolded by the Swami, which at that time I thought unwarranted, in many cases, and even felt mentally resentful, but as I recall some of them after a lapse of forty years, I realize they were real blessings in disguise. Now I wish I had had more of them. Perhaps that was the way the Swami wanted to suppress my ego.

When the Swami felt somewhat improved in health he decided to go to Puri and told me that this time I would be in charge of the party. The day was fixed and we went to the Howrah station to take the train. There were three ladies in the party. I believe many swamis and devotees came to the station to see us off. I was busy arranging the Swami's bed in the second-class compartment which was in the middle of the train. The ladies' compartment was near the engine and ours was in the rear. Remembering the incident about the ladies' clothes in Benares, I did not bother to look after them when we boarded the train. Some of the devotees took them to their compartment. At 10:00 p.m. the train stopped at Kharagpar and I ran to the Swami's room to inquire if he needed anything. He answered in a solemn voice that he did not. Early in the morning the train stopped at Bhuvaneswar and several Swamis of the local Ashrama came to the station. Again I ran to the Swami's room to find out if he needed anything. He asked me rather sternly to go to the ladies' compartment and see what they wanted. I brought them some water. The train finally arrived at Puri at about 10:00 a.m. Swami Sankarananda and a few devotees were at the station to meet us. I packed Swami's bed and arranged the luggage. Swami Sankarananda went to the ladies' compartment and helped them with their baggage. I believe Swami Saradanandaji, Swami Sankarananda and the ladies drove in a car to the Sashinketan where we would spend the vacation. We male attendants with our luggage came to the house in a horse-drawn carriage. I saw Swami Saradanandaji seated in the big living room with several devotees, taking coffee and smoking from the hubble-bubble. I took his luggage to his room on the second floor, opened the suit-cases and arranged his bed under the direction of another Swami who had lived a long time with Swami Saradanandaji. As I was a novice about these things the Swami asked me to make the night bed on a big couch and the day bed on the floor. When everything was ready I came downstairs and told the Swami that his room was ready. We came together to his room and without any apparent reason he scolded me for making his bed on the couch which was generally used by householders. His anger mounted up. His face and eyes showed it. He wanted to know who asked me to make his bed on the couch. For a few minutes I kept quiet and then asked him why he was so upset. I would be glad to bring down his bed to the floor. Somehow I felt that the real cause of his anger was quite different. Then he said: "I am very angry with you. I am surprised at your strange behavior. I cannot look after the ladies. As you know, I have gout. At the Sealdea station you did not at all pay any attention to the ladies. Other devotees took them to their compartment. At Bhuvaneswar you began to fuss about me and it was I who asked you to find out if the ladies required anything. At Puri you did not go near the ladies at all. Sankarananda helped them with their luggage. In Calcutta I told you that you would look after the whole party. If you purposely kept yourself away from the ladies because you are a monk, then you should not have come with me. Suppose your mother or sisters were in the party; would you have neglected them in that way?" I learned my lesson. I believe Swami Saradanandaji wanted to teach me to act according to time, place and circumstance.

Swami Saradanandaji used an ordinary cigarette can for his ashtray. All the articles in his room were not expensive but nice-looking. One day one of his wealthy disciples asked me if he could buy a gift for the Swami's room. I suggested a glass ash tray which cost perhaps half a rupee. I myself bought the article and put it near his bed at night. He saw it in the morning and asked me who had paid for it. I mentioned the disciple's name. He became angry and warned me not to ask householders to spend their money that way. He reminded me that we were monks and should be satisfied with simple things. He insisted that I return the ash tray and get the money back and if that was not possible to get ordinary soap used for washing his clothes. He then explained that he used the cigarette can for an ash tray so that the ashes wouldn't blow around.

At Puri Swami Saradanandaji revealed to me for the first time why he had asked me to come to Benares with him as one of his assistants. The Mohanta of the Emmar Math, a well-known monastery, used to drive to the beach in a beautiful phaeton with some of his attendants. He put on a gorgeous yellow robe and looked like a divinity. I saw the carriage almost every afternoon passing by our house. One evening Swami Saradanandaji was lying on his bed after supper. While I was fanning him I asked whether it was befitting a monk, especially the leader of a monastery, to drive in a beautiful carriage to enjoy the fresh air at the beach. The Swami suddenly became excited and said in an animated voice: "The Mohanta of the Emmar Math is an eminent person. He enjoys much respect and honor from his devotees and disciples. Is it an easy thing to digest honor?" Then looking at me he said: "I have been noticing you since you joined Mayavati. First you wrote the life of Sri Ramakrishna. Then you traveled extensively in northern and western India where you were entertained by several maharajas and other high officials. I heard all this and said to myself: "This young man wanted to be a sannyasin but he began his life in a wrong manner. He started writing books and giving lectures. He has not seen anything of a life of the sadhu. Before long he will be puffed up with vanity like a finger swollen into a plantain tree. He will never know the life of a monk." Then he added: "We at first practiced austerity and then we began to write books and to give lectures. I really felt worried about you. That is why I asked you, after your return from the lecture tour, to live with me, so you could see how a sadhu should live. I am sure you did not understand why I made you one of my assistants in Benares." I was overwhelmed by his compassion. Even now when I recall the incident my eyes become moist.

After the completion of Swamiji's birthday celebration in Benares, Swami Madhavanandaji wrote to Swami Saradanandaji asking him to call me back to Calcutta, as promised, so I could take care of the Center at Rajkot. The swami showed me the letter and asked me what I wanted to do. I felt that he really wanted me to stay with him for some time more otherwise he would have asked me to go to Rajkot. So I said: "I certainly would like to stay with you but if you order me I shall return to Calcutta." He told me to write to Swami Madhavananda that I wanted to stay with him. Swami Madhavananda was evidently annoyed thinking it was not really Swami Saradananda's wish but my own desire that was expressed in my letter to him. So Swami Madhavananda asked Swami Saradanandaji to write to him direct in his own handwriting about what he wanted me to do. The Swami then wrote that he did not feel any particular need for my going to Rajkot. He himself had visited the place many years before. People over there did not need a Swami who could lecture in English. He would rather like my staying with him. Now I realized how Swami Saradanandaji fulfilled my deeply cherished desire to spend some time living with a direct disciple of the Master.

I would like to finish these reminiscenses with another incident. Before we had left for Benares Swami Suddhananda asked him in front of me to finish the Cossipore chapter of the *Lila Prasanga*. He said that he had some notes but he was not well enough to write the article. Swami Suddhananda then said: "You can dictate it and Nikhilananda will write it." He said he would see what could be done. I believe he took his note book with him. As already said, he did not feel well in Benares, so nothing was done. When we were leaving for Puri Swami Suddhananda reminded him about the article and again asked him to dictate the whole thing to me. Then the Swami made the following significant remark: "When Holy Mother was alive I felt a great deal of inner strength and began to write the *Lila Prasanga*. She died and I felt as if all my powers were gone. Then I saw Swami Brahmananda and began to feel strong again. When he died I felt as if my brain was completely paralyzed. I simply cannot finish the book." Then he added: "When I began to write the *Lila Prasanga* I thought I understood the Master. But now I clearly see that the life of the Master is very deep. I was merely hovering over the top branches; the root is far beneath the ground."

There are many other incidents about Swami Saradananda. I often think to myself that if I could have applied even a fraction of his instructions in my life I would have been quite a different person.

Swami Saradanandaji's loyalty and devotion to Swami Vivekananda and the Ramakrishna Order were unique. I heard him say one day that after Swamiji's death, the monks of the Belur Math were naturally depressed and many of them wanted to lead a retired life. Swami Saradanandaji called a meeting of the monks and told them about the heavy responsibilities of the Ramakrishna Order which must be carried out. He asked who among them would be willing to help him, who was the Secretary selected by Swamiji, by devoting themselves to the activities of the Order and who would prefer to lead a contemplative life. He himself volunteered to work for the order for five years. I believe all the monks of the Order, with the exception of one, agreed to cooperate with him. Swami Saradanandaji did not quit the Secretaryship after five years; he carried on the work. After the first Monks' Conference at the Belur Math in 1926 the Working Committee was formed and competent Swamis were assigned various duties. I heard Swami Saradanandaji say that Swamiji had made him the Secretary of the Ramakrishna Math and Mission and he wanted to remain in that post as long as he lived. He asked the members of the Working Committee to carry on the active duties while he would remain as the nominal Secretary. At that time his health and vigour were declining, but he kept his promise.

It will be sheer presumption on my part to write anything

about Swami Saradanandaji's spirituality. He seldom mentioned his spiritual experiences, at least in my hearing. But the inner depths of this God-like man were seen only by the perceptive eyes alone. But even a casual observer could see from his ordinary conduct and way of life, his infinite patience, unhurried activities, unbounded compassion, deep understanding of human nature, total absence of any pretence, child-like guilelessness and unfailing courtesy. He fulfilled his onerous duties as General Secretary of the Ramakrishna Mission with complete self-effacement. Occupying such a responsible post, he had his full share of problems which he faced with wisdom and courage. He had to look after Holy Mother, who practically depended upon him for many things, and also her eccentric relatives. I believe wave after wave passed over him but he remained unmoved. Whenever I think of Swami Saradanandaji I remember the following verse of the Bhagavad Gita. "Not the desirer of desires attains peace but he unto whom all desires enter into as the waters enter into the ocean which is full to the brim and grounded in stillness."

When Swami Saradananda was stricken with apoplexy I was taking the cure for stomach ulcer from Dr. Aghore Ghosh. A telegram gave us the sad news. I hurried to Calcutta and stayed at the Udbodhan. One of his sides was completely paralyzed, but I felt his inner consciousness remained unimpaired. On the morning of his mahasamadhi two Swamis were changing the bed sheet. They needed a third person to hold Swami Saradanandaji on his side. I was asked to help. I sat on the edge of the bed. Swami's body was rolled to one side. I held it there so it would not fall back while they put on the sheet. Suddenly I felt him give me a special blessing, an experience too personal to narrate.

Swami Nikhilananda—April 1, 1966.

Swami Saradeshananda's Reminiscence

By the Lord's grace, I was very fortunate to meet Swami Saradananda for the first time in 1913 and hear from him of the greatness and glory of Holy Mother, Sarada Devi—consort and companion of Lord Sri Ramakrishna—and I became much attracted towards Her, very eager to meet Her, and very earnest to get Her Blessings and Grace.

Once a devotee in low spirits was telling of his deep sorrow to Swami Saradananda. He said: "I am a very unfortunate man—my life is useless—I was born in vain because I could not see Lord Sri Ramakrishna." Swami consoled him saying: "You are fortunate enough; you saw Holy Mother, touched Her feet, got Her Blessings! Lord Sri Ramakrishna and Holy Mother are one and the same entity." The devotee answered: "I have no such faith in Holy Mother and I cannot think of Her as a Divine Incarnation." Swami then admonished him with strong words and asked: "Do you think the Almighty Lord of the universe married a street-begger's daughter?" Hearing his emphatic and convincing words, I became much impressed.

After coming in close contact with Swami Saradananda I was astounded to see his immense faith, intense devotion, and his untiring spirit of service to Holy Mother. Neglecting all his own convenience, bearing all troubles silently, he tried his best to keep Holy Mother comfortable as far as possible. He was very sensitive and alert about allowing a person to go before Her for making obeisance or making "pranams," by inquiring thoroughly about that person's fitness beforehand. He himself hesitated many times when going before Her for his usual daily "Pranams," and asked himself whether it would create any inconvenience to Her. His wholehearted devotion and prostration at Her feet was a thing to be seen!

Once I begged his permission to go to Holy Mother's birthplace—Jayrambati. He told me, if I went at that time, there would be many inconveniences for me, so I should wait for sometime and that I should go there later, at a more convenient time. I said: "Holy Mother told me to go there now!" Looking at my face, smilingly he said: "Often, even I cannot understand whether what Holy Mother says is her wish or my own wish expressed through Her." I became much ashamed because, actually, hearing from me my desire and readiness to go there now—Mother affectionately gave Her consent but only to please me. From that day, I became much more cautious in talking with him—knowing his uncommon penetrative power.

Knowing my intention and my inclination for religious life,

Swami Saradananda kindly advised me to go and stay sometimes at Belur Math. He also wrote a letter of introduction in his own hand to the Swami-in-charge at Belur Math advising him to keep me there for sometime, and then he sent me there: that was the beginning of my monastic life.

Once, after Holy Mother's passing away at the time when the new temple was under construction at Jayrambati, I was staying there as a humble worker, and was suffering very much from malarial fever. My health was broken down very badly, my liver and spleen were enlarged very much, and my body became bloodless and emaciated. I also had throat troubles with constant coughing accompanied by restlessness. Everybody became worried about me, and I became a troublesome heavy burden to all. But, when I went to Swami Saradananda, seeing me in that state, he became very sorry for me and anxious about my condition, and assured me with an affectionate and tender voice that I should stay near him and he would arrange for my recovery, with the best treatment and everything. That very day, a good doctor was appointed, and the best medicine and nutritious food were arranged. His personal attendant Br. Kiran (later Swami Aseshananda) was instructed to look after me, and he, a very kind-hearted man, began to serve me devotedly. Slowly I began to improve, but after a few days, again I got an attack of fever. Then I became disgusted and thinking myself a burden to the noble Swami, I was anxious to leave the place and return to my native village. Knowing my intention, Swami Saradananda became very anxious for me again and he persuaded and insisted that I stay there for sometime more and continue the treatment until full recovery. I came to realize that he was expressing his anxiety for me and making me understand that if I went then to my interior remote village, my birthplace, where a good doctor and medicines were not available, my condition would become worse. My parents and relatives would be in trouble and very distressed. They would also blame the authorities of the Math saying: "Our boy went there healthy; they took hard service from him, and now he has become ill, they are driving him home to us!" Hearing this also from others, I became much ashamed and determined not to leave the place and thought that it was even better for me to die near such a large, kindhearted noble man.

By God's grace and swami's kindness and care, I slowly recovered and regained my health.

In boyhood, we were influenced by the National movement for freedom and progress of the Motherland. Reading Swami Vivekananda's books, we became determined to devote our life to the service of suffering humanity. At the beginning of monastic life that idea was predominant in our hearts. Coming in close contact with revered Swami Saradananda, one day I asked him his opinion of engaging myself in some form of activity for the upliftment of the backward poor people or some other kind of social work. He affectionately advised me first to mould and shape my own character properly, as without a good character, good work of any sort is not possible.

Once in front of him there was a discussion about a popular religious teacher. This teacher used to get ecstatic moods but his character was very bad, scandalous. Many people were attracted to him at first, but later on some of them after coming in closer contact with him and getting to know of his private life, began to circulate the true facts. One of our brother monks even then expressed his appreciation of the teacher's ecstatic moods, although he knew his character to be very bad. Swami Saradananda hearing the monk's praise, began to scold him with strong words. He said: "Do not think that only ecstatic moods indicate a very high state in religious life; pure character alone is the basis of religious life. Without pure character who can retain all these ecstatic moods? Ecstatic moods cannot endure without a pure good character."

Once the authorities of Belur Math decided to send out a young monk for his undisciplined and ill behavior. Disobeying instructions, he used to go out now and then. He came from a respected rich family and was himself highly educated and had held a high post in government service. His appearance was beautiful with a sweet voice and a good manner. When he first joined the order, he was loved by all, but slowly his weaknesses became apparent. He was not happy with coarse food and clothing nor with the hard work and strict discipline of the monastery. He began to go out to rich householder devotees' houses for good food and comforts. He also began to mix with other outside people. Trying to correct him, the authorities warned him again and again but he was unable to correct himself. Then it was decided that he should be sent back to his relatives. For this, the approval of Swami Saradananda was necessary and when the monk was taken before him, I was present there at that time. Hearing everything and seeing him, the Swami was moved very much. His heart melted with compassion, and like a mother, in a choked voice, and with much affection, he told the monk very tenderly, "You stay with me. My boy, where will you go? Where will you go? You stay with me! I will arrange all comforts for you, supply you with everything, there is no more need for you to go anywhere." Seeing Swami's affection for the guilty monk, his eagerness for his welfare and his attempt to correct him by keeping him near, I became overwhelmed and wondered how a man could be so kind and compassionate.

He encouraged me to study and perform spiritual practices, and he gave instructions accordingly. Also, he encouraged me to serve the needy saying, "What you do for your own enjoyment and happiness, that will be the cause of your bondage; but what you do for the benefit and happiness of others, that will lead you to the way of your liberation. I observed that he used to serve the needy neglecting his own comforts—sometimes even risking his health.

At the beginning of my spiritual practice once I sought his instruction, as to which would be more beneficial for me, concentration of my mind in a Divine form or discrimination, i.e., deep thinking on metaphysical finer truths—self-analysis. He affectionately told me that discrimination—and self-analysis would be more beneficial for me.

On another occasion I asked him the real meaning of "God Vision" realization; Is it seeing something with the physical eye outside or feeling something inside our inner self? He said, "It is the realization, feeling something inside our inner self, but you know when we see something with our eye or hear something with our ear, we become firmly convinced about its existence. But inner realization gives us an even greater conviction of the true eternal reality; That is realization—God Vision."

Once, seeing me spending leisure hours in useless gossiping and other activities, he warned me about such indulgences and advised me to utilize my spare time in reading Srimad Bhagavatam. Obeying his instructions, and reading the Srimad

Bhagavatam attentively, I was much benefited. Getting new light of knowledge, many obscure ideas on religious matters were made clear to me. Now, at the end of my life, Srimad Bhagavatam is my constant companion and consolation.

After Swami Saradananda's death, the 27 October 1927 Prabuddha Bharata *contained a fitting eulogy.*

Prabuddha Bharata Eulogy

What the Ramakrishna Mission is today is largely due to Swami Saradananda. The Mission, though it derived its ideals and inspiration from other sources, owes its present articulate form mainly to the endeavors of the departed Swami. It is he who worked at it from its very inception, giving the ideals concrete forms, linking them to the problems of the passing years, till it reached its present advanced state of development. The outside world has learnt to praise its philanthropic activities and its dynamic ideals, but it scarcely knew the man who primarily worked at the details of the machinery.

The Reminiscence of a Grandson of Jogin Ma

This letter was written by one of the grandsons of Jogin Ma, a disciple of Sri Ramakrishna. I have translated it from Bengali for the Western devotees of Vedanta because the letter is written in a simple tone which speaks from the heart. It has a charm and sweetness of its own which is untranslatable.

You have requested me to write to you whether we have discussed any religious or philosophical problem with Swami Saradananda. Although we did not go to him to solve any spiritual problem, still his memory brings to us the image of a person who loved us dearly, felt for us keenly since the day our

Mother had passed away. We have had many opportunities of enjoying his sweet affection and we will never forget them. His personality is bound to come in our talks because he was so intimately connected with us! But I cannot say whether the public will be interested in those talks. Besides, we do not know what spirituality is. We have never attempted to fathom the Swami's spiritual depth or evaluate his spiritual power. My older brother has rightly said, "I never looked upon Sarat Maharaj as a world-renouncing monk. I always thought of him as my mother." One cold winter night when I was sharing the same room with the Swami, he said to me, "Bhulu, the wind is blowing hard and the draught is coming. Will you be able to close the windows?" I replied, "Maharaj, please do it yourself. I am very sleepy." Immediately, he got up from his bed and shut the windows tight. Two events are coming to my memory. Sometimes I narrate them to others. Probably you remember that our Mother died in Benares. After her death we all moved to a house near Kedar ghat. One evening, perhaps you remember, all were out including yourself. I did not go because I was not feeling well. In the meantime the lady who cooked for us came. She needed a helper to flatten the dough. On other days my sister used to help her. Because she was absent and no one else was available, I volunteered to assist her. I was new to the job. I tried and tried but eventually each one began to take a peculiar shape. There was no uniformity. All on a sudden my grandmother (Jogin Ma) and Sarat Maharaj arrived. Grandmother began to tell her beads and was soon absorbed in her meditation. Sarat Maharaj entered the kitchen and enquired, "Hello, Monti, what are you doing?" I replied, "Maharaj, I am flattening the dough for the *chapati* (flattened wheat-bread)." He remarked, "Oh, fool, is this the way to flatten the dough? Each one looks so funny—out of shape and proportion. Give me the rolling pin. I will do the job for you." I was surprised and said to him, "Will you be able to do that? When did you learn it?" He answered, "Do you think I was always like this—the revered Sarat Maharaj, receiving honor and worship from people. At one time I was the cook of the monastery. I used to prepare *chapati* and a few dishes for forty to fifty people everyday." Saying this, he sat crosslegged on the floor with his huge bulky body and began to flatten the dough with the rolling pin until the last one was done, and each one of them looked so beautiful, was in good shape—a sight to see. I stood aside and watched the thing in gaping wonder. I was then only 14 years old.

Another event comes to my mind. When I was a student of the Engineering College at Shivapur, near Calcutta, I came to Udbodhan and said to the Swami, "Maharaj, I have got a scholarship for Rs. 15.00 for my performance at the annual examination." The Swami replied, "Go and relax." Then he called his attendant and said, "Entertain Monti. Prepare tea for him and give him biscuits, sweets and other refreshments for his satisfaction." Again, when I came to him, being unsuccessful in my final examination twice, I said to him, "Maharaj, I have failed," Even then he treated me in the same way as before and said, "Don't worry. Take it easy. Relax." He called his attendant and asked him to prepare tea and serve me with my favorite delicacies. He did not show the slightest difference in his attitude towards me, although the whole responsibility of supporting me during my studies in engineering college was mainly his. A lay devotee of Sri Ramakrishna, who sat next to him, listened to the talk and said, "Well, it all shows that you were quite indifferent to your studies. You were simply wasting your time—doing nothing." To this, the swami replied, "What has happened has happened. No need crying over the spilt milk. Monti, you better go from here and have some refreshments in the next room." Our grandmother, Jogin Ma, from upstairs, cried out, "Sarat, are you listening? Monti has failed again." With an unperturbed mind, which nothing could shake, the Swami answered, "Yes, I have heard, Yogin Ma. What is done cannot be undone. Let us forget about the past and give Monti another chance."

Glossary

advaita (advaita)   Nondualism, nondualistic.

ahamkara (ahaṅkāra)   The ego-sense, created by the knot of ignorance between spirit and matter, is attachment to "me and mine." The interpreter of sense impressions.

ajna chakra (ajna cakra)   *See* CHAKRA.

anahata (anāhata)   The center within the heart in which the yogis hear the unstruck sound called *Om,* the symbol of Brahman. *See also* CHAKRA.

antahkarana (antaḥkaraṇa)   The mind or "inner organ," comprising buddhi, chitta, manas, and ahamkara (which see).

antaranga (antaraṅga)   The inner circle of intimate disciples.

Antaratman (antarātman)   The Atman mixed with mind. The inmost self which is within the psychophysical personality of man. It is called the witness consciousness that remains unattached to all the thought waves of the mind as the silent screen remains unaffected by the patterns of light played on it. The sages designate the soul to be the enjoyer when the Atman is attached to the mind and the sense organs.

Antaryami (antaryamin)   The Indweller that knows everything that goes on within the mind, that gives power to the mind to think and power to the body to function. The immortal inner ruler seated in the heart who fulfills the desires of the sincere devotee.

apta purusha (āpta puruṣa)   An illumined soul. One who has obtained the realization of Brahmin by transcending maya.

aptavakya (āptavakya)   Revealed word, scripture. Words of an illumined soul who has seen the truth and, therefore, are charged with power.

asana (asana)   1. The prayer mat or carpet upon which a devotee sits for meditation at least twice a day—in the morning and in the evening. 2. The posture of the body during meditation—body, neck, and head erect.

Atman (ātman)   The Self, the aspect of God residing in the individual.

avatar (avatāra)   A divine incarnation, a son of God. God descended as man to help man realize his divinity.

ayurvedic (āyurveda)   A science of health or medicine derived from the teachings of the Atharva Veda. (Ayur means the span of life as determined by the healthy condition of the body.)

bhava samadhi (bhavasamadhi)   The vision of God in a transcendental state of consciousness in which the devotee maintains his individuality to enjoy the bliss of his Chosen Ideal. It is said to occur when the kundalini rises to the fourth chakra.

bhakti (bhakti)   Love of God.

bhiksha (bhikṣā)   Alms given to holy men practicing renunciation. Hence the practice of a monk to go out begging once a day for a few hours.

bhuta-shuddhi (bhūtaśuddhi)   Mental purification of the elements during ritualistic worship in which the worshipper offers his three bodies, gross, subtle, and causal, as oblations to the spiritual fire of Brahman and becomes one with the eternal spirit. It is a process by which the coiled-up energy of the kundalini is awakened and roused to travel from center to center until it reaches the thousand-petaled lotus in the head and the worshipper's individual soul becomes one with the universal soul.

bija mantra (bījamantra)   Literally, "seed utterance"; the letter or syllable of the mantra in which the essence of a particular aspect of God is concentrated in the form of a sound symbol. According to Tantric scripture by repeating the mantra with the seed, a spiritual aspirant will be able to purify his mind and ascend to the final goal of realization of God in His personal as well as His impersonal aspect. Seed mantras are not intellectually conceived. They are discovered by illumined souls in an exalted state of consciousness. They have tremendous power if the disciple has faith in the mantra and repeats it with meticulous precision and with sincere devotion, following the direction of the guru who must be an illumined soul.

Brahma-kundalini (brahmākuṇḍalinī)   Universal divine consciousness.

Brahmaloka (brahmāloka)   A heaven or sphere or plane of existence where spiritually evolved souls go after death to live in divine communion with a personal aspect of God.

buddhi (buddhi)   The discriminative faculty in the mind.

chadar (chadar)   A long piece of cloth draped on the upper part of the body as a part of the monastic dress of the Ramakrishna Order and is often used by Western devotees during meditation for warmth and to conceal the rosary.

chakra (cakra)   One of the six centers of consciousness located along the central spinal canal. The seventh chakra is located in the cerebrum. These chakras are often called lotuses symbolically and are said to bloom when the spiritual energy of the kundalini enters them. Located at the base of the spine, the muladhara is the lowest of the chakras. Next in order of ascent are the svadhishthan, the manipura; the anahata, near the heart; the vishuddha, in the throat; and the ajna, between the eyebrows. The sahasrara chakra, located in the brain, is associated with the highest samadhi, the realization of oneness with God.

chandraloka (candraloka)   Lunar sphere, a plane of existence that has less matter and more energy than earthly existence. Swami Saradananda translates it as lunar light.*

chhatra (chattra)   1. Literally, "sheltered," a student. 2. A place where monks are provided with simple free food once or twice a day to allow them to study and meditate.

chitta (citta)   The mind stuff, whose three components are manas, buddhi, and ahamkara (which see), retains the impressions of past experiences and forms the tendencies and character of the individual.

---

*See page 149.

devayana (devayana)   The way taken after death by the individual soul of a person who had lived a spiritual life but had fallen short of final liberation. Literally, the way of the gods.

dharma (dharma)   1. The way of life as determined by one's own past tendencies. 2. Religious duty. 3. The way of truth and morality. (Ethical rules belong to the world of duality. A liberated soul transcends morality but never violates it. To such a person morality becomes spontaneous like the fragrance of a flower.)

Dharma-vyadha (dharmavyādha)   Literally "righteous hunter." A famous hunter who did not kill animals but sold meat as a means to his livelihood. He attained wisdom through unselfish performance of his duties as a worship of God. A book is named after him known as *Vyadha Gita,* which speaks eloquently of him as a wise man filled with the aroma of the spirit.

dhoti (dhoti)   The traditional wearing cloth of a Hindu male that is tied to the waist and allowed to drape downward.

dhyana mantra (dhyānamantra)   The mantra memorized and chanted mentally during the time of meditation on the guru during ritual worship: I meditate on Sri Guru, who is two-eyed, with two arms, seated on the white lotus in my head, clad in white raiment, garlanded with white flowers, and adorned with sandalpaste. He is making the sign which dispells fear with one hand, and with the other hand he is bestowing his blessings on me. He is calm and is the image of mercy. He is smiling, gracious, and is the bestower of fulfillment of the desires of the aspirant. Another version of the dhyana mantra that is often chanted before meditation is: Salutations to the illumined guru who has made it possible to realize that supreme Being by whom this entire universe of movable and immovable objects is pervaded. The guru is Brahma (the creator); the guru is Vishnu (the preserver); the guru is the Lord Shiva (the dispenser); the guru is verily the supreme Brahman. To that illumined guru I offer my humble salutations.

dhyanasamadhi (dhyānasamādhi)   Samadhi through the discipline of raja yoga, the royal path [of meditation].

Gayatri mantra (gāyatrīmantra)   A sacred Vedic mantra: I meditate with an unwavering mind on the effulgent light of that Absolute Being from whom the universe has sprung. May he illumine our consciousness so that we may cross the ocean of worldliness and see His blissful form throughout eternity.

guru (guru)   A spiritual teacher. A spiritual aspirant should seek out for a guru only an illumined soul or one who is well advanced toward that goal, who teaches without regard for fame or wealth, and who can assume the responsibility for the spiritual life of his disciples.

Ishta (iṣṭa)   A particular aspect of God chosen by the guru as the most suitable for the student to meditate upon. Through constant practice of japa and meditation, the aspirant will be able to enter into a state of consciousness where the Ishta will become a living presence to grant the wishes of the aspirant. Ultimately the Ishta will be experienced by the aspirant as merging in Brahman; this is an experience which cannot be described in words.

ishvarakoti (īśvarakoti)   One belonging to a class of eternally free and perfect souls who are born on earth for the good of mankind.

Jagaddhatri (jagaddhātrī)   An aspect of the Mother of the Universe as protectress of the world.

Jagannath (jagannātha)   A name of Vishnu meaning the Lord of the Universe.

jagat (jagat)   The universe of name and form which is in a constant flux. Anything that belongs to the world of time, space, and causation comes under the category of jagat or the universe of becoming. It also means birth, death, and rebirth which moves like a wheel in an unending process. Buddha called it samsara.

japa or japam (japa)   The practice of repeating a name of God or one's mantra.

jiva (jīva)   The individual soul or the apparent self which has forgotten its true nature due to maya; its true nature is Brahman—eternally pure and perfect.

jivanmukta (jivanmukta)   One who has attained freedom from the bonds of maya by identifying himself with Brahman but still lives in the body doing good for all mankind as an instrument of God. He teaches not by speech alone but by his intense purity of character and a heart overflowing with love and compassion for the suffering of mankind.

jivatman (jīvātman)   The Atman manifesting Itself as the individual self.

kama (kāma) 1. Desire. 2. Romantic love. 3. Lust.

karma (karman) The chain of cause and effect operating in the universe. The sum of the consequences of an individual's actions in this and previous lives; the consequence of an act.

karmayogin (karmayogin) A spiritual aspirant who has chosen the path of work (karma yoga) as a means of realizing God.

kripa (kṛpā) God's grace.

kumbha mela (kumbha mela) A special festival, perhaps started by Shankara, in which monks and devotees congregate to take baths in the holy river and to discuss matters of philosophy and religion for the edification of their inner lives.

kundalini (kuṇḍalinī) The coiled-up spiritual energy lying dormant at the base of the spine. Spiritual practices such as japa and sincere devotion to God awaken this energy and stimulate it to rise up through six chakras, or centers of consciousness, which are located in the spinal canal. Through this process higher types of spiritual experiences emerge and finally when the kundalini reaches its final destination, the sahasrara chakra, the individual soul attains oneness with the universal soul in nirvikalpa samadhi.

Kuthi (kuṭhi) Residential quarters of the proprietors of the temple at Dakshineswar.

kuthir (kuṭir) A Bengali word for a small hut built on a hill-top or bank of a river where monks live away from the noise of a crowded city for a life of contemplation.

lakh (lakṣa) One hundred thousand.

madhura-bhava (madhurabhāva) A form of spiritual practice in the path of bhakti in which devotees look upon the Ishta as their beloved. To attain success in this path the aspirants must guard themselves from all deceptions of the mind and lead pure lives, free from the slightest taint of the world. Sri Ramakrishna practiced it and achieved wonderful results, calling this mood the culmination of all the moods in the path of devotion.

manas (manas) The recording faculty of the mind. Manas also carries out the orders of the will through the body.

manes   Ancestors. From Latin *manes,* the spirits of the dead. Hence, as a symbol of respect and to keep their memory alive, oblations to one's forefathers.

mantra or mantram (mantra)   A name of God, usually combined with a bija (seed)—a sound symbol of God—and possibly a devotional phrase, prayer, or form of address. See also bija mantra, dhyana mantra, and Gayatri mantra.

maya (māyā)   Brahman's power, the creative aspect of God (*See also* SHAKTI); the cosmic illusion that veils Brahman from man's eyes.

meru chakra (meru cakra)   The muladhara chakra; *see also* CHAKRA.

nadis (nādī)   Nerves. The subtle "veins" through which the vital energy circulates, which can be seen through the yogic eye or through the inner eye of wisdom.

nadi-shuddhi (nādīśuddhi)   Purification of the blood and nervous system through the method of self-control, repetition of the mantra, and the daily practice of meditation according to the instructions of a qualified guru.

neti (na + iti)   A method of obtaining discrimination by recognizing that everything changes and is illusory but God: neti, neti—not this, not this, only God is real, for He is changeless.

nirguna (nirguṇa)   Without attributes, pure.

Nirguna Brahman (nirguṇa brahman)   The unconditional Absolute; Brahman without attributes.

nirvana (nīrvaṇa)   Spiritual enlightenment or illumination; absorption in God.

nirvikalpa samadhi (nirvikalpasamādhi)   The supreme transcendental state of consciousness in which the spiritual aspirant becomes completely absorbed in Brahman so that all sense of duality is obliterated. The aspirant has gone beyond the realm of time, space, and causation; his soul has merged in satchidananda—existence, knowledge, and bliss absolute. This state has been described in the Upanishads: "There the sun shines not, nor the moon, nor the stars, not to speak of this mortal fire. He shining, everything shines after Him. By His light all things are lighted."

Om (Aum)   The sacred syllable representing Brahman as well as the personal aspect of God; the Logos. Om is the undifferentiated word that has produced all manifestation. An almost invariable part of a mantra.

parama (parama)   The highest order, the supreme.

paramahamsa (paramahaṁsa)   1. A title given to a monk who has achieved knowledge of Brahman. 2. A monk who belongs to a particular sect of Shankara's monastic Order.

Paramatman (paramātman)   The Supreme Self which is the essence of the universe and the real nature of man. In dualistic philosophy, the individual soul is distinct from the Universal soul, but in Advaita they are one in samadhi or the transcendental state of awareness.

pitriyana (pitṛyāṇa)   The way taken after death by the individual soul of a person who had lived a good life, but not a spiritual life based on renunciation of the enjoyment of the world. Literally, the way of the ancestors.

pranam (praṇāma)   A respectful salutation to holy persons with palms pressed together or by kneeling down and touching the forehead to the floor.

pranayama (prāṇāyāma)   Control of the vital energy—prana—through the practice of breathing exercises in a rhythmical way.

prarabdha karma (prārabdhakarman)   A particular type of karma which has borne fruit in the form of producing this body and which determines its span of life. It is like the momentum given to the wheel that stops at a certain time when the force is exhausted. An illumined soul is not affected by prarabdha because he has realized his true self which is absolutely distinct from his psychophysical personality.

prasad (prasāda)   Food or other objects that have been ritually offered to God. After the ritual, the prasad is usually given to the devotees, who accept it as a blessing of the Lord.

puja (pūjā)   Ritual worship following the method of the Tantras.

pujari (pūjārin)   The person who performs ritualistic worship.

puraka (puraka) The first part of pranayama—inhalation of the breath while repeating Om four times—for awakening one's spiritual consciousness.

purascharana (puraścaraṇa) The practice of performing japa systematically increasing the count a thousand times each day until the count reaches its climax of 15,000 times on a full-moon day. During this daily chanting of the mantra, the aspirant must not move from his seat until the count is complete. After the climax of 15,000 times has been reached, the process must be reversed, decreasing the number of japa by a thousand each day until the count reaches 1,000 chantings of the mantra. This practice symbolized evolution and involution, helping the worshipper to fix his mind on God under the dualities of pleasure and pain, exultation and defeat, health and sickness, life and death. This sadhana should only be done under the supervision of a qualified guru.

purushakara (puruṣakāra)   Self-effort.

rajayogi (rajayogin)   A spiritual aspirant who follows the eight-fold path of the great teacher, Patanjali. The central part of this method is intense meditation as a means of attaining samadhi, or transcendental consciousness. The goal of a rajayogi is kaivalya, or independence from the bonds of nature by discovering his true Self.

rechaka (recaka)   Exhalation. Part of the rhythmic breathing called pranayama; the aspirant repeats Om four times while exhaling, thinking that all the impurities of his heart and mind have been expelled.

rishi (ṛṣi)   An ancient Hindu seer to whom, while in a state of transcendental consciousness, the knowledge of the Vedas was revealed by God.

sadhaka (sādhaka)   A spiritual aspirant.

sadhana (sādhana)   The practice of spiritual discipline for realizing God.

sadhu (sadhu)   A holy man; a monk.

sahasrara (sahasrāra) The seventh and highest of the chakras (centers of consciousness) located in the cerebrum. It is symbolized in Tantric terminology as the thousand-petaled lotus. When the kundalini reaches this center, the individual soul becomes one with the universal soul in nirvikalpa samadhi. It is a superrational experience that cannot be described through words or comprehended by the dialectic of the intellect. This is the state of enlightenment by gaining which no other gain in this world will be worth attaining, as the Gita says.

sakara upasana (sākāraupāsana) Worship of divine forms.

samadhi (samādhi) A superconscious state in which the individual experiences the bliss of a sweet relationship with God. See also bhava samadhi, savikalpa samadhi, and nirvikalpa samadhi.

samvid (saṁvid) The full knowledge of perfect wisdom in Brahman.

samsara (saṁsāra) 1. The world of relative existence. 2. The ceaseless cycle of birth, death, and rebirth to which individuals are subject as long as they are ignorant of their identity with Brahman.

samskara (saṁskāra) An impression, tendency, or potentiality, created in the mind of an individual as a result of an action or thought. The sum total of one's samskaras produces one's character.

sannyas or sannyasa (saṁnyāsa) Monastic life; the solemn vows of monastic life.

sannyasin (saṁnyāsin) A monk who has taken the final vows of renunciation.

sastra (śāstra) A verse from the scriptures. Commandment of God as revealed in the scriptures.

sat-chit-ananda (saccidānanda) Absolute Existence, Consciousness, Bliss: the Formless One—Brahman.

savikalpa samadhi (savikalpasamādhi) A vision of God that occurs when the kundalini has risen to the sixth chakra.

Shakti (śakti) The power of Brahman, the Primal cosmic Energy, personified as the Mother of the Universe. *See also* MAYA. Sri Ramakrishna used to address that power as the Mother Kali. That reality in its relative aspects is Kali, the Mother of the Universe. In its absolute aspect the same reality is Brahman. Just as with fire and its power to burn, Brahman and Kali are inseparable.

shakti (śakti) Energy, the dynamic power of God as the cause of the world.

shanta-bhava (sāntabhāva) The peaceful attitude of the devotee towards his Ishta—of closeness and joy but of no definite personal relationship. This is the first state of love where intimacy has not been formed. As love grows, the attitude is transformed into a sweeter relationship which is called dashybhava, the attitude of a servant towards his Master—a servant expressing love through obedience, dependence, and faith in the words of his Master and complete surrender to his will.

sashtanga pranams (sāṣṭāṅga) Humble salutations in which the devotee falls flat on the ground and touches the feet of holy persons.

shraddha (śraddhā) Faith. According to Shankara faith in the teachings of Vedanta and the words of the guru, who is a living commentary of the scriptures. Faith in a spiritual aspirant is bound to be provisional, but the faith of an illumined soul is permanent because it is based on the personal realization of truth.

shraddha (śrāddha) A religious rite connected to a funeral ceremony in which a particular kind of food is offered to propitiate the ancestors. If God is invoked in the midst of the ceremony, it conveys the idea of remembrance and gratitude to Him, who is the Father of all mankind.

shrutidhara (śrutidhara) The possessor of an extraordinarily accurate memory, especially for verbal communication.

siddhi (siddhi) 1. Spiritual perfection. 2. An occult power. 3. An hallucinogenic drug.

sloka (śloka) A verse in an epic poem.

sushmna (suṣumṇā)   The passage near the spinal column through which the kundalini rises from its base in the muladhara chakra through the six other chakras to the seventh, the sahasrara chakra in the brain, during the process of realization. *See also* CHAKRA.

swarupa (svarūpa)   True self, true form.

tadakarakarita (tadākārakārita)   The stage when the Atman detaches Itself from the illusory personal self and remains absorbed in Itself.

tantradharak (tantradhāraka)   A ritual assistant who reads instructions to the pujari during a ritual worship.

Tat twam asi (tat tvam asi)   Literally, That thou art: implying the oneness of the individual soul with Brahman. A "Mahavakya" or great word of the Chadyoga Upanishad.

tithi (tithi)   A lunar day. Hence the actual birthday of a person according to the lunar calendar of the Hindus. As for example, Ramakrishna's birthday was the 2nd day of the bright fortnight in the month of Phalgun in B.E. 1242, which is equivalent to 18 February 1836 A.D. by the Gregorian calendar of the West.

Turiya (turīya)   1. The fourth state of consciousness—Superconsciousness. 2. According to Shankara, this is not a state but is the Atman which is the invariable background—like the unmoving screen that reflects the moving picture of a film—behind the three states of consciousness—waking, dreaming, and deep sleep.

vairagya (vairāgya)   Renunciation of the apparent self in order to realize the true Self, which is the mine of strength and the fount of infinite happiness. Through renunciation alone can immortality be reached, say the Vedas. Renunciation does not mean condemnation of the world but deification of the world. We renounce all that is untrue and discover all that is true, beautiful, and good. We renounce the temporary and fugitive joys of the world in order to obtain eternal and permanent joy that comes from the realization of God.

Vaishnavism (Vaisnavism)   Literally the following of Vishnu; a Hindu dualistic sect whose members follow the path of devotion to God in the form of Vishnu or one of Vishnu's avatars, especially Sri Krishna but also Sri Rama, and Sri Chaitanya.

vidyapitha (vidyāpīṭha)   A residential school where the teachers and students live together for the purpose of combining academic knowledge with moral and spiritual wisdom through the establishment of an unsullied character which will always remain true to the ideal of self-enlightenment and the service of God in man.

vija mantra (vījamantra)   See bija mantra.

Virat (virāj)   The Cosmic Person who thinks of the universe as his body. When he identifies himself with all minds, he is called Haranygarbha. Arjuna saw the universal form of the Lord and was struck with awe and amazement and prayed to Him to withdraw that form and appear in his sweet natural form. Unless the spiritual aspirant is qualified and his mind is very pure, the universal form creates fear, and the human soul cannot bear it. God has two aspects—power and sweetness. For a devotee the aspect of sweetness is more appealing: We want to feel that He will accept us in spite of ourselves.

Vyavaharika (vyāvahārika)   Historical truth: the level of everyday experience. This is contrasted with paramarthika, the level of Ultimate Truth experienced by realized souls.

Notes on Illustrations

Frontispiece: One of the most familiar of the Saradananda photos, this was taken after he had become the secretary of the Ramakrishna Math and a few years before his death in 1927.

2. This is the second of four known photographs of Ramakrishna, taken in December of 1881, when he was forty-five, at a studio in Calcutta.

3. A less common photo of Sarada Devi, one of the few of her taken in formal studio surroundings.

4. No photo of Sarada Devi was taken prior to her forty-fifth year (twelve years after the death of Ramakrishna). Here, she is probably in her early to mid fifties.

5. Swami Brahmananda, born Rakhal Chandra Ghosh, is still referred to by monastics and devotees of the Ramakrishna Order as Maharaj. Swami Saradananda is often referred to as Sarat Maharaj.

6. Narendra Nath Datta (1863–1902); Swami Vivekananda, known affectionately as Swamiji. This photo of him as a young man is a good example of how he appeared to Westerners on the occasions of his visits to North America and Europe.

7. This photo was probably taken on the occasion of the departure of Trigunatitananda or Turiyananda to the West to start a center in America.

8. Saradananda, shown here in a characteristic pose, seated in the small room at the entrance of the Calcutta residence of the Holy Mother (Sarada Devi) and the *Udbodhan* office.

9. This rare photo of Saradananda as a young man is the way he appeared to his North American and English friends. Note especially his use of the frock coat and cleric's collar to conform to Western custom (see also in photos 10 and 11) instead of the traditional *dhoti*, blouse and *chuddar* favored by monks of the Ramakrishna Order.

10. Saradananda photographed with an unidentified acquaintance in North America. Based on the presence of the unidentified individual (also shown seated next to Saradananda

in photo 11) these photos may well have been taken at the Cambridge (Mass.) Conference described on page 24 of this text.

11. Saradananda at an American gathering at about 1897.

12. Saradananda back in India, wearing more customary garb.

13. After Swamiji's death, Shivananda, Brahmananda, and Saradananda were spiritual and administrative mainstays of the Ramakrishna Order.

14. Girish Chandra Ghosh, the fiery, profligate Bengali poet and playwright, is pictured here at about the time of his first meeting with Ramakrishna. After Ramakrishna's death, Ghosh became friendly with Saradananda; the two men, besides having their love for Ramakrishna as a bond, both wrote extensively. At Saradananda's urging, Ghosh wrote his reminiscences of Ramakrishna in Bengali (which Swami Aseshananda has translated into English for this text).

15. Saradananda and Shivananda in later years, when they were Secretary and President respectively of the Ramakrishna Order.

16. One of the later photos of Saradananda; this is the way he appeared when Swami Aseshananda served him.

17. Swami Aseshananda, head of the Vedanta Society of Portland, Ore., and senior monk of the Ramakrishna Order in North America, as he appeared in a photo taken in the Summer of 1981 at Sarada Convent, Santa Barbara, Calif.